REWRITING CAPITALISM

Pitt Series in Russian and East European Studies

JONATHAN HARRIS, EDITOR

Rewriting Capitalism

LITERATURE AND
THE MARKET IN
LATE TSARIST
RUSSIA AND
THE KINGDOM
OF POLAND

Beth Holmgren

UNIVERSITY OF PITTSBURGH PRESS

Published by the University of Pittsburgh Press, Pittsburgh, Pa. 15261
Manufactured in the United States of America
Printed on acid-free paper
10 9 8 7 6 5 4 3 2 1

Library of Congress Cataloging-in-Publication Data
Holmgren, Beth, 1955–
    Rewriting capitalism : literature and the market in late
Tsarist Russia and the Kingdom of Poland / Beth Holmgren.
        p. cm. — (Pitt series in Russian and East European studies)
    Includes bibliographical references and index.

    ISBN 0-8229-4075-2 (cloth : acid-free paper)
    ISBN 0-8229-5679-9 (pbk. : acid-free paper)
    1. Russian literature—19th century—History and criticism 2.
Polish literature—19th century—History and criticism. 3.
Literature publishing—Russia—History—19th century. 4. Literature
publishing—Poland—History—19th century. 5. Capitalism and
literature—Russia—History—19th century. 6. Capitalism and
literature—Poland—History—19th century. 7. Literature,
Comparative—Russian and Polish. 8. Literature, Comparative—Polish
and Russian. I. Title. II. Series: Series in Russian and East
European studies.
    PG2981.P6 H65 1998
    891.709'003—ddc21   98-19706
                                                                   CIP

A CIP catalog record for this book is available from the British Library.

For Mark Franklin Sidell

contents

preface

IN 1996, IN A POST-SOVIET and seemingly post-Tolstoy Russia, the Vagrius Press ventured a sequel to the great novelist's *War and Peace,* drawing heavy fire from the critics and the avid interest of readers.[1] The novel's personalized title, *Pierre and Natasha,* recalls *Scarlett,* the sequel to Margaret Mitchell's *Gone with the Wind.* In both instances, publishers presumed that the general reader is ultimately more taken with character than concept. But the Russian sequel entailed taking a steeper step down the ladder of artistic value. *Scarlett* may be a less compelling read than *Gone with the Wind,* but the original novel fits squarely into the category of middlebrow literature. *Pierre and Natasha* takes a willing tumble from great Russian classic to a middlebrow status perhaps unprecedented in Russian culture. The sequel projects very different notions of writer, reader, and literature from those assumed by Leo Tolstoy over a century ago.

If *Pierre and Natasha* would reduce Tolstoy to romance, the phenomenal success of the romance genre itself in Eastern Europe signals an even more drastic decline. The Harlequins now being voraciously consumed have no pretensions to a "classical" heritage, but instead are produced and marketed explicitly as disposable commodities.[2] Their Polish distributors, for instance, have discovered the successful strategy of offering readers a book "every month, for just one month" in Harlequin's Romance, Super Romance, Desire, and Temptation series.[3] While Polish writers still balk at this kind of factory production, Polish readers have not disdained to buy translated Western imports, *asserting* their right to a literature that provides entertainment and comfort.[4]

It would seem that the postcommunist capitalization of Russia and Eastern Europe has toppled high culture into the marketplace. Ironically, but predictably, the freedom of expression so long sought by East European writers and readers has materialized into market control and consumer demand. Not only are writers free to write as they please, but also readers are free to buy as they please and publishers are free to anticipate or fabricate consumer taste. The reader's newfound purchasing power and the publisher's overriding concern for profit would seem to undo the writer's long-term advantage in Eastern Europe, an advantage both institutionalized and compromised over the decades of communist rule. For centuries, writers of "serious" literature in Eastern Europe had arrogated for themselves the role of social critics and spiritual leaders in the face of oppressive or sometimes foreign autocracies and on behalf of a vast uneducated populace. Soviet or sovietized cultural institutions, in turn, upheld the writer's privileged status and sense of moral mandate, even if the state attempted to enforce the writer's political allegiance; communist repression of dissident literature worked to the same effect, implying the outlawed writer's political power. In this dynamic, readers figured as a needy congregation rather than as a consuming public; writers both divined and dictated literature to them; and elite writers, readers, and publishers, who constituted a small fraction of the population, shared and imposed the judgment that only "serious" literature mattered.

Seen against this historical background, present-day developments could be read as the crude westernization of Russian and East European culture, for it was precisely this reverence for the writer and writing that for so long distinguished these literatures from their Western counterparts. Writers in the region prided themselves on their investment in the national cause and their independence from a bourgeois, profit-oriented West. Readers the world over marveled at the products of this independence and investment—awed, for example, by the philosophical and psychological depth of Russian realist novels or by the visionary sweep of Polish Romantic poetry that fueled an insurrection and sustained a nation in exile. In sharp contrast, the present ubiquity of the Harlequins and such "classic" sequels as *Pierre and Natasha* augur a Western invasion, or, as some critics baldly charge, a Western corruption of highminded indigenous literatures. Apparently, capitalism has paved the way for a cultural takeover, and soon Russian, Polish, Czech, and other East European literatures will copycat all the demeaning patterns of the Western book trade.

Yet before we resign ourselves to this hypothesis and define consumer culture in Russia and Poland as an inevitable Western transplant, it is essential that we review the evidence of a century ago, when the market had made strong, if temporary, inroads into the region's book publishing and mass-circulation press. It was during this period (roughly 1890–1917) that the mass-circulation press truly developed in Eastern Europe; publishers strove to materialize and capitalize on indigenous respect for books; "classic" writers were transformed into celebrities and packaged as status-enhancing commodities; and the new phenomenon of the bestseller reflected and promoted striking changes in authorship, readership, and (to a lesser extent) the very notion of "good literature." This fascinating and illuminating period of relations between literature and capitalism serves as the general focus of my book. I investigate, in selected examples, how Russian and Polish literatures attempted to rewrite capitalist role models and values that were already well established in the West, resisting or manipulating powerful market forces and thereby striving to retain some of their own distinctive worth. And I contend that this period yields valuable clues to the current transformation of literary culture in Russia and Eastern Europe.

I have narrowed my review to the literatures of tsarist Russia and the Kingdom of Poland or Russian Poland—that area of partitioned Poland under tsarist rule that has been most influential in Polish culture—because, of all the Slavic literatures in this period, these enjoyed the greatest prominence in general European literature.[5] Fin-de-siècle Russian and Polish literatures shared important contextual features and influences that distinguished them from Western models, and together illustrated a crucial and continuing tension in East European relations. By the second half of the nineteenth century, Russian literature had captured the attention of European readers. The novels of Leo Tolstoy, Ivan Turgenev, and Fyodor Dostoevsky impressed their European contemporaries as among the finest achievements of the tsarist empire, indeed, as the saving grace of what was perceived to be a benighted, backward, not-quite-European power. Polish literature did not enjoy the same rapid translation into other languages until the novelist Henryk Sienkiewicz took Europe by storm in the late 1890s. But the plight of Poland, dismembered by the Austro-Hungarian, Prussian, and Russian empires in the late eighteenth century, predisposed many Europeans to a ready sympathy for Polish culture, the product of an extraordinary international martyrdom. In addition, Poland's Western orientation, especially manifest in its close ties with France and Roman Catholicism, cast Poles in the role of Western favorite among the Slavs. In both cases, the European literary renown of Russian and Polish writers derived in large part from European perceptions of their unjust political context.

In both cases, too, Russian and Polish writers won great power and appeal in combating that context. "Serious" literature was mainly produced by an intelligentsia that, in Russia, functioned as an oppositional voice against the tsarist autocracy, and, in the Kingdom of Poland, struggled to preserve the Polish nation under tsarist occupation. Although writers were drawn from various classes, ranging from the landed aristocracy to educated urban workers, they self-consciously insisted on their function as a critical elite, a dictating vanguard. Like the societies they enlightened and exhorted, these self-styled leaders saw no possible consensus in a middle ground, no virtue in erecting a bourgeois bulwark against political tyranny. They could not and would not write as middle-class authors catering to peer demand, or at least so they declared. Their job was to navigate the straits between the Scylla of political oppression at home and the Charybdis of undesirable Western alternatives such as a self-complacent middle-class and a market-driven literature. When a new consumer culture began to flourish at the turn of the century, many of these writers apprehended it as a threat to their authority, prestige, and plans for educating the newly literate masses. It confronted them with the obverse of persecution—devaluation. My book considers how both "serious" writers and producers of consumer culture coped with such a drastic power shift, for, as it turned out, the social devaluation of literature was in no one's best interest.

At the same time, these tricky negotiations between high and consumer cultures were further complicated by the relationship between imperial power and subject state. Both Russians and Poles could and did claim the spiritual and moral superiority of their works over Western products, but projecting similar claims did not yield a pan-Slavic solidarity, much as the Russians might have wished. The Russians publicly assumed the role of protector of Slavic interests; the Poles, with understandable circumspection, overlooked the fact of Russian protection and flaunted their greater familiarity with the West, a culturally liberating cosmopolitanism. Thus, the three-way relationship linking Western Europe, tsarist Russia, and the occupied Kingdom of Poland produced some surprising displays of assertion and deference. Both Russian and Polish writers were avid for general European recognition—the Russians on account of their empire's "parvenu" status, the Poles in hopes of gaining Western support against their oppressors. More often than not, it was Russian writers, supposedly backed by imperial might, who manifested the greater insecurity and ambivalence toward the West. The Poles, in turn, self-righteously appealed to the West as wronged members of the European family. Wherever possible, my analyses trace how both sets of writers at once distinguished and, in a sense, *advertised* their nation vis-à-vis the other and with incessant regard for general European opinion.

My book argues that the literatures of fin-de-siècle Russia and its subordinate, the Kingdom of Poland, represent important variations on dominant Western models of interaction between culture and commerce because these literatures articulate (1) two *developing* European cultures similarly bifurcated between a politicized cultural elite and uneducated, or recently educated, masses; (2) two cultures similarly critical of and self-consciously distinct from the West; and (3) two cultures enacting the enmeshed politics of imperialism and national self-determination outside the European empire–non-European colony paradigm. Spanning a textual spectrum that ranges from "classic" literature to the mass-circulation press, *Rewriting Capitalism* registers how Russian and Polish writers, critics, and publishers sought to retain and generalize, with some major adjustments, high-culture notions of the writer and the writer's influence and message.[6]

Following an introduction in chapter 1 to the features of the publishing industry in fin-de-siècle Russia and the Kingdom of Poland, chapters 2 and 3 offer complementary readings of how "serious" Russian and Polish writers conceived of the capitalist in their powerful visions of national heroes and heroism—visions intended to both reflect and direct a questing intelligentsia. Chapter 4, still focused on literary texts, provides a bridge to the following section on the market by examining writing that constituted an intersection of high-culture function and market-proven formulas—a literature that I argue is comparable to, but not identical with, Western middlebrow fiction. Here I compare two best-sellers (Russian and Polish, respectively), *Keys to Happiness,* by Anastasiia Verbitskaia, and the *The Leper,* by Helena Mniszek, showing how they rewrite the predictable characters and plot of the popular romance to convey a "serious" national message and project a "serious" prestige. Finally, chapters 5 and 6 examine how the market, textualized in the mass-circulation press (and specifically in the Russian *Vol'f Bookstore News* and the Polish *Illustrated Weekly*), defined and packaged the entity of "literature," decorously commercializing and nationalizing the objects and practices of material book culture.

Chapter 7 reviews the collected evidence of the preceding chapters and speculates about the connection between the two end-of-the-century periods in Russian and Polish culture—that of a century ago and the present day. I anticipate that the current wildly fluctuating book market in today's Russia and Poland will gravitate toward the patterns of a century ago, promoting a consumer-savvy worship of the "serious" text for the sake of national distinction, although I see a fundamental difference in the intervening extreme politicization of the Soviet period.

In sum, this book offers selective readings of an important transitional moment in the evolution of Russian and East European literature and culture, to elucidate a relationship between high culture and consumer culture that has long been ignored or distorted by scholars on both sides of the Atlantic. Western historians established Russian popular culture as an important scholarly topic little more than a decade ago, and literary scholars have been rather hesitant to follow the historians' late lead, perhaps because they remain in thrall to high culture's legislation of literary value.[7] In Poland, studies of popular literature more or less began at home, but they too emerged quite recently and are still on a limited scale.[8]

It seems essential to me that scholars and teachers of Russian and East European cultures should represent these cultures in their complex entirety—that they not only survey a succession of "classic" works, but also integrate those popular and influential writings and writing contexts that "usually remain in the margins or beyond the scope of literary history."[9] This book explicitly promotes and contributes to a more inclusive literary history. It was also written to prompt self-reflection in its

Western audience. By learning more about the ways in which a capitalist market affected cultures quite distinct from our own—indeed, cultures that both criticized and contended with the West—we can better assess our own writings of capitalism and can complicate and enrich our sense of cultural value in the marketplace, our understanding of how literature both signifies and sells.

acknowledgments

THIS BOOK MATERIALIZED in a roundabout way, and, perhaps inevitably, it came to join together my various interests in Russian culture, Polish culture, gender studies, the relations between popular and elite cultures, and an ongoing comparison (more implicit here) of Western and Slavic attitudes and experiences. The initial project was funded by a postdoctoral grant from the Joint Committee on Eastern Europe of the American Council of Learned Societies and the Social Science Research Council with funding from the U.S. Department of State under the Soviet–East European Training Act of 1983. It focused on how the Russian and Polish mass-circulation press packaged the artist at the turn of the century, a period in which these quite distinct "national" cultures, so long dominated by elite production, had to adapt to a fast-developing print market. The last two chapters of *Rewriting Capitalism* carry out this project on a highly selective basis.

Once I began work on this project, I decided to expand its purview—in part to trace the fuller scope of this transformation, in part to analyze texts accessible to American students. That expansion paid off when I tested my approach and assigned some of these texts in a freshmen honors seminar at the University of North Carolina, Chapel Hill, in fall 1995. I am indebted to the students in this class for their terrific insights, enthusiasm, and occasional consternation as they responded to Russian and Polish "classics."

Because of the disparate subjects covered in this book, I also relied on the constructive criticism of a host of smart and generous readers—Paul Debreczeny, Galya Diment, Helena Goscilo, Madeline Levine, Louise McReynolds, Donald Raleigh, and Bożena Shallcross. These readers functioned more as "major donors" than "contributors" because all of them adamantly affirmed the worth of a comparative Slavic approach; their belief in my Russo-Polish project helped me resist mainstream pressure to "russify or perish." I had the great good fortune to find in the University of Pittsburgh Press a publisher who felt the same way, and I thank Jonathan Harris, editor of the press's Russian and East European series, for his keen support of the manuscript. Special thanks also go to Catherine Marshall, Niels Abboe, Eileen Kiley, Jane Flanders, and Ann Walston of the press for their expert handling of the book; to Justyna Beinek for her research on some of the Polish materials; to George Suboczewski for his loan of a hard-to-get source on Bolesław Prus's *Lalka;* to the excellent interlibrary loan staff at UNC and the unfailingly helpful librarians at the University of Illinois Slavic Collection; and to Fred Stipe of UNC's Photographic Services for his superb production of the illustrations. Two chapters have appeared elsewhere in somewhat altered form: "The Heart of the Matter: Nationalizing the Romance in Russia and Poland" ("Sedno sprawy, czyli unarodowienie romansu"), *Teksty drugie* 3–4 (1995): 68–86, and "Patronized Saints: The Cult of the Artist in Poland's *Illustrated Weekly,*" *East European Politics and Societies* 10 (fall 1996): 416–38. I am grateful to these journals for permission to reprint.

I thank the family and friends who saw me through my own production and marketing phases: Virginia Holmgren, Kenneth Holmgren, Jan Holmgren, Bill Brauer, Elizabeth McKay, Ellen McKay, Steve Levine, and Jane Peppler. My daughter Jessye generously offered to retype the manuscript on numerous occasions and has given me good advice about pink book jackets. Above all, I owe this book to my husband, Mark Sidell. He knows what this project cost me, and he shared that cost with enormous patience and generosity.

Note on Transliteration

The text uses the Library of Congress system of transliteration to render Russian words and names except in the case of such widely translated authors as Tolstoy and Dostoevsky, whose names and protagonists are familiar to nonspecialists in otherwise anglicized spellings. Lest the reader jump to psychoanalytical conclusions, I have also transliterated the first name of Verbitskaia's heroine in *Keys to Happiness* as "Manya" rather than "Mania."

REWRITING CAPITALISM

one

The Publishing Business in Fin-de-Siècle Russia and the Kingdom of Poland

BY THE TURN OF THE twentieth century, the publishing industry in tsarist Russia was booming, capitalizing on newly concentrated urban audiences and an increasingly literate population—estimated among young men in European Russia at 40 percent in the 1910s, and 70 percent by 1920.[1] Such publishing giants as A. F. Marks, A. S. Suvorin, and M. O. Vol'f had established their empires in the major cities and, to a more limited extent, by mail order and transportation lines.[2] One history of the Russian book trade observes that virtually every railroad station boasted a "Suvorin" book kiosk, and by 1916 Suvorin's firm alone was reported to ship out some 57,000 copies of newspapers and 320 copies of journals each day.[3] The "thick" journals that had once dominated the publishing scene with their prestigious offerings of "serious" literature and topical essays were now surrounded and sometimes eclipsed, in terms of subscriptions, by the diverse products of the mass-circulation press—dailies, weeklies, bi-monthlies, and illustrated magazines.[4]

By the late 1890s, newspaper circulation figures hovered between 50,000 and 70,000. By the 1910s, special promotional supplements to the popular "thin" magazines that accentuated news and entertainment peaked at the impressive figure of 800,000 copies.[5] Depending on their ability and income, Russian readers could choose from a wide array of texts, ranging from collectors' editions of the classics to kopeck novels, and from the arcane art journal to specialized magazines for new readers. By the early 1900s, for example, the sumptuously produced journal, the *World of Art (Mir iskusstva)*, complete with full-color reproductions, coexisted with the extraordinarily popular *Heartfelt Word (Zadushev-noe slovo)*, a children's periodical packed with fiction, pictures, puzzles, and letters from subscribers.[6] Recently formed professional associations produced their own publications, and city dwellers subscribed to news-papers that reported on their daily concerns.[7] In this era Russian readers shopped a print market that increasingly labored to anticipate and sat-isfy their needs.[8] When a new press law abolishing prepublication cen-sorship passed in 1905, in the wake of that year's revolution, the tsarist empire appeared to be taking "a great step toward the establishment of the principle of a free press."[9]

A similar, if more intensively developed, scenario emerged in the King-dom of Poland, that territory of the former Polish state under tsarist rule. Indeed, literacy levels rose somewhat higher there than in Russia proper—by 1920, roughly 60 percent of the total populace and 80 per-cent of Warsaw residents were able to read and write.[10] Technically a part of imperial Russia and also subject to the vagaries of tsarist censorship, the Kingdom of Poland nevertheless harbored the bulk of the Polish-language publishing industry and trade (an estimated 80 percent of the area's output) in the capital city of Warsaw.[11] With their main ware-houses and stores in Warsaw, big publishing houses such as Gebethner and Wolff purveyed books, journals, and newspapers to Polish readers throughout the partitions. Polish firms generated a tremendous number of new titles in the new formats of daily, weekly, bimonthly, and monthly publications. Periodical offerings almost doubled, increasing from 80 titles in 1885 to 140 in 1904.[12] Varsoviennes could read all about them-selves in such highly respected local dailies as the *Daily Courier (Kurier Codzienny)* and the *Warsaw Courier (Kurier Warszawski)*; by 1909 the latter could claim a whopping 33,000 subscribers in a city of over 800,000 inhabitants.[13]

Aside from the numerous commercial publications that cultivated them as consumers, Polish women possessed their own "intellectual" journal in *Ivy (Bluszcz)*, which boasted an almost all-female editorial staff as well as famous male contributors.[14] Much like subscribers to the "family-oriented" Russian-language magazine *Niva*, Polish families could count on a steady diet of traditional classics and mainstream contemporary literature in the generously illustrated journal, *The Literary Repast (Biesiada literacka)*.[15] And, for a brief period, a self-selected Polish elite could enjoy the rarefied contents, both verbal and visual, of Zenon Przesmycki's *Chimera*, an avant-garde journal similar to the Russian *World of Art* in its high production values and broad artistic focus.[16]

International Standards

How did this thriving, multifaceted industry compare with its Western counterparts? As in Western Europe and North America, the flourishing of the print market in Russia and Eastern Europe stemmed in large part from major technological advances. The invention of the linotype in 1885 and the development of more sophisticated and efficient modes of photographic reproduction (the line block, the halftone, the color reproduction) resulted in attractive, truly mass-circulating publications.[17] The development of visual elements—whether they reproduced beautiful art works or sensationally topical photographs—transformed print into a new kind of medium with far more powerful and wide-ranging appeal.

The visual attracted and aided newly literate readers in their consumption of the print text.[18] The photo specifically enticed readers with its novelty and up-to-the-moment reportage. As reproductions became more textured and sophisticated, they even conferred a respectability that was traditionally begrudged the visual embellishment of high literature throughout Europe, and perhaps most vehemently in Russia. The revolution in book illustration spearheaded by William Morris came later and less assuredly to tsarist Russia, where adornment of the book was believed to diminish its intellectual worth or moral purpose.[19] The superior quality and innovation of such high-culture publications as *World of Art* and *Chimera* did much to overturn this prejudice among elite readers. More broadly, the overall proliferation of illustrated books and magazines gradually conditioned Russian and Polish readers' expectations of and approach to the verbal text, cultivating a greater demand for illustrations as perfectly appropriate enhancement or documentary proof.[20]

Changes in the text's physical form made palpable the highly productive internationalization of the Russian and East European book trade. The geographical and political disjunction of partitioned Poland necessitated a multinational orientation and sophistication in terms of news coverage and distribution. That disjunction was cleverly worked to circumvent censorship. For example, the Polish weekly *The Country (Kraj)* attracted topnotch authors and even ventured political criticism because it was published in Saint Petersburg, where, paradoxically, censorship of Polish publications "was less severe than in Warsaw."[21]

Very often publishing firms were international ventures in terms of staff and experience, if not ownership. Some of the biggest Russian publishers were immigrants with a West European background in the book business: S. M. Propper, the founder of the standard-setting *Stock Market News (Birzhevye vedomosti)*, came from Switzerland, and the publisher of the ultra-popular *Niva*, A. F. Marks, was German. Non-native as well as non–upper-class entrepreneurs injected a vital stimulus into the trade, for they cared more about marketing innovations and less about offending native prejudices against entertainment and fancy packaging.[22] They flaunted the same sort of upstart bravado and business imagination that scholars have observed among immigrant publishers in early twentieth-century America.[23] Adventurous Russian and Polish publishers imported not only the visual techniques pioneered in Western Europe and the United States, but also the building blocks of successful commercial fiction. Just as improved printing technologies made possible more attractive illustrations and layout, so commercially proven formulas— adventure story heroes and detective novel plots—standardized a kind of mass entertainment literature previously unexploited in Russia and Eastern Europe. In management, form, and content, book production crossed national boundaries with impunity, to an extent defining the tastes and requirements of the Russian and Polish markets even as they emerged.

Such international standards were also readily adopted by the Russian and Polish publishing industries because the urban centers controlled their distinctive marketing territories, insofar as they were able, concentrically and centripetally. Throughout the tsarist empire, publication and distribution tended to concentrate in the largest cities, and even there the network of stores and vendors expanded somewhat erratically.[24] The extensive railroad network built in tsarist Russia and the Kingdom of Poland throughout the latter half of the nineteenth century mapped the potential boundaries of a reading public, with bookstores offering travelers reading material at major points of embarkation and freight lines facilitating mail-order distribution.[25] Yet however mobile their wares, publishers continued to abide by one of the chief tenets of the tsarist administration and, for that matter, the high-culture establishment—that the center should dictate intellectual and material standards to outlying regions. To a large extent, mass production and mass distribution reinforced the power and prestige of the major publishing cities—Moscow and Saint Petersburg in Russia, and Warsaw and Łódź in the Kingdom of Poland.[26] Readers all over tsarist Russia and partitioned Poland were thereby assured of high-quality products whose purchase brought enhanced status: buying books published in Saint Petersburg or Warsaw signified that they were keeping abreast of the latest and most sophisticated developments in culture, science, and civic life.[27]

Market Differences

At the same time, a centrifugal effect was also evident. The many publishing firms being established in rapidly growing and diversifying urban areas attempted to reflect and anticipate the interests and capacities of their increasingly varied audience.[28] In so doing, the publishing industry registered the breakdown of power monopolies and changing group identities—the rise of the professions, the birth of the proletariat—generally at work in late nineteenth-century Russia and the Kingdom of Poland. In Russia, the intelligentsia's control over the printed word had eroded as the intelligentsia splintered into a wide range of ideological positions, new professional associations pursued their own special interests in the press, and altogether new social groups acquired reading skills and access to print. In his indispensable book, *When Russia Learned to Read*, Jeffrey Brooks chronicles in great detail the rise of literacy among the lower social strata after the emancipation of the serfs in 1861 and the concomitant development of publishing firms cultivating this new readership. A modest trade in *lubki* (satirical woodcuts) and some translated popular tales branched out into the production of best-selling kopeck novels (the equivalent of American dime novels), popular series such as detective stories and romances, and a broad variety of mass-circulation periodicals.[29]

Many of these products were issued by publishers who themselves rose out of the lower estates of Russian society—the peasantry, lower-class urban workers—and knew the clientele firsthand. For instance, Nikolai Pastukhov, the son of lower-class provincials, worked his way up as a liquor wholesaler and beer-hall owner to become publisher of the influential newspaper *Moscow Leaflet (Moskovskii listok)*. I. D. Sytin's spectacular trajectory from a peasant childhood to publishing prowess stands as the most legendary example.[30] There were, of course, attempts by those whom Brooks dubs "culturalists"—both established intelligentsia and "upwardly mobile people of common origins"—to educate and uplift new readers.[31] Such enterprises as the Society for the Dissemination of Useful Books, or the Tolstoy-sponsored firm Intermediary (Posrednik), hastened to make cheap editions of literary classics and moral tracts available to a mass audience. But, as Brooks forcefully argues, "culturalist" efforts presumed to dictate, yet failed to contain, the directions and products of the commercial book market.[32]

Brooks traces "culturalist" presumption of control all the way down the social ladder "to the middle ranks of Russian society, including such people as schoolteachers, priests, civil servants, and technicians in industry, agriculture, and local government."[33] This middle was more professional than entrepreneurial and shared the traditional intelligentsia's deep sense of social responsibility, opposition to the state, and antipathy to the market.[34] It is essential, however, to note that even those middle-rank readers who aspired to intelligentsia status deviated from the "classics" in their reading choices. Their professional commitments and orientation prescribed a different life style, one geared toward reading that was efficient, informative, and occasionally entertaining. These readers subscribed to the still prestigious thick journals, but they relied on professional publications for career advancement and general newspapers for their daily needs.[35] As I discuss at greater length in chapter 4, these "middle ranks" never cohered into a Western-style middle class before the Bolshevik revolution redrew the class map altogether.

Despite their ready emulation of the traditional intelligentsia, readers from this much-varied middle expressed significant differences in taste and desire, revering the classics even as they admitted an interest in the adventures of popular fiction heroes and heroines.[36] In a sense, they sought at once the spiritual credentials of the intelligentsia and the material satisfactions of the middle class, expressing a fascinating tension between "culturalist" aspiration and materialist gratification. Louise McReynolds credits mass publishing in Russia with creating the middle as a wedge between the intelligentsia and the tsarist government.[37] These readers' consuming habits suggest, however, that such a wedge figured more as a tentative bridge than a dividing line between middle and elite. To a certain extent, their response echoed the avidity and anxiety with which a Western bourgeoisie embraces the works of a legitimizing high culture, yet differed in the emphatic moral and political function of Russian high culture and its producers: Russian readers embraced a high culture that contained a ready critique of and moral counterweight to middle-class complacency.[38]

The Kingdom of Poland experienced much the same market expansion and diversification, although (as we shall see) scholars do not agree about the extent of the intelligentsia's control over the commercial market. Certainly that market enjoyed very favorable conditions, for in the aftermath of the 1863 revolt—a largely aristocratic rebellion against the tsarist government in the kingdom—most publishing passed into the hands of merchants and entrepreneurs, socioeconomic groups that profited from the tsarist crackdown on the insurgents. Yet in the Polish case any conflict between a dictating intelligentsia and an often defiant reading public was muted by national concerns. The mass-circulation press remained one of the few above-ground refuges from increasing russification, a policy the tsarist government perpetrated by eliminating the Polish language "from all levels of administration and the courts" and from all internal correspondence of legally registered associations; by russifying the names of Polish towns, streets, and buildings; and, most devastatingly, by limiting admission to and russifying the curriculum of the kingdom's schools.[39]

Different social groups also joined forces involuntarily. As I describe more fully in chapter 3, tsarist economic repression after 1863 to a certain extent obliterated the distinction between the intelligentsia and the professional middle ranks, because so many of the gentry were dispossessed and forced to earn a living. This blurring of distinctions was particularly true of the publishing world, which employed the most significant proportion of these mandatory new professionals. The developing mass-circulation press provided them with an indispensable, if not entirely adequate, economic lifeline.

Moreover, the Positivist movement that cautiously boosted national morale after 1863 with a program of economic development and general education actually promoted the notions of a bourgeois democracy and an enlightened middle. Despite the fact that this Polish middle tacitly included large numbers of Jewish and German professionals and entrepreneurs, it attempted unity, at least during the enthusiastic initial phase of Positivism, for the sake of the nation.[40] That coherence surfaced and for a time succeeded in print as a strange combination of capitalist and moral exhortation. Significantly, from the 1870s on the "classic" often coincided with the popular. Some of the best-selling writers of the period—Bolesław Prus and, especially, Henryk Sienkiewicz—wrote quite specifically with the market in mind, yet they enjoyed tremendous national prestige.[41]

The Polish middle continued to expand over the latter half of the century, absorbing both upper- and lower-class members, and inevitably fragmenting in terms of ideology and taste. By the turn of the century, publishers and critics had detected a sizable clientele of new readers that one scholar rather condescendingly classifies as "quarter-intellectuals" (*ćwierćinteligent*). Much as in Russia, these readers aspired to the only positive role model available—that of the cultured intellectual with a keen social conscience and an abiding love of country.[42] They rejected boulevard trash (*literatura brukowa*) and sought engagement with contemporary politics and culture in their reading.[43] But their capacity and desire for literature were quite different, and the timing of their cultural initiation was problematic. They needed and preferred simpler, more entertaining narratives in a period when the aesthetic experimentation of modernism presumed an extreme sophistication among readers. As Jacek Kolbuszewski concludes, these aspiring readers were even attracted to modernism because it sanctioned individualistic pleasures (eroticism, the cult of beauty) in a culture that largely preached hard work and self-sacrifice, yet they required a guide through its arcane labyrinth.[44] In a curious way, a modernism intended for elite readers paved and approved the way for a "classier" commercial product, a literature that sugarcoated weighty concerns in the familiar, attractive forms of romance, melodrama, sentimental tale, or detective story, and was qualified as respectable and even distinctive for its consumers.[45]

It would seem, then, that Russian and Polish publishers and their audiences were poised on the brink of wholesale Western transformation, a transformation involving both market organization and social self-image. Historians of print culture in the West insist on the link between book production and class configuration, most often concluding that a flourishing mass-circulation press reflected and abetted the growth of a middle class, the "inevitable" outgrowth of a newly educated and aspiring lower class. Elizabeth Eisenstein characterizes the general development of printing as a movement toward social egalitarianism and individual autonomy.[46] For Benedict Anderson, "print capitalism" signaled the birth of the bourgeoisie, a class he maintains could coalesce only in the replicating and imagined forms of print rather than the established customs that had once cordoned off the aristocracy.[47] The burgeoning publishing industry in the West seemed bent on erasing or destigmatizing class distinctions, at least those between the upper and middle classes, and dispersing an authority previously concentrated at the top of the social hierarchy. At the same time, that industry refigured writing and publishing as commodity production, as purchase instead of privilege. Although the book had always been to some degree a product of leisure culture, "a rare possession," it now became a truly disposable artifact and its author more and more subject to the laws of the industry, required to write quickly and in great quantity.[48] In effect, what buyers gained in autonomy and prestige, producers and their products partially lost to the vaunted demands of the market.

Of course, the publishing industry in the West did not level the quality and access of print culture, in the main because the reading communities it served were neither uniform nor united. Indeed, as Roger Chartier points out, the market's seemingly democratic push often forced a splinter group reaction, as readers joined by class or taste demanded specifically tailor-made publications.[49] It is no coincidence that the notion of the "highbrow"—a genteel upper-class aesthetic—took shape in late nineteenth-century America, when the phenomena of immigration, urbanization, and industrialization were perceived to undermine a "genteel definition of character and culture," just as the mass-circulation press threatened to engulf the American reading public.[50] This exemplifies a predictable sort of elite backlash, one that has recurred in Western publishing history and has textured rather than stunted the growth of the print market. Consequently, readers who insisted on "highbrow" fare simply attracted and financed their own niche of writers and publishers; they did not succeed in censoring or stopping other publications.

But theirs was not the only reaction. As I discuss more fully in chapter 4, a "middlebrow" culture also evolved in the perceived vacuum between "highbrow" elite and "lowbrow" mass cultures in twentieth-century America, and this kind of production was plied as avidly and endorsed as wholeheartedly as any elite art. In the West, print culture reflected and encouraged differences made acceptable by notions of earned leisure consumption and customer satisfaction. This meant that the elite could not dominate or dictate, and the middle was not effectively stigmatized, but socially approved and commercially irresistible. To reformulate Anderson, I contend that print capitalism announced the birth of an unabashed bourgeoisie and a positive declaration of consumer rights.

Thus, even given increased class mobility and differentiation in fin-de-siècle Russia and Poland, the Western-style commodification of literature promised nothing less than a revolution in the relationship between writer and reader. As I have sketched briefly in the preface and will elaborate in the respective national surveys of chapters 2 and 3, throughout modern Russian and Polish history the high-culture writer has exercised and received tremendous moral and national authority. High literature in Russia had functioned as a de facto opposition—a relatively autonomous site of judgment and directive—in the absence of a multiparty government, a teaching church, and a free press. Great realist novelists such as Tolstoy, Dostoevsky, and Turgenev had literally spelled out the ideal of the Russian writer as the independent conscience, chronicler, and seer of the nation—although these very different men by no means shared a radical or even internally consistent ideology; the contradictions between Dostoevsky's conservative journalism and his all-questioning fictions best illustrate this point. The not always sanguine interplay between Russian realist writers and radical critics in the nineteenth century further conditioned readers to decipher their works as encoded political messages or a diagram of national distinction and future greatness. Writers and critics did not agree in their conceptions of the truth, but they were unanimous in assuming literature's mandate to seek and script it.

Polish literature had performed an even more vital political act, affording the most revered and accessible expression of nationhood after Poland's political erasure in the late eighteenth century. The great poetry and drama of the Romantics—Adam Mickiewicz, Juliusz Słowacki, Zygmunt Krasiński—reinforced the equation of high literature with national glory. Mickiewicz's poetry in particular was believed to be the catalyst for the failed 1831 insurrection against the tsarist occupiers, and his works written in Parisian exile were deliberately composed and desperately heeded as divinations into Poland's supranational destiny, with their visions of Polish martyrdom and eventual resurrection. Słowacki's and Krasiński's texts conveyed other world-altering, if far more self-critical, national messianisms. Yet whatever their specific ideology and despite their publication in exile, the Romantics' writing fired and generally shaped Poles' nationalist aspirations (and literary expectations) at home. In both the Russian and Polish contexts, the writer's prominence and the reader's patronage were founded on the bedrock of literature as social conscience, political profession, and national prophecy, not on any consumer dynamic, in which commercial profit ranks above cultural service.

Moreover, the modernist movements that vied for the educated reader's attention at the turn of the century with opulent effects, erotic explicitness, and the privileging of aesthetic form over social commentary did not undo these respective national paradigms, but reconceived their effect and address. The Russian symbolists and poets and dramatists of the neo-Romantic Young Poland movement defied what they dismissed as a formally dull, thesis-heavy realism or Positivism, yet they assiduously cultivated their predecessors' belief in the high mission of art. Although the emphases on beauty and the flesh in modernist works could be and were construed as a license for high-flown consumption, their stylistic intricacies and dense cultural references presumed an elite audience and were deployed to prompt the reader's reflection and even spiritual metamorphosis.

The intrusion of a consumer-oriented, multileveled publishing industry into these paradigms would effect a reversal of status whereby the reader would be entitled and empowered as consumer, the writer would hustle to attract reader interest and investment, and literature would serve the gradated needs and desires of various self-defined and self-satisfied audiences. Nowhere would this reversal be more apparent than in the writers' and publishers' battle for the reading middle—what I have already indicated to be a highly fragmented, varied, and untested clientele. Did the fin-de-siècle market ultimately demote the writer in Russia and the Kingdom of Poland? Did it concomitantly divest literature of its political and spiritual power? Did it duplicate the Western hierarchy of "highbrow," "middlebrow," and "lowbrow" to accommodate and mirror a new, layered audience? Did the literature produced in this period and inevitably sponsored by the market promote new capitalist heroes and visions?

This book analyzes specific examples of response, rather than attempting a comprehensive answer to such questions. What these selective, yet wide-ranging, examples consistently show is that a capitalist revaluation was not valorized in fin-de-siècle Russian and Polish literatures. The capitalist model of writer-producer, reader-consumer, and literature-commodity was not endorsed by writers, readers, or even (indirectly) publishers, and the protagonists and plots that writers drew from their capitalizing societies rarely succeeded and certainly did not endure as heroic models and designs for living. In both Russian and Polish texts, it seemed essential that writers and publishers rewrite the scripts of capitalist progress as well as the formulas for successful marketing in order to assert and advertise national distinction.

My readings suggest, moreover, that these national cultures eschewed an openly stratified market that acknowledged an audience stratified in education, taste, and desire, and instead more broadly divided literary production into "serious" and "popular" categories. Just as the Russian and Polish middles remained incoherent in form and self-definition, so Russian and Polish literatures named no categories, even in the market, for those hybrid works the middles so avidly consumed. Acutely uncomfortable with the concepts of a middle class and middle-class culture, these literatures and their developing markets instead opted for a continuous remapping of the "serious"—either a rigid definition that sharply limited and segregated "truly serious" works from the mass of "boulevard literature," or (more often) an elastic and expanding definition of what could constitute elite art. Whatever the composition or provenance of the literary product in these cultures, its worth appeared to depend absolutely on its designation as "serious" by writers, publishers, or critics, who in some cases professed to be taking their cues from the discerning reader.[51]

As I noted in the preface, the following chapters will illustrate this reaction to the market on a variety of texts that describe a kind of sociocultural descent from "classic" prose to ad copy. That line of descent serves a double purpose in my analysis—both to explore the social extent of the reaction and to underscore the sociocultural values and aspirations these very disparate texts share and repeatedly express. In part I, "Literature on the Market," I begin by examining works universally deemed "serious" in fin-de-siècle Russia and the Kingdom of Poland, which together mounted perhaps the most powerful and certainly the most complex self-defense against capitalist revaluation.[52] I have chosen "serious" texts that largely reflect realist and Positivist, rather than modernist, traditions because these engaged most explicitly and accessibly with their contemporary societies.

I

LITERATURE ON THE MARKET

two

The Problem of the Merchant
in Russian Literature

The Merchant's Image

IT IS A MOST CURIOUS FACT THAT the image of the Russian merchant never radiated the power of the tsarist empire. Unlike the English
merchant-explorers written up as the British empire's advance guard and
"civilizing pioneers," the Russian merchant did not figure in tales of
imperial expansion.[1] The absence of the merchant estate in large part
reflected its marginality in the building of the Russian empire, which
proceeded more by military action than economic colonization and bat-
tened on the economic integration rather than the subordination of conquered peoples. "Russian merchants had not kept pace with the march of
empire," Alfred Rieber explains, because "the division of the commercial groups in Russia along cultural-territorial lines impaired the development of a single all-Russian capitalist class."[2] It would seem that the
Russian merchant stood neither in the front ranks nor even at the center
of the Russian empire. As a real-life leader and heroic reflection, he was
eclipsed by the soldier, the high-ranking bureaucrat, or the "classless"
intelligent.[3]

The merchant's marginalized and frequently ambiguous image in literature also derived from inequities and slippages in Russia's peculiar social organization by estate or *soslovie,* a term that came to designate a category of people joined (somewhat variously) by kinship, occupation, legal status, distinctive culture, and social identity.[4] By the early nineteenth century, the merchants had emerged as a separate group in an estate system generally descending, in terms of privileges and rights, from gentry to clergy to townspeople *(meshchanstvo),* and finally to the heavily taxed and restricted peasantry. The somewhat amorphous category of the estate yielded "an exceeding complex and variegated" social structure and did not equate to "class."[5]

Membership in an estate, moreover, guaranteed neither individual status nor group solidarity. In wealth and occupation Russian merchants ranged from mighty industrialists to pawnbrokers and were subdivided into three guilds, with the first and second including the more affluent and the third offering membership to well-to-do peasants. It was the merchant's individual fortune that determined his ranking between the gentry and *meshchanstvo.* As Richard Pipes observes, "The middle estate thus became a kind of half-way house for those moving up and down the social ladder."[6] Only the merchant who had amassed enough capital could enjoy some of the gentry's advantages—basic civil rights, exemption from a stigmatizing poll tax, and financial well-being. And merchants could escape their "half-way" estate altogether by marrying into the gentry.

Furthermore, the merchant's economic prowess did not readily translate into sociopolitical power, for under the tsarist autocracy this depended on education, professional and high society connections, and a talent for public action. The merchants as a group were long unable or unwilling to control their own public image, especially through the important forum of "serious" literature. Tending to be religiously conservative Russian Orthodox or Old Believer sectarians, they did not encourage a secular education and, as a rule, did not attempt or desire contact with the sites of Russian high culture, its salons and literary circles. Their isolationism was remarkably persistent, despite the flowering of a national culture in the nineteenth century; according to Edith Clowes, "Until the 1880s literature [was] anathema even for the highest reaches of the merchantry.[7]

In the nineteenth century, an increasingly hybrid intelligentsia drawn from the gentry, the clergy, and those "without rank" *(raznochintsy)* did most of the talking and writing for educated Russian society, and they usually passed a negative verdict on their nation's emblematic businessmen. Writers both above and below the merchant in estate rank stereotyped him as

> a man of old-fashioned views and virtues (if any), conservative in dress, opinions, and way of life, a philistine interested in nothing but business, money, and the strict observance of church rites, a tyrant at home and at work. . . . A typical specimen of this sort was a man of distinctive appearance, wearing a beard, his hair fairly long and cut so as to hang just below the nape of the neck. Usually he wore a peaked cap and was dressed in a long caftan with a stand-up collar hooked at the throat and baggy trousers tucked into top boots.[8]

Writers from among the gentry not only imparted their ignorance of merchant life through stereotypes, but also conveyed their ambivalence about the merchant's unenlightened "Russianness" and their leisure-class scorn for the profession of doing business. In their case, the tense, often antagonistic relations between the aristocracy and the bourgeoisie in Western Europe were exacerbated by the marked external differences and clannishness of merchants, traits that embarrassed and frustrated a gentry bent on acquiring some degree of westernization. Alfred Rieber asserts, "As the tastemakers of society, the nobility legitimated and spread these derogatory attitudes until the merchants became highly sensitive and openly defensive about their social role." The gentry's (mis)representation of the merchant forms an interesting complement to their mythologization of the peasant. In both cases, the portrayal reflects very partial knowledge, and their judgments may have ministered to their own class complexes. Just as they tended to cast the victimized peasant (the gentry's one-time slave) as a saintly savior, they tended to consign the alien merchant (the gentry's not so infrequent creditor) to the background as a minor villain.[9]

Raznochintsy, or members of the intelligentsia who lacked the means and status of the gentry, evinced, if anything, a greater antipathy toward the merchant and the business world. Their self-made identity as intellectuals, their commitment to radical social reform, and even their clerical pedigree (many were the disaffected children of Russian Orthodox priests) ensured their dissatisfaction with mere money making as a vocation and a disdain for the "petty-bourgeois" culture of money worship and tasteless consumption—a culture they were economically positioned to share. Indeed, for the gentry and educated commoners alike, the very notion of bourgeois character was stigmatized as an attribute of the lower-ranked *meshchanstvo*. By the late nineteenth century, the related epithet *meshchanskii* broadcast the pejorative, petty-bourgeois meanings of "vulgar, bigoted, greedy, and philistine."[10] The nineteenth-century *intelligent* of whatever estate muddied the distinction between the well-to-do merchant and the poorer *meshchanin* (townsman), ascribing to both the potent political-cultural negatives of conservatism, materialism, willful ignorance, and tastelessness. This antagonism was only reinforced by the conservative merchants' generally "sluggish" response to the social and political reforms implemented in the latter half of the century.[11]

Russia's "serious" writers were certainly not unique in their disdain for the merchant. Even in the United States, the supposed homeland of the Puritan work ethic and capitalist zealotry, highbrow writers did battle with indigenous fast-talking traders and a utilitarian mind-set that in their eyes threatened to corrupt the nation's moral fiber and subvert the value of artistic production.[12] What distinguished the Russian situation, however, was the fact that "serious" writers wielded unchallenged moral and social authority. Because they alone articulated a kind of opposition in their authoritarian society, their judgments dictated the outlook of the most influential segment of the population. In tandem with the government restrictions that economically disadvantaged the native merchant in favor of the noble or foreign industrialist, their negative representation effectively denied the merchant social cachet and any sort of oppositional clout.

A curious American book printed in 1937 takes this power play as its target. *Russian Literature and the Business Man* (the author deems businessman a "more comprehensive term" than merchant) is a published dissertation by Louis Perlman, a Russian émigré who received his doctorate from Columbia University. Perlman purports "to examine the descriptions of the business man as they appear in Russian literature from the time of the heroic epic poem to the modern day." Its "examination" is actually a counterattack: Perlman's own bias surfaces in his conclusion that "the merchant's struggle for a place in Russian society was a courageous one against great barriers" of what he construes as class antagonism.[13] His author-by-author appraisal therefore reads like a settling of accounts in which he faults most writers (those "of noble parentage") for their class-bound hatred and lauds occasional exceptions (those born into a merchant family) for their equally class-bound tolerance. As Perlman generalizes in his preface:

> The sentiment of the aristocratic writer toward the rising middle class of merchants was not kindly. He looked upon the merchant as the innovator of a vulgar, noisy, and loathsome commerce, etched him as a barbaric lover of money, dishonest and devoid of culture, a danger to the well-defined class distinctions of serf and landed gentry. The harsh concept of the merchant was not softened during the process of social evolution that lifted him from petty commerce to a position of financial power and high cultural attainments. A petty trader could be treated with gentle scorn and ridicule, but a merchant prince was another thing. Fear and jealousy strengthened the dislike of the aristocrat for the merchant.[14]

Perlman's book represents a fascinating attempt at accommodation to American values, as it transforms the merchant into the American "equivalent" of the businessman, refines him into a martyr of the upper class and an unambiguous example of the middle class, and presumes a sympathetic hearing in a nation where business and the businessman usually flourish. His vociferous defense seems understandable against the attacks of such powerful writers as Dostoevsky, Nekrasov, and Saltykov-Shchedrin. Yet Perlman is far too partisan in his judgments and reductive in his reversed readings to provide a definitive survey. Dubbing the merchant a martyr of the gentry, he not only whitewashes his subject, but also misses how it challenged and complicated the "serious" Russian writer's constant self-critique and search for a meaningful existence. Perlman mistakes the merchant for the intelligentsia's scapegoat rather than its tellingly ambiguous alternative.

A Hierarchy of Heroes

As Rufus Mathewson observed almost a half century ago,

> Russian imaginative literature—perhaps more than any other of the
> world's great literatures—has been concerned with the celebration of
> emblematic literary heroes. . . . And the degree to which nineteenth-
> century Russians read their own spiritual history in the lives of their
> literary heroes is a unique feature of the whole national literary expe-
> rience.[15]

Of course, by "nineteenth-century Russians" Mathewson implies the
tiny minority of educated writers and readers who were alienated from
the vast majority of the population. For this isolated and politically dis-
enfranchised intelligentsia, the production of fictional scenarios and especially fictional heroes served as a primary means for working out their
own place and function in a thoroughly bureaucratized and deeply unjust autocracy. Given the bare subsistence of most Russians, there was
much for the intelligentsia to do, yet given the government's regimented,
autocratic structure, there were very few effective professions through
which one could get things done. The literary hero increasingly explored
and tested these options.

Throughout the nineteenth century, the writing intelligentsia, divided
into camps of liberal or conservative writers and radical critics, debated
the possibilities of a viable positive hero, and their debate yielded rather
selective, if still imperfect, heroic categories. The radical critics insisted
on "a deeply affirmative ideological hero" and advocated its creation in
the rational man of action, but they narrowly defined that action as car-
rying out revolutionary programs and putting radical ideas into practice.
Action was made heroic through ideological dedication. Although the
writers also aimed to construct an effective hero, they tended to dismiss
the rational man of action as simplistic, immoral, or lacking in credibil-
ity, and in his stead they developed a series of magnificent near-heroes
too introspective and self-aware to commit themselves to a single cause
or to attempt major change. Predictably, these variations on the so-called
superfluous man, a type coined in the first half of the century and characteristically "alienat[ed] from other human beings and from purposeful

activity," elicited scorn and polemical essays from the critics.[16] But such dreaming, reflecting, searching protagonists, immured on their estates or stifling in government service, also impressed readers as noble failures who possessed greater intellectual and spiritual depth than the men of action. Inaction or too modest action was also the result of lofty preoccupations.

In sum, only men of the intelligentsia proved eligible for the roles of simplistic hero and complex near-hero, for in the context of "serious" Russian culture, heroism generally presumed a character's intellectual abilities and investigations as well as a commitment to solving society's problems. Unless a merchant had graduated into the ranks of the intelligentsia, a phenomenon widespread only at the end of the century, he could not qualify for the role. In this sense, although the heroes of nineteenth-century Russian literature ranged in economic terms from Dostoevsky's destitute Raskolnikov in *Crime and Punishment* to Tolstoy's wealthy Prince Bolkonsky in *War and Peace*, and although they encompassed the *raznochinets* as well as the noble, they formed a quite exclusive club. The stray peasant who gained entrance was more like a visiting speaker than a regular member. And the merchant was regularly blackballed because he was not deemed a thinker, a leader, or a virtuous man.

The haughtily guarded division between spirit and matter, between political ideology and mere business, also indirectly compromised the merchant as a dealer in material goods. In inverse proportion to the altruism and intellectuality ascribed to their heroes, nineteenth-century Russian writers tended to deemphasize or problematize the pleasures of consumption. Aleksandr Pushkin's celebration of earthly delights (champagne, roast beef, a shapely foot) in *Eugene Onegin* (1833), a work often cited as the first portrait of the superfluous man, was quickly overshadowed by Nikolai Gogol's "dead-souling" of human appetites. In such works as "The Old-World Landowners" and his famous novel, *Dead Souls* (1842), Gogol lavished attention on the consumption of food, implying that gluttony was the highest desire of his spiritually impaired protagonists. Gogol's outlook, although extreme, was basically adopted by succeeding realist writers. The lure of consumption represented a particularly dangerous temptation for noble heroes equipped by income and status to consume conspicuously, yet self-appointed to do good and live right. Tolstoy's heroes methodically wean themselves from such consumption; Dostoevsky's heroes neglect or punish it in their feverish pursuit of ideas; Turgenev's heroes settle for moderation.[17]

The merchant stood in implied contrast to these self-abnegating heroes, for his very profession entailed the satisfaction of appetites, the circulation of goods, and the accumulation of property. Gogol made his dilemma abundantly clear in *Dead Souls:* If the novel's de facto merchant-protagonist Chichikov wishes "to attain redemption," then he "must, metaphorically speaking, learn to curb his enormous appetite," his all-consuming "acquisitiveness" *(priobretatel'stvo).*[18] Provision and consumption were flip sides of the same soul-shrinking sin of materialism, and the merchant was thereby doubly damned.[19] It is no accident that Raskolnikov, a rational man gone to extremes, decides to kill a usurer to enact his own revolutionary idea, or that Rogozhin, a merchant's son distinguished by passion rather than intellect in Dostoevsky's *Idiot* (1868), is doomed to the hackneyed role of mad murderer.[20] Almost three decades later, Tolstoy managed to redeem a self-made merchant in *Master and Man* (1895) only by driving him to an inexorable and self-sacrificing death. The *intelligent*-hero thus remained peripatetically above or beyond the making of money, while the merchant character, whose whole life revolved around this endeavor, was largely relegated to an unheroic role or self-destruction.

Not surprisingly, the Russian hierarchy of heroes was restricted to men, although writers often created "strong" or "terribly perfect" female characters of the gentry and the intelligentsia to accompany and expose their inadequate "leading" heroes.[21] Female merchants or members of merchant families were featured much more rarely, perhaps in part reflecting the patriarchal restrictions of the merchant household and women's consequent absence from public life. Negative stereotypes of the venal proprietress and the crass conspicuous consumer did recur, as exemplified in Raskolnikov's greasy-haired usurer and Nikolai Leskov's horrifyingly voracious merchant's wife, the protagonist of *Lady Macbeth of the Mtsensk District* (1865), who commits three murders in her single-minded quest for passion and wealth.

But, to some extent, images of merchant women, like heroines of the gentry, were enhanced by their victimization. This tendency is manifest in Nikolai Dobroliubov's famous and obtuse valorization of the fearful, superstitious suicide in Aleksandr Ostrovskii's play, *The Storm* (*Groza*, 1859); his review insists that Katerina, an unhappy merchant's wife who kills herself after confessing to an adulterous affair, is protesting the merchants' unjust world.[22] This tendency may also explain the vogue in the 1860s for the writings of Aleksandra Kobiakova, an exceptional merchant's daughter who documented and protested her oppressive estate for educated readers.[23] Yet the female character's victimization, however poignant and ennobling, led to the same dead end as the male character's self-destruction. The merchants' positive image, it seemed, required the denunciation of their estate or their literal transfiguration.

In those rare cases where the merchants were ceded protagonist status, they appeared somewhat off the beaten path of "serious" literature and often evolved from ethnographic subject to heroic material. For example, the prose works of Pavel Mel'nikov (the pseudonym of Andrei Pecherskii, 1818–1883), largely drawn from his ethnographic studies of the Nizhnii Novgorod region, furnish exotic portraits of the merchants who belonged to the dissident religious sects of the Old Believers. Mel'nikov-Pecherskii's artistry failed, however, when he ventured to concoct positive heroes rather than recreate observed types. The "virtuous, honest, educated, Westernized, tolerant, Old Believer–nurtured merchants" he envisions in *the Woods* (*V lesakh*, 1874) and, especially, *On the Hills* (*Na gorakh*, 1881) seem pale and tendentious in contrast to his other rich characterizations.[24]

The playwright Aleksandr Ostrovskii (1823–1886), more than that of any other nineteenth-century writer, explored and developed the merchant as protagonist, although he did so on the stage in a literary era dominated by narrative prose.[25] Like Mel'nikov-Pecherskii, Ostrovskii came to focus on this group through personal contact and observation— specifically, of the Zamoskvorech'e (Beyond-the-river) business district in Moscow and of provincial Volga towns. Such early plays as *A Family Affair* (*Svoi liudi—sochtemsia*, 1849), *Stay in Your Own Lane* (*Ne v svoi sani ne sadis'*, 1853), and *Poverty's No Vice* (*Bednost'ne porok*, 1854) represented dramatized physiological sketches of the Moscow merchant milieu, displaying a somewhat confounding array of characters—the heartless, deceitful, and successful lovers in *A Family Affair,* the wise and kindly father in *Stay in Your Own Lane,* and the failed merchant as sympathetic drunkard and victim in *Poverty.* Ostrovskii's bullying merchant types, epitomized by the figures of Dikoi and Kabanova in his most renowned play, *The Storm,* would become famous as examples of the *samodur,* an unenlightened tyrant who wields absolute power at work and at home, yet it bears noting that *samodurs* of other estate backgrounds also populate his dramas.[26]

Notwithstanding his iconic *samodurs,* Ostrovskii never demonized the merchant, for, over time, this figure proved to be an important catalyst and eventually a possible hero in his work. Perhaps because his staged and therefore heavily censored plays could not afford to indulge in the political allusions that charged contemporary Russian prose, Ostrovskii depended on the drama particular to the merchant's world, the plots of big and small business, of characters enslaved by poverty or driven by greed. As he observed from the changing world of Russian big business in the late nineteenth century, the merchant did not always function as the greedy, parochial villain, but regularly yielded that role to dispossessed, parasitic aristocrats, weathering their machinations to emerge a more positive alternative in the end. Therefore Ostrovskii's later works assay portraits of relatively virtuous, sympathetic, and more fashionably dressed *businessmen*—the hard-working nouveau riche Vasilkov in *Easy Money* (1870) or the magnanimous, if socially awkward, Belugin in *The Marriage of Belugin* (1878), a play Ostrovskii co-authored with Nikolai Solovev. Yet it is telling that Dobroliubov, the same influential critic who misread *The Storm,* also powerfully and inaccurately fixed Ostrovskii's reputation as a painter of the merchant's oppressive "dark kingdom."[27] Admittedly, Dobroliubov did not live to see the playwright's later dramas, but his radical politics obscured the variety and ambiguity already evident in Ostrovskii's early work and long prevented a more nuanced appreciation of his evolving representation of "old" and "new" merchants.[28]

In the dominant genre of the realist novel, the most comprehensive and well-written challenge to contemporary definitions of heroism versus nonheroism appeared in Ivan Goncharov's *Oblomov* (1858).[29] The novel's title character, a nobleman who served briefly as a government bureaucrat, displays certain prerequisites of the superfluous man—intellectual ability and artistic sensibility, dissatisfaction with his professional options, and a critical stance toward his society. The novel follows his almost perpetual state of reverie, which climaxes early in his recollection of childhood on the family estate. Yet in lieu of focusing on a near-hero clashing with his inadequate context, this text dwells on the protagonist's specific and seemingly insuperable class conditioning. With extraordinary frankness, Goncharov insists on the very real costs of being a "thoughtful" nobleman, delineating Oblomov's utter physical dependence on his serf, without whom he cannot feed or dress himself. The novel exposes the *indulgence* of his dreaming and thinking made possible by enslaved servants, estate income collected and skimmed off by dubious intermediaries, neglect of friends and surroundings, and almost complete inertia. However appealing Oblomov's sentimental dreams may be, they cannot ennoble or vindicate his inaction. His passivity is shown to stem from his class privilege, not a hamstringing Hamletism.[30]

This distinctly unlofty *intelligent*-protagonist is further weighed down by his habits of consumption. He neglects his property and rejects the dreary bustle of doing business—possible signs of asceticism—but creature comforts serve him as both life support and artistic subject. On close inspection, his dreams prove to be made of anticipated physical pleasures, projecting an artful catalogue of picturesque sights, delicious meals, and a permanent sense of holiday. The charm of Oblomov's remembered childhood mainly derives from the "vegetable life" of the routines, rituals, indulgences, and feasts that mark time on his parents' estate. When Oblomov conjures up a rosy future, he can distinguish his idyll from his ancestors' pedestrian round of making jam, pickling mushrooms, and boxing maids' ears only by its more refined consumption, its incorporation of "music, piano, elegant furniture," and a "chef trained at the English Club."[31] Over the (rather short) long run, Oblomov settles for the baser stuff of his comfort-lined dreams, forfeiting the love of an inspiring but demanding woman, relinquishing control over his affairs to con men, and marrying his amply endowed cook and housekeeper, Agafia

Matveevna. Oblomov's failure in love, the one force that might have up-lifted him, seals his destiny as a mere consumer. His subsequent few actions and conversations focus solely on eating and celebrating:

> In March cakes were baked in the shape of larks according to custom, in April the double windows were taken out, and he was told that the Neva had thawed and spring had come. He walked about the garden. Vegetables were planted out in the kitchen garden; the spring holidays came, Whitsuntide, the first of May, and were celebrated with the traditional birches and wreaths; there was a picnic in the copse. Early in the summer conversation began about the two great festivals to come: St. John's Day—Ivan Matveich's nameday and St. Ilia's Day—Oblomov's nameday; these were important events to look forward to. When the landlady happened to buy or to see in the market an excellent quarter of veal or to bake a particularly good pie, she said: "Ah, if I only could buy such veal or bake such a pie for the namedays!" They talked of St. Ilia's Friday and the annual walk to the Powder Works, and of the feast at the Smolensky Cemetery in Kolpino. The deep cluck of the broody hen and the chirrup of a new generation of chicks were heard under the windows; pies with chicken and fresh mushrooms, freshly salted cucumbers, and then strawberries and raspberries appeared on the table. "Giblets aren't good now," the landlady said to Oblomov. "Yesterday they asked seventy kopeks for two lots of quite small ones; but there is fresh salmon—we can have cold fish soup every day if you like." (392–93)

Ironically, once Oblomov has drifted to the bottom, his well-fed, well-tended person becomes his housekeeper's ideal. Ever the sharp observer of class relations, Goncharov assigns the socially inferior Agafia Matveevna to provide for her clean, fair-skinned gentleman, who in exchange does nothing whatsoever. Oblomov's example unmasks the noble superfluous man as an appealing parasite, a carnal rather than a spiritual character.

In place of the discredited noble hero, Goncharov actually proposes a successful businessman, Oblomov's childhood friend Andrei Shtolts. Shtolts sports a hybrid ethnic pedigree of German father and Russian mother, which singles him out as a happy "middle man," a character biologically equipped to balance crude bourgeois German industry with refined noble Russian indolence; interestingly, his characterization elides German with *burgher* and Russian with *aristocrat*. His father trains him to be practical and assertive, while his mother anxiously tempers and cultivates his taste and appearance. As a result, Shtolts turns out to be a thinking, cultured businessman, a merchant who circumvents the merchant's ghetto and breaks the nobility's stranglehold on heroism, or so the narrator hopes:

> Such a character, perhaps, could not be formed without the mixed
> elements of which Shtolts was made up. Our men of action have
> always been of five or six stereotyped patterns; lazily looking round
> them with half-closed eyes, they put their hand to the machine of the
> State, sleepily pushing it along the beaten track, treading in their pre-
> decessors' footprints. But, behold, their eyes are awakening from
> sleep, bold, lively footsteps can be heard, and there is a sound of ani-
> mated voices. . . . Many Shtoltses with Russian names are bound to
> come soon! (165)

For the time being, however, Shtolts reappeared only in the pages of his author's subsequent novel, *The Abyss (Obryv)*, and Goncharov's contemporary novelists did not recreate his likeness elsewhere. Indeed, in yet another famous and class-biased analysis, the critic Dobroliubov pronounced Shtolts at once premature and inadequate—at least for "the educated section of society, which is capable of loftier strivings; among the masses, where ideas and strivings are confined to a few and very practical objects, we constantly come across such people."[32] To make matters worse, Shtolts was judged to be not only premature as a character type, but also unconvincing and ultimately uninspiring, read as "a lifeless abstraction."[33] Goncharov, critics generally charged, had fashioned his hero too abstractly, and even so, his final sketch proffered nothing more impressive than an *honest* businessman.[34] In a tantalizing and somewhat frustrating conclusion, Dobroliubov posits that Ol'ga, Oblomov's disappointed fiancée and Shtolts's happy wife, successfully incarnates "the highest ideal" of intellectual development in "our present Russian life" and comes closest to achieving a positive heroism. Yet while he recognizes that this wife of the businessman, freed from the business of business, at once embraces action (theoretically) and resists complacency and narrowly defined goals, he does not claim leadership for her. As Goncharov characteristically makes plain, Olga's sex severely limits her educational and professional opportunities, and she is left on its pages as a "questing" wife and mother.

The Merchant's "Articulate Sons"

Goncharov's experimentation with a businessman-hero clearly did not resonate among other mid-nineteenth-century Russian writers. The debate over true heroism continued to reflect the intelligentsia's perspective, mesmerized by the revolutionary rather than the capitalist, and concentrated on "necessary" relations between *intelligent* and peasant or *intelligent* and worker. Perhaps Dobroliubov had guessed right about Shtolts's poor timing and unconvincing class provenance. There were as yet few writers and readers, at least of "serious" literature, who could identify with a hero posed between the merchant and the *intelligent*. Even Perlman, who welcomes Goncharov's class outlook (the writer was born into a merchant family), recognizes the then embryonic state of what he calls the middle class, noting its lack of political and social vision.[35] For Perlman, the middle class did not come of age until the late nineteenth century: "The character of the merchant was, of course, modified when his sons became articulate and of cultural importance in Russia."[36]

This is an apt observation, if somewhat simplistic. Although class background did not guarantee class sympathy, a cross-class perspective proved to be crucial to the breakup of the solipsism of the intelligentsia, its charmed circle of self-absorbed authority. The merchant's access to representation improved only with the education of his heirs, in part because of the intelligentsia's monopoly on cultural expression, in part because the gap between merchant and gentry actually widened in the nineteenth century, with "a massive influx of trading peasants" entering the merchant's estate.[37] The merchant's sons and daughters had to "pass" fully into the intelligentsia-dominated arena of Russian literature and culture in order to signify and be heard.

As Rieber and other scholars have shown, a select group of wealthy heirs had attained enormous "cultural importance" by the turn of the century, redressing the merchant's traditional low self-image in the process:[38]

> It became increasingly difficult to speak of "the merchants" as a class or even as a homogeneous group or, indeed, as "merchants"; "industrialists" would have defined them better. Sharp and sharpening differences in the scale and nature of business enterprise, in income and education produced corresponding differences in manners and

habits, attitudes and ways of life. As in other countries in transition from an agricultural to an industrial economy, Russia's social structure was breaking up. The tradition of *noblesse oblige* was, in John Bowlt's phrase, being replaced by *richesse oblige,* and the upper reaches of "merchant" society led the way, probably more so in Moscow than elsewhere. The patronage of the arts was taken over by the new class of business tycoons, and their achievement is best, but by no means exhaustively, recalled to this day by the Moscow Art Theatre and the Tretyakov Gallery, named after its founder and familiar to every tourist in Moscow.[39]

In a high culture newly shaken by the development of a popular market, many of these cultured heirs eschewed the profit motive and functioned as sophisticated, influential patrons, maintaining costly artists' colonies, amassing collections of fine art, and financing galleries and theaters and esoteric publications. Self-made gentry by virtue of their acquired tastes and their altruism, they countered the restrictions of government sponsorship and, in many cases, supported with their financial clout projects undertaken by the intelligentsia. Yet although these wealthy Russians had abandoned long beards and caftans for Western dress, a significant majority committed their money to the production and preservation of specifically Russian culture, thus supporting "an alternative to obscurantism and backwardness, on the one hand, and crass materialism and foreign domination on the other."[40]

With their patronage of a nationalist highbrow art, at least one group of heirs managed to connect their merchant Russianness with their acquired nobility.[41] John Bowlt speculates that the Moscow merchants' particular attraction to contemporary art reflected their own "presumptuous and avant-garde" social position.[42] Nevertheless, this mapping of a possible middle ground remained a tricky business even (or perhaps especially) for those who could "pass." It is striking that the new generation of merchants scored their greatest public relations successes behind the scenes as collectors and patrons or in those artistic venues (painting, theater) that were relatively neglected by the nineteenth-century intelligentsia. For wealthy heirs venturing onto the debating ground of "serious" literature, becoming "articulate" did not automatically empower them to project a positive self-image and family portrait. Here they faced deeply entrenched stereotypes of their past and the intelligentsia's deeply divided outlook on the present.

At the same time (as I will discuss in greater detail in chapter 4), "serious" literature was becoming more inclusive and responsive to readers. The omnipresence of the mass-circulation press and all that it entailed —a multifaceted and self-serving metropolis, a very involved reading public, the premise of verbal "coverage" of the empire—fundamentally transformed the "serious" writer's eligibility and approach. The press increased the public's appetite for the topical and broadened the scope of its knowledge.[43] Writing in the wake of globe-spanning reports and daily editorials, even the most esteemed authors could no longer claim the same authority, universality, and attention. In this period, we see a blurring of the boundary between the writer and the journalist—indeed, between writing for a living and a number of other professions—and more and varied candidates for "serious" authorship were admitted into print. While some critics deplored such inclusiveness as a sign of the devaluation of literature, it clearly indicated the greater accessibility of literary production for both writers and readers and the emphasis the Russian reading public placed on real-life experience and immediate relevance.[44]

Still committed to the mandate of Russian realism to provide social commentary and increasingly compelled to report the "news," quite a few fin-de-siècle writers generated panoramic novels of Russian society that "covered" all classes and most regions, and their sagas naturally gravitated toward the dramatic rise of the new merchants. Novels by such prolific writers as P. D. Boborykin (1836–1921) and Aleksandr Amfiteatrov (1862–1938) straightforwardly asserted the new "cultured merchant" to be a hero—a hero, moreover, of the Moscow urban scene already privileged in the mass-circulation press.[45] Amfiteatrov's *People of the Eighties* (*Vosmidesiatniki,* 1908) and *People of the Nineties* (*Deviatidesiatniki,* 1910) approve the rising fortunes and industrious good works of Moscow merchant families, and Boborykin's *Chinatown* (*Kitaigorod,* 1882, named for the Moscow business district), *Vasilii Tiokin* (1892), and *Watershed* (*Proezdom,* 1894) fictionally elaborated his journalistic conclusions about the new merchant-leader:

> The nobility's streets are fading, there are no more grand receptions,
> there is no move even to keep up appearances of its former luxury

and magnitude. . . . But the millionaire-industrialist, the banker, and the warehouse owner not only occupy public office and become directors, councillors, and representatives of private firms and charitable organizations, but also are beginning to fund intellectual and artistic programs, found galleries, buy expensive works of art for their studies and salons, establish stipends, sponsor schools, learned societies, departments, painters and poets, actors and writers. In the last twenty years a kind of little Florence has emerged in Moscow, with its own de Medici, its own class of moneyed patricians and patrons.[46]

What was most striking about these proliferating merchant heroes was their derivative character. As Boborykin's comments indicate, the merchant became a literary hero by stepping directly into the shoes of the affluent intelligentsia; in these traditional, if topical, novels, the concept of the hero remained aligned with the upper class in content, form, and function.[47] Such fiction formulated the merchant group as a surrogate aristocracy-cum-intelligentsia, not a distinctive new class. My analysis in chapter 4 delineates how Anastasiia Verbitskaia's *Keys to Happiness*, perhaps the most popular novel of this period, relied heavily on nineteenth-century models of the *intelligent*-hero, whether the protagonist is a Jewish millionaire or a barefoot female dancer.

Yet other, less derivative fin-de-siècle portraits of the merchant appeared in this period, the most interesting and original of which were penned by two "articulate sons" of tradesmen if not bona fide merchants —Maxim Gorky (1868–1936) and Anton Chekhov (1860–1904).[48] Their works merit our close attention for both their contemporary innovations and continuing endurance in the canon of "serious" Russian literature. Rieber also singles out these two writers for distinction in his quick survey of the merchant's literary fate: "In Gorky's strong hands, the merchant emerged as an energetic, often violent, and ruthless entrepreneur whose moral sensibilities suffered under the weight of his twin urges to transform the world and fill his own pockets. Chekhov gave us both sides."[49]

Of the two, Gorky, born into a *meshchanstvo* family that soon became destitute, began with the greater handicap; but both first saw Russian society from a markedly plebeian and trade-oriented perspective

—one from behind a shop counter (Chekhov's father owned a grocery store) and the other cruising the streets for saleable junk (Gorky resorted to this as their fortunes plummeted). Both, too, passed successfully into the ranks of the intelligentsia by way of the mass-circulation press. Once their literary talent was recognized, they were embraced by "serious" literati and enabled by their writing to lead the life of a comfortable *intelligent*.[50] Both resolutely avoided glorifying either their past or their present condition, albeit in very different ways.[51]

One can argue, in fact, that the *problem* of inheritance dominates Gorky's oeuvre, for it mirrors his own family dilemma and search for a vocation.[52] Making his debut as a writer in 1892 after years of odd jobs and hard labor, Gorky did not attempt his life story for several decades, but his early works already reveal his preoccupation with the fate of the son, or more generally the fate of the talented, disaffected individual struggling against the determinism of money, class, and family practice. Although the Soviet literary establishment later tidied up its literary father's paradoxical views, Gorky tended to favor the extraordinary individual over any given class representative, a preference evident in his amoral nonideological tramp protagonists or *bosiaki*.[53] As demonstrated by the eponymous hero of his 1894 story, "Chelkash," Gorky accentuated the positive traits of "vigor, determination, and independence," but did not overlook his hero's criminality and ruthlessness; subsequent tramp protagonists display other negative features.[54] As social outcast and social rebel, however, the tramp afforded Gorky the broadest critical scope on Russian society, indicting the greed of both the owners (merchants, industrialists, the gentry) and the equally money-grubbing and land-starved peasants. It is characteristic that even in this early stage Gorky resists romanticizing the peasant, the darling of the intelligentsia.[55]

The intelligentsia as a group fare no better in Gorky's fiction, and their unexceptional types irritate as weak ineffectual complainers against a dreadful status quo.[56] In a number of works—most fully in his mammoth postrevolutionary *The Life of Klim Samgin* (begun in 1925)—he flattens the *intelligent*-protagonist into a mere lens through which great events are observed. Gorky implied that weakness and passivity were the hallmarks, if not the exclusive properties of the intelligentsia, and such disqualifiers created an important vacuum where the hero was supposed to be, suggesting to one critic that Gorky's exceptional tramp represented the final degeneration of the superfluous man.[57] Soviet critics, predictably, championed the protagonists of his anomalously programmatic novel *Mother* (1906) as his alternative to the weak *intelligent,* and Gorky's own subsequent pronouncements about the socialist realist hero again tidied up a very interesting confusion in his work, implying that he would reproduce the man of action in the committed revolutionary.[58]

Yet Gorky's incessant quest for a hero and his documented dissatisfaction with *Mother* indicate that the old prototypes of the intelligentsia could not serve, even when primed by a new Bolshevik order.[59] More surprisingly, despite his amply informed critique of capitalist excess and brutality, the drudgery of labor, and the devaluation of human and artistic values by commodity culture, Gorky's distaste for the weak and the ineffectual individual prompted him to experiment with merchant protagonists, especially those self-made types who evinced attractive energy and initiative.[60] For example, the merchant father in his early novel, *Foma Gordeev* (1899), makes a striking impression:

> Strong and handsome, far from stupid, he was one of those people
> who are always successful—not because they are talented and hard-
> working, but because, endowed with enormous stocks of energy,
> they do not spurn—are, in fact, incapable of spurning—any means
> that leads to the achieving of their end, and recognize no law save
> their own desires. Sometimes these people speak with awe of their
> consciences, they may even endure real torture struggling with
> them. But only a weak man is unable to conquer his conscience; a
> strong one easily subdues it and makes it serve his purpose. He may
> sacrifice several nights of sleep to the struggle; even if his conscience
> wins out in the end, his spirit is not broken by defeat and he goes on
> living just as vigorously under its rule as he did before.[61]

The wry Darwinian narrator explicitly presents Ignat Gordeev's flaws—his ruthlessness and moral compromising—as the necessary components of a strong man's character. The value Gorky accorded such strength, at first colored by his admiration for Nietzsche and always posed as a countermeasure to a vaunted Russian "meekness," enlightens other such ambiguous portraits. In fact, on account of his heroic dimensions (rather than heroic consistency), the merchant Ignat Gordeev has been compared to the Russian folktale warrior or *bogatyr'*.[62] Barry Scherr also claims this figure as "the precursor . . . of essentially good entrepreneurs who appear in some of the plays Gorky wrote during the 1910s."[63] All of these "good entrepreneurs" represent trading peasants who energetically worked their way into the merchant estate, and whom Gorky viewed, according to Scherr, "as people of talent and determination who possessed the ability not just to accumulate wealth, but also to improve the lot of others."[64] Yet not all of Gorky's merchants display this redeeming charisma. *Foma Gordeev* itself features two other distinct types—the sly, cynical hereditary merchant, Iakov Maiakin (Foma's godfather), and the still rustic blend of seer and brute, the lumber baron Ananii Shchurin—and these two-faced figures further complicate the portrait of the successful merchant.

Nonetheless, it is significant that Gorky, whose first approach to literature was forever charmed by his grandmother's folktales, expressed an abiding fascination for the almost fantastic energy, appetites, passions, and thoughts of the self-made Russian businessman.[65] Like his exceptional tramps, Gorky's exceptional merchants are impressive for their eccentricity and rebelliousness (even to the point of self-destruction), and they outstrip the tramps in their greater capacity for getting grand things done. The externalized Russianness that so put off writers of the intelligentsia positively distinguished the merchant in Gorky's eyes, for his blend of "the eccentric and the playboy" and bouts of nihilistic despair manifested a depth and an appeal that was lacking in the Western businessman.[66]

Almost invariably, however, these fascinating characters are the fathers or elders in Gorky's writings, and their already troubling image bequeaths a much more troubling legacy. In some instances, their heirs are simply unfit to inherit. They are born weaklings, or they incarnate the abuses of their hard-living parents, having been crippled in the womb by the all-too-common practice of wife beating.[67] Yet poor nurture rather than nature is more often the cause of their degeneration. For if Gorky's fictional parents are able to build a financial empire, they do so at the expense of family feeling and nurturing their children, and they amass no spiritual capital to pass on to the next generation. Even the likeable Ignat Gordeev mistreats and neglects one wife because she produces no male heirs to carry on his business, and his instructions to his beloved son amount to tough business advice. While most of these inept parents are men, an occasional merchant mother fails as well. The title character of Gorky's play *Vassa Zheleznova* (1910, first version) is mainly portrayed as a smart, unscrupulous businesswoman, revealed only intermittently as a loving mother.[68]

Materially pampered and emotionally deprived or abused, the merchant's heirs in Gorky's fiction tend to have absorbed their parents' cynicism rather than their ability, and they are at a loss to know what to do with themselves once they come of age. *Foma Gordeev* plots this dilemma to tragic extremes as the son, Foma, wanders aimlessly through his adult life, seeking and staging sometimes cruel sensations and eventually denouncing the spiritual emptiness of his own estate—for which behavior he is clapped into an asylum. Vassa Zheleznova's crippled son, Pavel, frustrated by an unloving wife and reduced to whining and violence, is finally shut away in a monastery. The children seem doomed to endless dissatisfaction, alienation, and destruction.

However melodramatic the particular plights of Gorky's characters may be, they resemble the portraits of other such heirs in American literature. In both cases, inheriting wealth either enervates or repels the children, and the parents' exertions are not appreciated. In both cases, too, the children may suffer from a debilitating class confusion, embarrassed by their past status and still unsure of themselves among their social betters.[69] This dilemma seems particularly acute in the Russian texts, however, because of the chasm separating the merchant estate from the gentry. Once again we encounter the no-man's-land of the middle, hemmed in by lower-class brutality and upper-class self-hatred. Here Gorky's characters generally lose their way and, in some instances, wholly disappear from view. Yet Gorky did imply one possible path "up" and out in the practice of his autobiography. Although he did not see and therefore could not prescribe the development of a positive, progressive middle class, he could offer the powerful story of one exceptional individual as affective inspiration.

Begun in 1913, well after Gorky had won fame for his fictional portraits of the merchant, his autobiographical trilogy indirectly chronicles the misfortunes of a petty tradesman's family.[70] The author's maternal grandfather, Kashirin, had industriously worked his way out of serfdom and forced labor (hauling barges on the Volga) into owning a dye shop in Nizhnii-Novgorod, but his business crumbled away during his lifetime due to poor investments and the ineptitude and greed of his sons. The young Gorky, returned to his grandparents' household after his father died of cholera, involuntarily occupied a ringside seat at the spectacle of generational dissolution. In his recounting of it in *Childhood* (1913), the first volume of the trilogy, Gorky depicts his grandfather as an ambiguous figure and a successful tradesman (shrewd, energetic, authoritarian, violent); his uncles as classic degenerates (lazy, greedy, alcoholic, wife-beating); and his mother as a painful enigma, remote from him and the family squabbles but ultimately crushed into poverty, apathy, and early death. The one truly positive family member, his storytelling grand-mother, largely eludes the family curse because she is deeply and cheerfully religious and does not care about class status and the family fortune. Yet even she copes with her brutalized life by lapsing into passivity and drinking. Doubly victimized by the men's greed and the women's passivity, the young Gorky character is ejected from the family altogether at the end of *Childhood,* facing class demotion rather than the dilemma of upward mobility.

Although the tradesman's immediate heirs in Gorky's life story inherit much less than nothing, there are hidden blessings in this horrific family for the autobiographical hero. Not only is he one generation removed from his tyrannical grandfather, and thus predisposed to watch rather than to act out against him, but also he possesses a more promising heritage (or so he writes) in the person of his father. The naturalistic opening scene of *Childhood*—a grim tableau of the father's corpse, the keening mother, and the curious son—equips the narrator with the orphan's physical loss and imaginative gain: the freedom to make myths of the dead. Part of Gorky's way out thus involves reinventing his family, a strategy most evident and sustained in his portrayal of his father, but also implicit in his portraits of his grandparents, his mother, and special friends. The impulses of the storyteller and the hero-worshiper help him to dictate his past and reconstitute his legacy.[71]

Not surprisingly, given the focus of Gorky's fictions, the idealized characters in *Childhood* are presented as exceptional individuals—more, as individuals who exempt themselves from the Kashirin family dynamic of greed and brutality and who form particular valorizing attachments with Gorky himself, recognizing *him*, in turn, as an anomaly in the Kashirin family. Aside from his grandmother and father, these characters are distinctly nonfamilial and on their own: Grigorii, the dye shop's foreman; Tsyganok, a valued and martyred worker; Good Idea (Khoroshee delo), an intellectual boarder at the Kashirins; and the boys who go scavenging with Gorky in later years. In positive counterpoint to the perverted family relations he is forced to witness and endure, Gorky highlights his voluntary association with an invariably hardworking and benevolent few. Their examples reinforce the value of autonomy and of self-creation—crucial lessons for an author who wishes to redeem his childhood self from family identification. Scherr argues that the second half of *Childhood* describes the hero's shifting allegiance from his too-accepting grandmother to the imagined model of his father, envisioned "as a person always alone, an embodiment of the independence [the hero] seeks."[72] His father, the solitary and forever incorruptible hero, incorporates the grandfather's initiative and work ethic without the taint of materialism; he actually renounces the family business he married into to make his career elsewhere.

While Gorky conveys a role model of industry, self-reliance, independence, and benevolence through these singular characters, he does not glorify their particular labors. More often than not, hard work leads to envy and exploitation rather than material reward. His father is almost killed by his jealous brothers-in-law, and Tsyganok dies after volunteering himself for heavy physical labor. In the subsequent volumes of his trilogy, *In the World* (*V liudiakh*, 1914–1916) and *My Universities* (*Moi universitety*, 1923), the autobiographical hero mainly underscores the drudgery and meaninglessness of his many jobs. In his depiction, the life of the worker cannot provide a truly positive alternative to the merchant's life, for it is crushed by poverty, exhaustion, and monotony. In *My Universities*, the hero recoils from the prospect:

> I needed only to sit an hour outside beside our gate to see that all these people—cabmen, yardmen, workers, officials, merchants— lived their lives differently from me and from the people I befriended; that they were moved by different desires and aspired to

different goals. And the people I respected and believed in were strangely alien, alone, unwanted outsiders to the great majority, who in their dirty, cunning, ant-like labor meticulously built up the heap of life, which seemed to me thoroughly stupid and deadly boring. And not infrequently, I found that people who talked of mercy and of love went no further than words and when it came to deeds, they yielded quite unconsciously to the general trend of life.[73]

Nor does entry into the intelligentsia guarantee a sure course for the hero, as he discovers in his contacts with the young intellectuals in the university town of Kazan'. Their esoteric and often naive thinking betrays their ignorance of a life Gorky knows too well; their reported perversities in the local brothels threaten to undermine the spiritual power he ascribes to them. It is intriguing that Gorky's autobiographical observations repeat the double indictment of the nobility found in *Oblomov* —the charges of self-absorbed dreaming and demeaning consumption. The autobiographical hero does find exceptions to befriend, admire, and commemorate among the intelligentsia as well, but he is quick to note any signs of hypocrisy or crudity in his spiritual "superiors."[74]

Nonetheless, despite the fact that Gorky's autobiography generally trains on the "anthill" of life inhabited by merchants, workers, and intellectuals alike, the text's very existence proves that he has himself enacted a viable alternative to the lives and life styles of merchant and *intelligent* by developing into a certain kind of writer. Throughout the trilogy, the hero professes an overwhelming love of books and stories that links him to both the lower and the upper classes. Through the narrative, Gorky functions as a translator in either direction, retelling the plots of Russian and West European classics to his fellow workers and preserving in print his grandmother's folk legends for his book's educated audience. By openly cherishing both his grandmother's stories and the classics he manages to obtain, he asserts his joint folk-highbrow pedigree as a writer, his example as an autodidact, and his catholic taste for all kinds of verbal art. While the hero occasionally admits that he glosses over prosaic details in the classics, he corrects this omission in his own narratives and still validates colorful characters and romantic legends.[75] In contradistinction to his merchant characters consumed by business and to his intelligentsia blinded by dreams and undercut by hypocrisy, his carefully constructed *self-image* stands firmly on the ground, with eyes alert for signs of injustice, deceit, or heroism, and pen poised to condemn or celebrate. Throughout his works, but especially in his trilogy, Gorky's narrator functions as the reader's guide among the people, as the advance scout for heroes who merit recognition (hence literary representation) for their *action* rather than submission.

Thus, although Gorky opted for the traditional profession of the *intelligent* over the professions of his father or grandfather, he indicates that his writing did not so much signify renunciation of his past as a curiously distilled blend of past and present group values. On the one hand, Gorky took up themes championed by writers of the intelligentsia, their concern for the oppressed and their quest for heroes, and he shared their desires for a more altruistic life style and a beautiful art. On the other, he reevaluated the estates in his works, dethroning the idolized peasant, attacking the intelligentsia's embrace of a corrective suffering and humility, and openly admiring the merchant's strength, initiative, and capacity for action. To a certain extent, his writing emulated such action. Gorky set himself up in the business of collecting and assessing Russia's many character types for "inexperienced" readers of the intelligentsia, less for pay (although this of course was important to him) than for the cause of moral education. He propagandized the image of the writer as a "tough and fearless literary warrior" and proselytized the young writers in his literary circles to follow him into battle.[76] His alternative therefore combined altruism and pragmatism, romanticism and real-life observation, recreative imagination and activism; and his image as an "articulate son" wedded the worker with the writer.

I use the category *worker* advisedly: Gorky's model absolutely eschewed identification with the middle class in the Western sense of the term.[77] While Gorky resisted stooping to worship the lowly peasant, it is remarkable that most of his charismatic characters (including his autobiographical persona) tend to dwell in, or emerge from, the lower depths of Russian society. His vagabonds truly embody this tendency; his most attractive merchants are newly minted self-starters from the peasantry; and he himself is saved from bourgeois compromise by his family's impoverishment and his early experience as a street urchin. Gorky's characteristic view from the bottom up reconnected the merchant with Russian folkways but avoided any romanticization of his transformed self and progeny—that is, of Russia's embryonic middle class.

Anton Chekhov, Gorky's contemporary and mentor, offered a rather different and more far-reaching perspective. The grandson of a serf and the son of a shopowner, he qualified as a modest version of the "articulate son" (or stepson, given his family's poverty), but he did not suffer Gorky's extreme hardships and unrelieved family gloom. Although his father played the despot at home and went bankrupt, like Gorky's grandfather Kashirin, Chekhov possessed more protections against adversity: a devoted mother, good relations with his five siblings, and a great deal more formal schooling.[78] Whereas Gorky worked at many thankless jobs before he found a livelihood and a vocation in journalism and creative writing, Chekhov first approached writing with less seriousness (if not less financial need), contributing pieces to the popular newspapers as he studied medicine in Moscow. Not only was Chekhov able to pursue a higher degree, an opportunity denied Gorky (see *My Universities*), but also he began his writing career at the cultural center of the Russian empire, where he could exploit the best connections with both the popular press and the elite literary establishment.

In a sense, then, Chekhov himself was a product of this nebulously defined middle, for he was born into a shopkeeper's family and pursued the education and career of a white-collar professional. His early writings, in turn, linked him with the new literary market rather than the literary intelligentsia. The market met his financial needs and those of his family, and to a certain extent it shaped his product, encouraging brevity, tight organization, a ready repertoire of effects, and a breezily mocking narrator.[79] Yet Chekhov's class background and popular writing in no way prohibited his entry into the world of "serious" culture, especially after he moved to Moscow. Through family ties, he became close to such incipient luminaries of fin-de-siècle culture as the architect Fiodor Shekhtel' and the artists Isaak Levitan and Konstantin Korovin.[80] The humor magazines to which Chekhov contributed, despite their presumably popular readership, introduced his work to influential writers and, more important, to publishers. Chekhov's case illustrated a fluid rather than stratified world of publishing, for he truly managed the leap from "popular" to "serious" literature through the sponsorship of Aleksei Suvorin, another upwardly mobile literary man of peasant stock who built up a newspaper and book empire in the late nineteenth century.[81] Suvorin's offer of support, enhanced by various highbrow writers' recognition of Chekhov's talent, testified to Chekhov's *general* circulation and galvanized him to invest in his work as "serious" art—to stop producing "for a deadline" and to commit himself emotionally and aesthetically to his writing.[82]

Chekhov's development from popular into serious writer was accretive rather than contrastive, a pattern evident in both his style and themes. The brevity, tight structure, and parodistic impulse of his early works carried through, if his chatty narrator did not. Although his early stories "faithfully portrayed the tastes and interests of the petty bourgeoisie," they neither championed nor sentimentalized this group.[83] Even his production for popular consumption exercised a kind of critical distance which he refined in his later work. Whether he wrote for clerks or intellectuals, Chekhov's class experience resulted in a rather equitably directed class critique, not a fixed class allegiance. Like Gorky, Chekhov cherished no delusions about the innately virtuous peasant and saw through the beautiful mirages of the intelligentsia. Grateful for his admission into the ranks of "serious" writers, he nonetheless resisted certain almost prerequisite highbrow beliefs, just as he resisted the critics' subsequent pressure to deliver "answers" in his fiction.

Chekhov's consistently different perspective did not settle in the lower depths, however, but tended to survey characters of all types who confronted their limitations, delusions, and paradoxes, who realized a situational complexity that binds. Chekhov replaced a class-inflected definition of character with an almost universally applicable sense of restriction and frustration—a sense that nearly equalized peasant, merchant, and nobleman but precluded Gorky's glorious heroism of the exceptional individual and the prospect of a better world. I would even venture to say that Chekhov generalized for all classes and characters his own orientation as a member of a talented, yet prematurely jaded, "middle."

Thus Chekhov provides a sharp contrast to Gorky in his relative neglect of the rising merchant class in late nineteenth-century Russia. He may have extrapolated from his own example, but he never explicitly told his life story and he never highlighted merchants and tradesmen as a special class. His attention to this milieu surfaced rather late in his work and was largely concentrated in a handful of narratives—the two short stories "A Woman's Kingdom" ("Bab'ie tsarstvo," 1894) and "A Case History" ("Sluchai iz praktiki," 1898) and the novellas *Three Years* (*Tri goda,* 1895) and *In the Ravine* (*V ovrage,* 1900). His final play, *The Cherry Orchard* (*Vishnevyi sad,* 1904), also features a merchant, the good-natured Lopakhin who began life as a poor peasant. Of these, only the numbly horrific *In the Ravine* trains on lesser tradesmen, and while it echoes Gorky's categories of brutal entrepreneurs and a meek folk, the narrative eschews Gorky's judgment and even character involvement. There is no hope in this story, in which the avaricious Aksinia gets away with murdering her infant nephew, the obstacle to her inheritance, and there is no attempt to connect the reader with an empathetic, educated character, the sort of interpreting consciousness typical of Chekhov's later work. These peasant shopkeepers and their family circle remain alien villains and alien victims, and their business spawns only greed, hypocrisy, mental illness, and death.

Chekhov's other portraits of merchants are more inclusive, sympathetically demonstrating how the merchant's heirs, supposedly paragons of class mobility and progress, lead lives of double binds and doubled self-consciousness.[84] Significantly, two of these portraits focus on the heiress rather than the heir. Instead of tracing Gorky's disappointing line of descent from strong father to weak son, Chekhov chose a perceiving subject who would be least initiated and invested in the father's example and therefore most sensitive to the strangeness of her position. The protagonists in "A Case History" and "A Woman's Kingdom" are both daughters bereft of their fathers and somehow troubled by their inheritance; in fact, the premise for "A Case History" is a doctor's diagnosis of the daughter's mysterious illness. The reluctant ruler of "A Woman's Kingdom," Anna Akimovna Glagoleva, might be said to suffer from an excess of good health, for she cannot find a socially acceptable outlet for her normal sexual appetites.

Anna's story, presented from her perspective but told in Chekhov's characteristic third-person narrative voice, represents the more elaborated portrait, spelling out what the visiting doctor in "A Case History" could only glimpse. The narrative appropriately opens with Anna's reflections on a pile of money she has somehow received and must somehow spend:

> There was a thick wad of banknotes. They were from the timber plantation, from the manager. He wrote that he was sending her fifteen hundred rubles, the proceeds of winning a court case on appeal. She disliked and feared such words as "proceeds" and "winning cases." She knew that legal proceedings were necessary, but whenever her works manager Nazarych or her timber bailiff—great litigants, those two—won a case, she always felt abashed and rather guilty. And now too she felt embarrassed and ill at ease, wanting to put these fifteen hundred rubles out of sight.[85]

In telling contrast to Gorky's *Foma Gordeev,* Chekhov's text forgoes establishing portraits of Anna's industrious father and hard-nosed uncle, opting instead to place the reader immediately in Anna's complex situation—her coping with a dubiously gotten wealth, her reliance on suspect intermediaries, and, perhaps above all, her unrelenting, if vague, awareness of her guilt and discomfort. The continuing assertion of that awareness, a recurring strategy in the text, is key to maintaining the character's appeal. We are not only made privy to Anna's interior perspective, but also reassured that our heiress is neither sheltered nor complacent. Anna is wise to unscrupulous middlemen as well as to hard-drinking and self-pitying workers, stung by the anonymous letters that denounce her as an exploiter, and ashamed in advance of her inadequacy as a benefactress. Her own ability to embrace several perspectives at once and her consequent self-critique predispose us to sympathy and even identification, not condemnation.

In addition, Anna, like Gorky's persona, differs from her well-bred reader in having a working-class childhood. That experience equips her with a curiously double vision: "If . . . some resident from town had driven past, he would have noticed only dirty, drunken, swearing people. But Anna Akimovna, having lived in these parts since childhood, now seemed to see her late father or her mother or her uncle in the crowd" (60). In her short lifetime, Anna has undergone, through no exertion of her own, a fantastic transition from life in the factory workers' slums to a pampered existence in a mansion with butlers and governesses. She is portrayed not as a grasping nouveau riche, but as an involuntary traveler who cherishes the landscape of her first modest home. For the most part, her vision of that home is positively colored by memories of lost family happiness and security. Her "easygoing" father and the mother with whom she "shared a blanket" are both dead, and the satisfying childhood routines of washing, ironing, and running errands have been replaced by a confusing, tedious round of official visits and obligations. Anna's nostalgia for an impoverished past, her attraction to the homier "downstairs" of her mansion, and her uneasiness in a still alien and intimidating upstairs reverse the orientation of either a nouveau riche or a privileged reader acclimatized to drawing rooms and repelled by the opacity of "dirty, drunken, swearing people."

Anna thus seems ill-prepared and poorly advised to navigate, let alone rule, a new world of money, and the narrator repeatedly indicates the relaxation of the "old order" through her newly "womanned" kingdom. The household servants, for example, enjoy the fact that "they could do anything they liked without fear of being kept up to the mark" (83), and the workmen feel at ease around Anna's surviving aunt, the senior member of the family, because she had once "dressed like an ordinary peasant" (70). This relaxed kingdom is largely devoted to the leisure pastimes and consumptions of lower-class women—to eating, drinking, gossiping, fortune-telling, and playing card games. Yet while one reading of this story condemns Anna's "nonrule" and her submission to a downstairs ethos of "superstition, gambling and fatalism," Chekhov's narrator suggests no positive alternative in the upstairs world designated for receiving "the quality and educated persons" and in which Anna is required to be upper-class and adult.[86] Over the course of the Christmas holiday, she presides as a formal hostess before a steady stream of official well-wishers, a ceremony that "neither could nor did give her a minute's happiness" (74).

For all its pretensions to refinement, the upstairs world is no less focused on physical appetites than the comfortable downstairs. Anna's aunt, the downstairs mistress, may be plump enough to balance "a samovar and a tray of tea cups on her bust," but the useless factory lawyer, Lysevich, Anna's favored upstairs guest, is exposed as a superior sort of glutton, a "sleek, rich, remarkably healthy" man who relishes good food, recondite expressions, Guy de Maupassant and Jules Verne, and a touch of immorality in women. The narrative pointedly alternates between descriptions of the upstairs Christmas dinner and lengthy quotations from the lawyer's thoughts on literature and life styles. At every turn, Lysevich urges the beautiful Anna to consume—to "plunge into flowers," "choke in musk," "eat hashish," take lovers, and "squeeze the juice out of each line" of Maupassant. Although Anna rebuts him by stating her downstairs desires for a working-class husband and children, his example clearly sways her, for she is mainly "pleased to have spoken so well, pleased to be reasoning so honestly and stylishly" (79). Indeed, she essentially pays him for the pleasure of his company, awarding him the "distasteful" fifteen hundred rubles which she had intended to give to the deserving poor and which he pockets with "lazy elegance."

The upstairs world embodied in Lysevich might be conveniently classified as "the spiritually void and amoral monied world of the rising bourgeoisie" and Anna's act construed as "capitulation to the bourgeois ethos."[87] But Lysevich's blend of connoisseur and glutton and Anna's irresponsibility are not class-specific. Rather, they lay bare damning correspondences between the classes. The lawyer's refined talk, the calling card of the intellectual, is clearly dependent on his full belly; his carefully masked consumption is not so very different from the behavior of Spiridonovna, a pious downstairs visitor who devours caviar and salmon "while scowling at everyone" (84). Anna's irresponsible generosity characterizes the behavior of another Chekhov character, the estate owner Madame Ranevskaia in *The Cherry Orchard,* who lavishes the remains of her fortune on whoever inspires her momentary pity.[88] Ultimately, Anna's concluding fit of self-disgust and self-pity resonates on all levels, linking her with a host of alienated and compromised superfluous men, and also with her weeping maid Masha, whose beloved, the pompous butler Misha, rejects her as an unfit wife. Like these echoing characters, Anna suffers on account of her own weakness and her complex situation.

In "A Woman's Kingdom" and in other portraits of the new merchant, Chekhov effected a very significant revision of the traditions fostered by the intelligentsia, outlined above. Rather than caricature or color the merchant as occupying a different order of being, Chekhov included this figure in a valorized human constellation, insisting on the equation of the merchant with the peasant and, most important, the *intelligent*. He did so in part by exploring and respecting the merchant's thoughts and spiritual longings. He conferred on the merchant those capacities for self-reflection and philosophizing that had singled out the intellectual for heroic status in "serious" literature. We have seen how Anna Glagoleva's featured consciousness and self-critique make her a sympathetic near-hero. The ailing merchant's daughter in "A Case History" also appeals to the doctor, our proxy judge, because of her projected sensitivity and sadness; she seems always on the verge of "wanting to say something special, something vital, something for his ears only."[89]

Furthermore, in spiritualizing and intellectualizing the merchant's image, Chekhov scrupled to map his specific psychological makeup. Chekhov's merchants do not simply represent differently dressed or more recently monied gentry. Just as he probed the mental deterioration of the small-town intelligentsia in such works as *Ward No. 6*, so in the novella *Three Years* he represented the particular abuse, servility, and paranoia that characterized the traditional merchant family. This text chronicles three years in the lives of three heirs—Nina (Lapteva) Panaurova, terminally ill and married to a spendthrift, philandering nobleman; Feodosii Laptev, whose self-abnegating service to his father brings on mental illness; and Aleksei Laptev, the main protagonist who protests, yet ultimately shoulders the burden of the family business. As if to guarantee an authentic self-assessment, Chekhov yielded Aleksei the right to articulate his class psychology. Arguing with his dutiful brother, Aleksei bitterly denounces their shared past and his own character:

> "An illustrious house—fiddlesticks!" Laptev tried to contain his irritation. "An illustrious house! Our grandfather was always being kicked around by the gentry, and the most wretched little clerk would slap his face. Grandfather beat Father, Father beat you and me. What did your 'illustrious house' ever give either of us? What kind of nerves and blood have we inherited? For nearly three years you've been maundering on like some canting cleric, mouthing miscellaneous claptrap. As for what you've just written—why, it's the ravings of a flunkey! And what of myself? Just look at me. . . . I lack adaptability, audacity, a strong will. I'm as scared of taking the smallest step as if I risked a flogging. I quail before nobodies, imbeciles,

and swine, my utter inferiors intellectually and morally. I fear hall porters, janitors, policemen of all kinds, I fear them all because I was born of a mother who was hounded to death and because I have been beaten and terrorized since infancy. We'd do well not to have children, you and I. Oh, God grant that this illustrious merchant house ends with the two of us."[90]

Aleksei's self-hatred resembles that of Foma Gordeev, yet it is significant that Chekhov's character, unlike Gorky's, continues to cope with his situation for the sake of his incapacitated father, insane brother, dependent wife, and orphaned nieces.

On the one hand, therefore, Chekhov invested the merchant with psychological depth and particularity, and equipped him or her to serve as an empathetic character for an educated readership. On the other hand, Chekhov managed this revision without divesting the merchant of materiality. Rather, he declassed and, to a certain extent, destigmatized the merchant's connection with material goods and consumption. Anna Glagoleva enjoys fine clothes and good food, and Laptev buys art works energetically and indiscriminately, but both are depicted as trapped rather than reduced by wealth, and their "business" almost invariably consists of giving money away. Infusing a modicum of "nobility" into the likes of Anna and Laptev, Chekhov proportionately fleshes out other characters. His unredeemable gluttons hail from every social stratum: Lysevich the professional man; Panaurov the noble who squanders money with "a special flair" and collects "cups, glass-holders, studs, ties, canes, scents, cigarette-holders, pipes, dogs, parrots, Japanese wares, and antiques";[91] and, most intriguing, the madeira-guzzling governess in "A Case History." This last character actually consumes *for* the merchant's widow and daughter, who in their simplicity and enmeshed solicitude (the daughter's illness from guilt, the mother's anxiety for her daughter) cannot bring themselves to live within their means.[92]

Most often, Chekhov simply underscores the habit of consumption, thereby confounding any character who presumes to rise above his or her human needs. This view finds classic expression in *Ward No. 6*, when the supposedly stoical Doctor Ragin, having resigned himself to incarceration in the town's insane asylum, demands freedom in order to get his customary beer and cigarettes. Perhaps more than any other nineteenth-century Russian writer, Chekhov demonstrated that talk, especially the grandiloquent philosophizing of the intelligentsia, is neither cheap nor altruistic. With his unflinching focus on the intelligentsia at play—eating, drinking, flirting, resting, and incessantly talking—he made a point of exposing the material base of their "antimaterialist" life style. Those characters who disregard this material connection are often forced off their property. The high-minded Prozorov sisters, for example, relinquish their home to their grasping sister-in-law (another self-indicting consumer) in *The Three Sisters*, and the irresponsible gentry in *The Cherry Orchard* lose their lovely estate at a public auction. Although in both instances a nouveau riche encroaches on their space, their displacement also stems from a kind of delusional self-indulgence, from too much talking and dreaming and too little action.[93]

In their juxtaposition of fading gentry with the ascending nouveau riche, *The Three Sisters* and *The Cherry Orchard* together represent a fascinating continuum that reworks the class commentary of Ostrovskii's later dramas.[94] Both men chose to explore these late nineteenth-century social tensions in their work, although the older playwright seemed more willing to cast the gentry as schemers and cheats and to settle for openly calculating, mercenary protagonists. Thus, in *Easy Money* the relatively more positive Vasilkov does accept his society-belle wife, Lidiia, who has blatantly used him for his wealth, but on the chilling condition that she serve him as a frugal housekeeper. In *The Girl Without a Dowry* (*Bespridannitsa*, 1879), the poor aristocrat Larisa abandons the petty official she had pledged to marry for financial security and indulges in what turns out to be a fling with the equally poor, but dastardly, aristocrat Paratov.

Chekhov's treatment of the gentry in conflict with the "middle" seemed more sympathetic, but his indictment proved to be more subtle and incremental. The figure of Natasha in *The Three Sisters* clearly manifests the *poshlost'*, the vulgarity masquerading as lofty idealism, that also regularly appears in his narrative accounts of provincial life. Portrayed as tasteless, acquisitive, selfish, and cruel, she abuses the servants, dislodges her sisters-in-law, and is eventually condemned by her once loving husband as a "mean, blind, thick-skinned animal."[95] Countering Natasha's negative traits with their sensitivity, magnanimity, and high culture, the three sisters cannot help but emerge as the superior, albeit tragic, protagonists. Yet Chekhov also suggests some unsettling parallels between the vulgar Natasha and the noble trio in the latter's solipsism, sharp judgments, and unabashed adultery.[96] Furthermore, the sisters' beloved brother, the future "professor" and the embodiment of their lofty hopes, is incapable of realizing their dreams and instead abides by Natasha's pettier domestic and careerist ambitions, reprising, in grimmer terms, Oblomov's "descent" from Olga to Agafya.

The Cherry Orchard, in turn, levels the playing field more completely. In a plot that hinges on the necessary sale of property to a "new" merchant, Chekhov develops complex characters who are not villains, heroes, or even clear victims. Both gentry and merchant are elaborated in Chekhov's characteristic self-involved, self-indicting, and "unheard" monologues. The former peasant and merchant Lopakhin is made no less self-aware and sympathetic than the frivolous Madame Ranevskaia and her brother Gaev. Unlike the social-climbing Natasha, he is the first to reflect: "But you can't make a silk purse out of a sow's ear. I am rich, I've got a lot of money, but anyone can see I'm just a peasant, anyone who takes the trouble to think about me and look under my skin."[97]

Although Ranevskaia repeatedly dismisses as "vulgar" Lopakhin's proposal to transform the cherry order into lots for summer homes, she admits her devastating and sometimes tawdry material improvidence, and the childishly self-indulgent Gaev declares, "They say I've eaten up my whole fortune in sweets."[98] Indeed, Chekhov keeps his audience's sympathy in constant flux in this final play, shifting from Ranevskaia's and Gaev's moving tears over their lost estate to their criminal neglect of their old retainer, Firs, and contrasting pronouncements about Lopakhin's "fine, sensitive soul" with exclamations about his tactlessness (he is having the cherry orchard chopped down before Ranevskaia can depart). And while Lopakhin revels in the triumph of the peasant over the gentry, he continues, in his bumbling way, to serve as the gentry family's friend. In the end it is clear that both parties are at fault in the cherry orchard's destruction, but we are also left with the carefully mixed impressions of a charming and wasteful gentry and a boorish and well-intentioned "new" merchant.

Chekhov's careful balancing acts of class with class and spirit with matter upset many contemporaries accustomed to a set class allegiance and behavior for its heroes. His work proved even less palatable to a new Soviet state that imposed its own class cosmology and had to "adapt" Gorky's oeuvre for its purposes.[99] Most telling, however, is the fact that Chekhov's consistent highbrow popularity in the capitalist West has elicited widely divergent views on his class bias. W. H. Bruford, writing in the late 1940s, pronounced Chekhov "a spiritual aristocrat" who "was repelled by the coarse, hard life of the peasant and 'black' worker on the one hand, and by the self-satisfied lazy life of the bourgeois intelligentsia on the other."[100] His "bourgeois" epithet curiously reverses the traditional notions of a lofty intelligentsia and a self-indulgent aristocracy. Forty years later, Gary Saul Morson pays Chekhov "the compliment of being a petit-bourgeois writer" who upheld "sober living and careful thinking, hygiene and honesty" against the intelligentsia's example of laziness, muddleheadedness, and self-dramatization.[101] These very different placements of Chekhov on a class spectrum reflect in part the elusiveness of class definition, but mainly speak to Chekhov's own elusiveness. It seems that Chekhov wrote from out of the middle at once for and against the middle; that he eschewed philistinism, but espoused good work habits; that he scorned a sentimental positivism, but equally scorned a sophisticated fatalism.

Sketching new merchants, aspiring professionals, and impoverished gentry forced into dreary jobs, Chekhov did provide a composite, if fragmented, picture of Russia's socioeconomic middle at the turn of the century. As it happened, this picture, together with Gorky's boldly colored portraits, comprised a logical end point in the "serious" depiction of the tsarist Russian merchant. Both Gorky and Chekhov complied with the long-standing documentary duty of the "serious" writer, recording the new phenomenon of the "new merchant." Themselves representative of changes in the elite establishment, both brought their own class experience to bear on the material, and this resulted in a revaluation of the intelligentsia's concept of class hierarchy and especially its hierarchy of literary heroes. Writing in a period of greater tolerance for class mobility and blending, Gorky and Chekhov restored the merchant's connection to both validating ends of the social spectrum: Gorky traced the merchant's roots in the lower class, and Chekhov demonstrated the "upper-class" intelligibility of the merchant's intellect and soul.

Nevertheless, the merchant did not cease to be a problem in their works.[102] Although these late-to-become "serious" writers did not embrace the intelligentsia's solipsism and narcissism, they readily accepted its self-conscious and self-critical habits. If Gorky and Chekhov would not glorify either *intelligent* or peasant, neither would they glorify a group between that evinced upper- and lower-class flaws as well as virtues. The mixed results of capitalism did not dispel their sense of being a privileged minority in a giant nation of the poor. Hence they painted portraits of brutish go-getters and clueless philanthropists in lieu of merchant princes and endowed their sympathetic protagonists with much of their own awareness and anguish. Perlman's hopes for the merchant's literary vindication, therefore, would have to wait out the radical reorganization of Russia's class structure, with the redesignation of victims and villains in the Soviet period, to the point of predictable counterreaction. It was only in post-Stalin literature, after all, that the fin-de-siècle "new merchant" was allowed to sire that supreme idol of the intelligentsia, the Russian poet.[103]

three

The Doll-Nation
of Polish Capitalism

Polish Heroism and the Partitions

GIVEN THE IMPORTANT SIMILARITIES between "serious" Russian and Polish literatures at the end of the nineteenth century, one might presume that the image of the "new merchant" would pose for Polish writers problems of association and inspiration similar to those confronted by their Russian contemporaries. In Poland, too, the politicized and much-valued territory of literature had long been governed by an intelligentsia no less convinced of its interpretive authority, but even larger and more gradated in its class composition. At least until midcentury, heroes who advanced in this territory also mirrored their makers as intellectuals and political visionaries, and they functioned as absolutely essential proxies for readers who could look only to literature for national fulfillment. As Norman Davies remarks, in an era of non-nationhood, "Polish Literature could always supply the nation's needs whenever Polish politics was found wanting."[1] Just as the Russian realist hero focused on the issue of social justice, so the Polish Romantic hero, a palpable influence throughout the modern period, trumpeted the cause of national sovereignty as his raison d'être and inspired many a Polish reader to incarnate his model. The main distinction between the two lay in their location of evil: whereas Russian writers generated conscience-stricken dreamers and revolutionaries against an unjust internal order, Polish writers envisioned prophesying mystics and rebels against foreign domination.

Not only diminished by upper-class myopia, the good image of the merchant in Polish literature was also tarnished by hybrid ethnicity. The middle stratum that emerged in the Polish lands in the latter half of the nineteenth century contained large percentages of Germans and Jews. The Jews in particular played a crucial role in the capitalist development of partitioned Poland.[2] If Russian writers, bent on equality with Europe, scorned their merchants for manifesting an obscurantist Russianness (or a Russian obscurantism?), then Polish writers, intent on preserving an oppressed European nation, scorned their merchants for not being primarily Polish. When the standards of Polish literary heroism prescribed passionate patriotism and Polish blood, a German or a Jewish merchant could never quite qualify.

Yet, in spite of these considerable obstacles, late-blooming Polish capitalism and its "new merchants" enjoyed a more positive literary representation than their Russian counterparts, and the secret of their qualified success stemmed from the no less important differences between the Russian and Polish political contexts. I have sketched how the tsarist empire and its literary conscience ghettoized the Russian merchant. The conditions of the Polish partitions in the Russian Kingdom of Poland delimited the merchant and his or her literary reflection in both negative *and* positive ways. Poland's dismemberment and occupation at the end of the eighteenth century had fomented a series of unsuccessful uprisings which, in turn, provoked more severe repression by the governing powers and a reassessment among Poles of how to cope with the ongoing occupation. Tsarist repression and Polish reaction were especially extreme in the January 1863 uprising; principally involved were the supporters of rebellion—a "'society' composed of the gentry, the Catholic clergy, the Westernized intelligentsia, and the urban middle class."[3] The harsh reprisals against these upper- and middle-class elements—which included execution, deportation, heavy taxation, and confiscation of property—

reshaped the position and self-image of the hero-makers, Poland's "serious" writers.[4]

In a sense, the economic bottom dropped out of "serious" literary production in Poland, and Polish authors were forced to grapple with the dilemma of professionalization several decades before Russian writers such as Chekhov and Gorky resorted to the mass-circulation press. According to Henryk Markiewicz, a leading scholar of this period, formerly affluent and independent authors

> became professional writers and treated their work as a livelihood, most often in conjunction with another profession. A writer might also work as a journalist (approximately 50%; both professions were denoted by the same term of *"literat"*), and sometimes as a teacher, professor, bureaucrat, lawyer (around 25%) or, more rarely, a landowner.[5]

As a result of the writer's changed conditions, "serious" literature in Poland reflected a variety of professional (as opposed to political) experiences and evinced a greater sensitivity to the needs and sometimes the desires of the lower classes. The professionalization and commodification of literature broadened its access for both writer and reader. This meant that the writing profession was opened up to most educated people who were willing to accept its hard terms, an openness that resulted most noticeably in an increase in women writers.[6] It also meant that the writer's new dependence on a flourishing mass-circulation press dictated a product-oriented approach to writing, with predictable emphases on quantity (for installment publication) and reader appeal. For the first time in Polish history, production of literature of all types apparently succumbed to the laws of the market.

But the market itself succumbed to the laws of the partitions. The same press that exploited the writer also served as a vital sanctuary for Polish language and literature, the remaining signifiers of a nation conquered and divided.[7] Its mass circulation and wide-ranging format (encompassing "serious" literature and daily news) equipped it to be a de facto national institution, a venue for preserving and promoting national awareness. Although the press definitely operated as a business, writes Markiewicz, its "most ambitious [publishers] tried to harmonize [its commercial aims] with national and social obligations."[8] This intriguing "harmony" of commerce and national service resonated for writers as well. Impoverished and stripped of the material privileges of class, they nonetheless behaved in print as national educators and guides. They projected a perspective that was above class, nonpartisan, and all-Polish.[9]

Their perspective might appear to reprise the lofty visions of the Polish Romantics, but, in keeping with conditions after 1863, it was trained on a more modest and workaday horizon. Deliberately setting themselves apart from the Romantics, writers in this period tailored their own version of Positivism, one that discredited attempts at rebellion and hopes for salvation from the West and instead espoused "organic work using legal means to preserve the nation and to build up its economic and cultural might."[10] They urged their readers to pursue concrete action and attainable goals, "to develop industry and trade and to foster education" rather than waste their lives on the vain dream of nationhood.[11] Writing, even literature, constituted such action, as long as it provided useful (read scientific) knowledge and inculcated good morals. The writer correspondingly served as a hardworking activist instead of a flamboyant visionary, keeping one step ahead of the reader by gathering and disseminating new information.[12] In the writer's always influential self-image, the pragmatic displaced the romantic and national aspirations were "responsibly" concealed.

This shift of emphasis and life style proved surprisingly salutary: the Positivist program of economic betterment struck gold in the Russian-ruled Kingdom of Poland. As noted in chapter 2, the tsar's incorporation of the Kingdom of Poland (demoted to "Vistula Land," Privislanskii Krai, after 1863) helped to stimulate the extraordinary economic growth of the region—indeed, to assure its primacy in the empire.[13] Afforded a vast imperial market, Poles could wield considerable economic power if they competed successfully with German and Jewish merchants in the region. The Positivists' pragmatic reformulation of political romanticism seemed to pay real dividends, at least for a short time, and economic power served as a temporary surrogate for national independence.

Thus the sociopolitical context of a post-1863 Russian Poland fundamentally redefined what could be heroic and who could be a hero, and writers obligingly produced the new scripts. In the flush of initial optimism about capitalist promise, such writers as Józef Kraszewski, Eliza Orzeszkowa, and Michał Bałucki cleared away the detritus of previous generations—the gentry's old baggage of reckless passion, self-indulgence, and dreamy impracticality—and set up their heroes in business, industry, and various other productive pursuits. These new heroes were still largely drawn from the upper class, but the plots of the newer works reflected the post-1863 exigencies of professionalization and economic recuperation. Recurring types included aristocrats who managed to save and cultivate their estates, either through scientific farming or industrialization—see Orzeszkowa's *Wacława's Testament* (1871) and Kraszewski's *Resurrecturi* (1875); aristocrats who lost their estates yet found other employment as estate steward, shopowner, or artisan—as in Orzeszkowa's *The Brochwicz Family* (1876); and professionals such as doctors, lawyers, engineers, and scholars—as in Orzeszkowa's *Last Love* (1867) and Bałucki's *The Shining Poor* (1870).[14] Positivist support of capitalism and its broadening focus on all the new "workers" in Polish society also ushered more positive Jewish characters into "serious" literature. Although the price of admission was assimilation—Jews were required to resemble other Poles as much as possible in values, allegiance, and appearance—it is significant that a Jewish merchant could attain the rank of hero in this period, a transformation perhaps best demonstrated in Orzeszkowa's novel *Eli Makower* (1874).[15]

The Positivists propounded their world view and maintained their new heroes for approximately fifteen years before the inequities and brutality of capitalism, terribly manifest in the 1880 Warsaw labor riots, forced them to reconsider their approach. In the last two decades of the nineteenth century—the literary era termed by Polish critics *mature realism* —writers did not necessarily abandon their hopes for an educated, industrious Polish society, but they admitted the real problems of capitalism.[16] They moved toward the same ambiguous position on capitalism that the Russians had reached by the turn of the century—only from the opposite direction of initial approval and, hence, with certain distinctive hesitations. Nowhere is the Polish ambivalence toward capitalism more comprehensively drawn than in the magnum opus of this later period, *The Doll* (*Lalka*, 1890), by Bolesław Prus (the pen name of Aleksandr Głowacki). Prus's mammoth text amply illustrates Poland's "serious" engagement with and approach to capitalist culture at the end of the century. The problems of capitalism, as Prus delineates them, invoke and compound problems of national heroism, national psychology, and national worth.

Capitalism and Representation in *The Doll*

The Doll's reflections of and on Polish capitalism carry particular value because the novel is in so many ways a product of its time. Prus, who followed the most circuitous and complex "path to literary success" among all the Positivist writers, wrote the novel after he had grown disillusioned with a chiefly economic resolution of Poland's oppressed and depressed condition.[17] Locating his work in the economic boom period of the late 1870s, Prus drew his characters from his own life experience and professional observation. He shared many of the same formative episodes with his hero, Stanisław Wokulski, a one-time revolutionary and scholar turned shopkeeper. Both spent their early years in an impoverished genteel family; both participated in the 1863 uprising; and both were exposed to Warsaw's Main School (Szkoła główna), the training ground for Positivists. Prus partially based the character of Ignacy Rzecki, Wokulski's right-hand man and the novel's intermittent narrator, on a real-life prototype.[18] The novel as a whole is saturated with the realia of Warsaw life, an achievement stemming from Prus's many years as a Warsaw journalist and feuilletonist.[19] (His famous *Weekly Chronicle [Kronika tygodniowa]* ran for four decades in the newspapers.) Indeed, the novel's concentrated focus on Warsaw highlights one of the three major urban and economic centers in the Kingdom of Poland.[20] As one Polish scholar concludes, the accuracy and amplitude of detail in *The Doll* qualify it as a kind of sociological study, a nonfictional fiction.[21]

Valuable as both document and interpretation, *The Doll* clearly imprints the impact of capitalist culture in its genre, structure, and discourse. The Positivist ethos in post-1863 Poland, writes Czesław Miłosz, favored the already ensconced realist novel "as the literary genre best suited to the needs of a writer-citizen and most able to convey the greatness of industry and technology."[22] In its attention to the prosaic and in its pragmatic philosophizing, the Positivist novel rebutted at length the enraptured poetry of first-generation and especially second-generation Romantics.[23] Although the Polish Positivist novel undertook more pragmatic problem solving than its Russian realist counterpart, its evolution in this period resembled the Russian model in its growing formal and ideological complexity and decreasing tendentiousness.[24]

Yet even the most esteemed and complex writers had to contend with the habits of consumption inculcated by the omnipresent press, exploiting the novel form's capacity for entertainment and prolonging its excitement over a lucrative run of installments. As one of the few authors who managed to make a living solely from his writing, Prus was keenly aware of his work's commercial value. When he describes the genesis of his book, Prus admits that *The Doll*'s great length was, at least in part, a commercial strategy:

> A few months before I began writing and after I had mapped out
> the whole text, I asked Mr. W [Józef Wolff, the editor of *The Daily
> Courier*] if I was to write expansively or concisely. He said I should
> write as expansively as possible, and that resulted in three volumes. If
> he had given me less space, I would have reduced the whole thing to
> one volume.[25]

Paradoxically, while *The Doll* was liberally injected with Prus's trademark humor and "written expansively" to sell papers, contemporary critics found fault with its extended intricate structure.[26] They argued that Prus's characters harbored too many paradoxes and that Prus, "a poet of the lower depths," could not rise above the welter of details and proffer a higher vision, a workable program.[27] Their criticism targeted the pluralism of his text, complaining that Prus had packed too many *different* traits and perspectives into his novel without attaching a clear-cut inventory. As Stanisław Brzozowski, one of Prus's early champions, explained in 1906:

> Prus was a humorist, a teller of funny anecdotes. . . . A society that
> adored Sienkiewicz was unable to appreciate much more in Bolesław
> Prus. His work was not crystal clear like Sienkiewicz's. In Prus's
> works, perspectives were constantly changing and there was a constant progression of thoughts and emotions. Of all the writers of our

era, Prus made the greatest effort to understand the social transformations taking place all around him. . . . Prus has a Balzacian sense
of social sets. Every one of his characters bears the sign of his social
stratum. . . . [Prus] creates an entire society that transforms itself and
develops, shaping individuals.[28]

Later critics have reversed these early negative judgments, finding psychological truth in his characters' paradoxes, declaring his shifting perspectives to be innovative and lauding the text's structure as a successful
amalgam of chronicle, social cross-section, and synthetic novel.[29] With
the benefit of hindsight and Mikhail Bakhtin, we can see that *The Doll*
evinces that polyphony of viewpoints characteristic of the nineteenth-
century realist novel.[30] More to our purpose, however, is the fact that
the novel's "unsuccessful" structure—its ever-branching plot and plural
perspectives—exhaustively maps the complex features of capitalist culture in the Polish context.

To begin at its foundations: the novel's primary plots struggle unsuc-
cessfully with the problems of materializing the ideal and idealizing the
material. They elaborate Wokulski's pursuit of the beautiful and almost
bankrupt aristocrat, Izabela Łęcka, her maneuvers in accepting him, and
the attendant ruminations and naive machinations of Rzecki, a career
clerk with a passion for politics and the Napoleon dynasty. Wokulski
aims to buy himself a new image and marriage to an "angel," only to dis-
card his goddess (and his business) once he is convinced that she is used
goods. A spoiled young woman in desperate financial straits, Łęcka
contrives a marriage of convenience in which her rich husband would
finance her "platonic" passions for handsome men, yet she is ultimately
abandoned by all her prospects. Rzecki tries in vain to save his friend
Wokulski from financial and moral ruin by arranging a marriage into the
ready-made family of the hardworking and beautiful Mrs. Stawska.

These main plot lines generate many secondary plots, largely through
the idiosyncratic circulation of Wokulski and Rzecki, the tradesmen
heroes, whose actions blend business (making deals, buying property,
serving customers) with sentimental or romantic altruism (philanthropic
gestures, passionate self-sacrifice). The resulting subplots highlight different angles of the misalliance of idealism and materialism. Some involve the decorous veiling of money making with noble phrases—a

gesture characteristic of the wealthy aristocrats who invest in Wokulski's cooperative ostensibly to help their "unfortunate country" but who in fact earn an unprecedented 15 percent interest. The opposite effect obtains in other plots: a character's blatant materialism proves to be the consequence of prior victimization, a fact usually revealed by a helpful spokesperson. This is the case of Mrs. Meliton, a woman taught by harsh experience to cash in her ideals and request payment for any service rendered.[31] The same scenario applies to many of the Jewish characters in the novel, who are often portrayed as both mercenary and victimized.

Perhaps most provocatively, the pursuit of sexual love is almost always portrayed as a material transaction, probably as a response to its elevation by the Romantics. The only love affairs that flourish in *The Doll* involve an indulgence of sexual appetite (if only in exchanged glances) and provide choice entertainment for onlookers. The fact that the lovely rich widow Wąsowska seems to have an almost voracious demand for admirers does not at all detract from her position as a pillar of Warsaw high society. Few are intrigued by Bela's eventual betrothal to Wokulski (although this betrothal improves her social value), but society enjoys the sideshows of infidelity and jealousy it generates. The venality of passion-as-rarefied-consumption is best revealed in Bela's cultivation of the touring virtuosos Rossi and Molinari, exposed by her idealistic lover Wokulski. Whereas Wokulski willingly carries out Bela's instructions to orchestrate a spontaneous tribute to the actor, Rossi, he recoils at the very sight of her "drugged" infatuation with the second-rate violinist and ladykiller, Molinari (572).

All of these plots, to varying degrees, imply the ambiguous, inexorable power of money and the provisional, delusive, and often self-indulgent nature of idealism. In *The Doll* Positivist teleology grinds to a human halt and diffuses into chaos. Instead of the joint progress of economic and ethical betterment predicted by the Positivists, Prus charts a whole series of individualized plot lines that rupture, dead-end, double back on themselves, or veer off on mysterious tangents. Its positive characters do not achieve well-deserved happy endings, and by the end of the novel, which is triggered by the death of the kindly Rzecki, society is poised on the verge of riots and pogroms.

Prus fragments and layers his narration to similar effect. The omniscient, editorializing narrator favored by the Positivists is displaced here by the voices of an informed, ironic observer and the well-meaning but shortsighted Rzecki. No one character or voice, therefore, is positioned to settle questions of value or purpose, a fact best demonstrated by the constant vacillation of Wokulski. Yet almost all of the characters are written to mouth a language of business and commodification—either in spoken dialogue, quoted thoughts, or the extensive monologues of certain key figures (Rzecki, Wokulski, Wokulski's Jewish friend, Dr. Szuman) who deliver larger analyses of their society. The narrative regularly eavesdrops on a chorus of voices who represent public opinion and report the latest "word" on a given character's social rating. Such choruses function, in effect, as a kind of social stock market. In aristocratic circles, the discourse of business may be refined as euphemisms or nonchalant asides (talk of marriage matches or murmurs about "gambling" debts) or relegated to private exchanges (as when the Łęckis' shrewd Aunt Hortensia speaks frankly about their financial plight [308–10]). Curiously enough, this discourse also presents human psychology and emotions in commodified terms. Wokulski, for example, analyzes his obsessive love in terms of "natural" capitalist law:

This is how nature is revenged for violation of her laws. As a young man, you despised your heart, you mocked love, you sold yourself as husband of an old woman—and now look at you! Your capital, hoarded over many years, is coming back to you with interest today![32]

Even the characters' visions come prepackaged by a commodified culture, a phenomenon that particularly applies to their visions of women. Both Wokulski and Rzecki, whose perspectives are most privileged in the text, spy obsessively on pretty women. In fact, one might posit that Wokulski's love for Bela, his "ideal," originates as window-shopping, aroused by glimpses of her in a variety of staged public settings (the theater, the church, the salon). Rzecki's noble effort to wed Wokulski to Mrs. Stawska, the woman he most loves, similarly derives from his delight in her beauty and requires that she be displayed before his friend. Romantic love represents a dressed-up continuation of shop trade. Through their appreciative gaze, the shopkeeper and the clerk transform the very women who patronize their store into elevated objects of desire, objects they do not wish to see cheaply displayed and for which they would sacrifice far more than money. Rzecki's dreams for Stawska evolve from initial delectation into ardent service and fears for her abuse; he anguishes over the fact that Stawska and her mother invite malicious voyeurism when they sit before the open windows of their apartment. Wokulski, too, ultimately breaks with Bela as a result of his recurring vision of her posed with her philandering cousin Starski. The image of Bela and Starski together, intimating a tawdry flirtation and Bela's descent into "common-ness," drives him to attempt suicide.

The Doll thus portrays a world dictated and prefigured to a great extent by money talk and commodified vision. But it also questions this world view, albeit intermittently and surreptitiously. Its characters tend to conceal what is spiritually most meaningful to them, because such feelings have little overt value in their capitalized context. Wokulski's passion for Łęcka rules his life, but he is mortified, at least in the early stages of his pursuit, when anyone speaks openly of his love. One of the most powerful and self-assured aristocrats, the wealthy duchess, refuses to divulge the tragic love story of her youth in public. (She had been in love with Wokulski's uncle, but her family's wealth and rank prevented their marriage.)[33] Yet the narrative is layered to disclose these secrets through intimate conversations, interior monologues, daydreams, other hallucinatory or premonitory visions, and Rzecki's ongoing "Memoir of an Old Clerk." It is no coincidence that those experiences identified by one critic as the most beautiful and noble in the novel—Rzecki's participation in the 1848 Hungarian campaign and Wokulski's post-1863 Siberian exile—surface only in the characters' ruminations and late-night talks.[34] In this fashion, *The Doll* traces a tentative, half-conscious, and inconclusive debate with Positivism and capitalism, a debate that takes place both tête-à-tête and in the characters' vacillating thoughts.

Dolls, Dreamers, and Clerks

Just as plot, perspective, and discourse reveal the uneasy coexistence of idealism and materialism, inchoate desire and shrewd calculation, so the characters in *The Doll* act out the varied and often contradictory options open to individuals in a capitalist Poland. Prus heightens the pathos of their situation by focusing on individual psychology. This focus not only sidelines ideological considerations, but also, conveniently enough, marginalizes any description of doing business. Prus concentrates on the psychological repercussions of commodification, not on its technology or its political ramifications; and Wokulski, a former revolutionary and present-day businessman intent on personal happiness, exemplifies that approach. Unlike the successfully adaptive heroes of early Positivism, Prus's "heroes" are rendered as living paradoxes who embrace what might seem to be the mutually exclusive roles of visionary and shop clerk, dreamer and doer, consumer and consumed. The title figure of the doll serves as a touchstone for these contradictions, for it evokes quite different and self-revealing responses from each of the characters. By way of analyzing this complexly drawn cast, I focus here on its main players—the female protagonists, Łęcka and Stawska, and the three male "idealists," Wokulski, Ochocki, and Rzecki.

Although I will argue that both female and male characters are consumed in the capitalist labyrinth of *The Doll,* the women are most susceptible to commodification by virtue of their restricted professional and social position. As I have noted, Prus frequently puts women on display, implying that their beauty and charm are purchaseable goods. The spectrum of female characters reveals the degrees of their commodification, from the open prostitution of Marianna, a fallen woman sponsored by Wokulski, to the aristocratic Bela's fluctuating value as a marriage partner. They all are (or were) dolls for sale and, like the trademarked doll that vindicates Mrs. Stawska's reputation, they are to be imprinted with the name of their legal owner.[35] Even the affluent "independent" women (the duchess, Mrs. Wąsowska) have to marry to acquire their wealth.

On the other hand, virtually all of these women exercise the considerable privileges of the consumer, whatever their obligations as paid-for wives and fiancées. No one is more adept in this role than Izabela (Bela) Łęcka, the object of Wokulski's obsession, and her patterns of consumption reveal much about a "top-heavy" Polish world view. Born into the upper aristocracy, possessed of exceptional beauty, Bela is raised in a most refined "dream world" of consumption in which the specifics of time, place, and weather are erased by unvaried pleasure:[36]

> A veil shielded her from the wind, a carriage from the rain, furs from
> the cold, a parasol and gloves from the sun. And thus she lived from
> day to day, month to month, year to year, above other people and
> even above the laws of nature. (38)

Elaborating the mentality of Bela and her set with barely veiled sarcasm,
the narrator defines her as the epitome of the conspicuous consumer, an
upper-class daughter who fulfills her family duty as totemic and discriminating shopper and who sincerely believes that life consists of eternal
delectation and always obliging servants.[37]

Despite her pampered upbringing, Bela is resigned to marrying well
rather than happily. Yet she justifies both her incipient commodification
and her current consumerism as sacrifices to the ideal of maintaining the
aristocracy. Prus draws Bela's ways of thinking and consuming to reflect
the particular mentality of the Polish upper class—a sense of God-given
feudal privilege enhanced by a peculiarly romantic, self-indulgent glorifi-
cation of the supposedly noble past. Bela's lodestar is not Mickiewicz,
the bard of tragic love and national revolt, but her "distant cousin,"
Zygmunt Krasiński, who, in her misreading of him, unambiguously beati-
fied an embattled aristocracy in his famous play, *The Un-Divine Com-
edy* (1833). Bela's ideal not only expiates her sale in marriage, but also
sanctions her sumptuous life style, her aristocratic consumption for the
enjoyment and edification of her "inferiors."[38]

The values of beauty, pleasure, and piety therefore commingle in
Bela's mind. She sees no contradiction between self-sacrifice and self-
adornment, serving God and going shopping. In one characteristic episode, her reading of the religious tract, *The Act of Resignation,* convinces
her "that her prayers have been heard, that she will have the most beautiful dress and the smartest church for the Easter collection."[39] Her devotion consists of making pretty vestments and accessories for the church
(e.g., a cord for a church bell) and gracing worship services with her well-
attired presence. Bela's conflation of beauty with piety is the more con-
sonant because she dissociates beauty from fleshly desire. Her one great
love is a statue of Apollo (she managed to obtain a "fine copy" for her
boudoir), and she herself figures as an angel or a goddess to her would-
be lovers. In Bela's assessment, the doll as either desired object or as a
reflection of herself is an art work to be cherished.

It is no wonder, then, that even an impoverished Bela refuses to sell herself into bondage and abide by what Wokulski claims are contractual obligations. She interprets marriage as provision, not purchase, and she presumes that her husband will allow her to circulate freely and to consume whatever pleasures she desires, including that of another man's company. In a sense, she conceives of herself as a treasure to be collected and given proper public display. She asserts her rights before her presumed "patrons," flirting with her cousin Starski while betrothed to Wokulski and subsequently pining for Wokulski (in the company of a sympathetic admirer) when she is almost engaged to a rich old marshal of the nobility.

Predictably, Bela's suitors do not share her philosophy. They insist on possession or at least exclusivity rather than patronage, and they interpret her circulation "crassly" as common use. Pained by his angel's fall into the flesh, Wokulski even likens her to "a restaurant napkin which anyone may use to wipe his mouth and fingers" (661). Once Bela is abandoned by her patrons, she must drop out of circulation altogether; her father dies of apoplexy (his maintenance depended on her sale); and she is last reported to have entered a convent. This final act is wonderfully appropriate. Since Bela cannot be assured patronage in a commodified marriage, she chooses to array herself among the other beautiful objects in a safely spiritual sanctuary. Although she can no longer consume at will, she need no longer fear her own possession, and she is still counted among beautiful things, albeit in a less worldly way.

Like so many characters in *The Doll,* Bela can be paired with a number of illuminating doubles—the wealthier and more visceral consumer, Mrs. Wąsowska, or the inept consumer commodity Evelina, who is divorced, disinherited, and shamed by her aging former husband. Helena Stawska figures as Bela's true antipode in this commodified schema. Stawska also attracts attention with her "spiritual" beauty when Wokulski first spies her in a church. Stawska is also constantly displayed before and coveted by men. In a curious twist, her pretty little daughter actually enhances her value, for her male admirers clearly relish the thought of making both mother and daughter their own.[40]

Yet Stawska's commodification is prevented by her unclear marital status (her husband is a fugitive from justice) and by her paradoxical efforts to remain both self-sufficient and altruistic. Deprived of a provider-husband, Stawska barely supports her all-female household with piano lessons. Her awareness of her admirers' attention produces only confusion and blushes; in lieu of purveying herself as commodity or treasure, Stawska opts for the very relative autonomy of paying her own way. Thus, her attempt to purchase an expensive doll in Wokulski's shop in part underscores her earned rights as worker and consumer. A working mother and a single parent, she specifically buys the doll to give pleasure to her little girl.

Like Bela, Stawska resists the baldly materialistic implications of a commodity culture, but she counters Bela's aristocratic self-gratification with compassionate self-sacrifice. Despite her own straitened circumstances, Stawska blends work with charity. She earns to serve others. Wokulski notices that she is "never concerned about herself" (555), and Rzecki astutely surmises that she would serve as Wokulski's true helpmate in contrast to the trophy wife he intends to marry. Stawska's angelic nature, unlike Bela's angelic looks, is rooted in familial devotion and solicitude, striking virtues against the novel's general background of failed marriages and families wrecked over money concerns.

Of course, the altruistic Stawska would probably not survive but for the intervention of Wokulski, who secretly subsidizes her purchase of the doll, defends her successfully from charges of theft, and provides her with lucrative work. As I will elaborate in my analysis of Wokulski, Prus softens the harsh edges of capitalist culture with the individual and sometimes incredible philanthropy of his characters. Yet what remains intriguing about Stawska's case is her peculiar path to salvation. She is not only able to combine paid work with good works, but also, as a beautiful woman destined for purchase, she is vouchsafed autonomy and a wider scope for her virtue through the bequest of a shop. Warsaw society may gossip that Wokulski's benefaction attests to their illicit relations, but his acts are designed to vindicate and empower her. He first hires her as a cashier, demonstrating that this accused thief merits his trust, and he ultimately finances her own store, thereby transforming her once and for all from potential commodity into owner. That Stawska sets up shop in the holy city of Częstochowa may be sheer coincidence, but this location symbolically reinforces her connection of business with goodness. In any event, Stawska appears to suffer none of the disillusionment that causes Wokulski to forsake his trade, and she remains to the end a shop-keeper, married a second time to one of Wokulski's most talented and handsome clerks.

Just as the characters of Bela and Stawska defy certain gender stereo-types (neither is ultimately sold), so the male protagonists in *The Doll* experience some of the mistreatment traditionally allotted to women. The conditions of commodification level them all. It is particularly significant that the novel's hero sells himself into marriage and consents to being his rich wife's doll, escorting her to parties and the theater and indulging her emotional whims. Moreover, Wokulski resorts to none of the loopholes utilized by Bela and Stawska (the presumption of worship and/or auton-omy), for he interprets his sale as a binding contract and abides by its conditions to the letter.

Wokulski's commodification, along with the other hardships he en-dures, provides him with a crucially affective pedigree, a point of empa-thetic engagement with the reader. Prus makes his hero a victim many times over. Wokulski belongs to a genteel family that has lost its wealth and rank; his efforts to educate himself elicit ridicule from his peers; his participation in the 1863 uprising results in his imprisonment and exile; his failure to find work necessitates his sale into marriage; and his ill-starred pursuit of Bela utterly devalues his business success. Therefore, although this businessman hero does not redeem himself through na-tional service, his individual strivings and sufferings conveniently divest him of the stigma of the mercenary. And his business dealings take place discreetly in the wings. Prus's contemporary, the Positivist journalist Aleksandr Świętochowski, was quick to discern how Prus glossed over the possibly dirty details of how Wokulski made and kept his money. In their stead, Prus deploys certain characters to defend the hero's honesty and industry before the insinuations of the crowd.[41]

In fact, as sporadically represented, Wokulski's business dealings seem almost entirely motivated by romanticism and altruism. The shopkeeper is born of the dreamer; money making is always a means, not an end. Wokulski first prostituted himself in order to stay alive, and he atoned for his loveless marriage by dedicating himself to the cause of his wife's business. After her death, when he was on the verge of returning to sci-ence, his first love, the sight of Bela compels him to bring home a fortune,

much like the quest hero winning his bride. He succeeds in business, in
large part, through friends with whom he shared harder times and higher
ideals—the Russian merchant Suzin, whom he met in Siberian exile, and
his trusty lieutenant Rzecki, who housed him when he was poorest and
talked politics with him when he was most stifled by his marriage.

In tandem with, and often in consequence of his romantic quest,
Wokulski becomes a random philanthropist. Wandering lovestruck about
the city, he happens on various individuals who awaken him to pity and
action: the prostitute Marianna, the destitute carter Wysocki. When he
buys the Łęckis' building to save Bela's face and dowry, he proves to be
a most benevolent and enlightened landlord, lowering the rents of the
virtuous and tolerating the residence of madcap students who pay no
rent at all. While some of these gestures are calculated to improve his
social standing and further his quest, for the most part they represent
genuine acts of kindness and ennoble his image as a mere "tradesman."
Yet, unlike Stawska, whose altruism seems all-pervasive, Wokulski cannot function on good deeds and conscientious behavior alone. Although
he agonizes over his selfish and financially extravagant love for Bela, he
recognizes it as his primary motivating force, one that overwhelms even
his love for science.

Because Wokulski incarnates the paradox of an unmaterialistic pur-
veyor of material goods, he can never quite reconcile his ideal of Bela
with Bela's ideal of conspicuous consumption. His interior monologues
conduct a constant self-critique as he wastes money on "show" and assiduously cultivates the ways of the nobility—buying and racing horses,
learning English, fighting duels. He castigates himself in part for divert-
ing resources that would be better spent on the poor, in part for aping a
code he does not really respect. Like his money making, his consumption is devoted to the cause of romance. He makes many of his purchases
(the Łęckis' dinner service, their building) behind the scenes in order to
save Bela's reputation; when he consumes for show, he buys to surround
Bela with the proper tribute, even to the point of outfitting himself as
her proper escort. In a telling admission, he likens his spending to Bela's
various ploys "for self-advertisement and marriage":

> "Or take such a trivial thing as a carriage. . . . If I had one, I could
> have sent her home with her aunt in it, and another bond would have

formed between us. It would cost a thousand roubles a year, but that can't be helped. I must be prepared for all eventualities. . . . A carriage, English lessons . . . more than two hundred roubles for one Easter offering? And I am doing all this, I who despise it. However, what am I to spend my money on, if not to ensure my own happiness? What do theories of economics mean to me when my heart aches?" (96)

In sum, Prus's businessman hero keenly feels both the power and the limitations of money. In a world where virtually all achievement (including class status) is achieved financially, Wokulski's fortune constitutes a prodigious feat that can and does generate other feats—helping a family to survive, redeeming a prostitute, maintaining dependent friends, funding important scientific work. New to his own wealth, Wokulski constantly marvels over the good his money can do, and the burden of its moral potential weighs heavily on his conscience. Yet in relying on the power of money, Wokulski comes to wield it as the sole instrument for achieving his ideals—a strategy that ultimately dooms him, the dreamer and the rebel, to the vicious circle of consuming and being consumed. Once his ideal topples from her imagined pedestal and divests his commercial dealings of their "higher" goal, this seeker descends into a carnal sphere of sheer physical satisfaction, sleeping and eating heavily, leafing through picture books, armchair traveling, and lusting after pretty women, with only the vague dream of scientific endeavor (appropriately presided over by an inventor named Geist) to aerate his venal existence.[42] Although Prus leaves his hero's fate deliberately unclear, it is significant that Wokulski physically disappears, whether by suicide or flight abroad, and his sole legacy is money in the form of bequests to others. In the end, the extraordinary businessman who worked his way up from one kind of dollhood and dreamed beyond the materialism of his trade is reduced to speculative legend and the impersonal circulation of cash.

Whereas Wokulski enacts the grandest and most dynamic model of the dreamer merchant, Rzecki, his humbler companion and the novel's second narrator, offers a significantly different experience and perspective. In choosing to be a career clerk, Rzecki might well suggest the terrible limitations of Nikolai Gogol's subhuman Akakii Akakievich or Herman Melville's blighted Bartleby. But Rzecki fascinates us in the ways he manages to wed his clerking and the life of the shop with a persistent, if often somewhat ludicrous, idealism. He warmly evokes the shop through childhood memories and family feeling, a connection manifest in opening and closing scenes in which the clerk happily plays with the dolls and toys on display. Rzecki has retained a childlike enjoyment of the shop's merchandise that dates back to his boyhood observations:

> I had known Mincel's shop for a long time, for my father used to send me there to buy paper, and Aunt for soap. I would always hurry there with joyful curiosity to look at the toys in the window. As I recall, there was a large mechanical Cossack in one window, which jumped and waved its arms by itself, and in the doorway were a drum, a saber and a wooden horse with a real tail. (17–18)

Rzecki enters the trade after his father's death makes him an orphan, and the shop owner, Jan Mincel, along with Jan's mother and two nephews, soon function as the clerk's surrogate family and school. Old Mincel not only disciplines him in shop values (his object lesson is not to steal), but also introduces him to the world through its commodification, teaching him geography, science, and math by way of explaining the source, use, and price of the goods he sells: "We would go through each drawer in the shop and he would tell me the story of every article" (21). Shop and shop owner shape Rzecki's sense of space, time, and human nature, and inculcate in him the values of daily routine, service, and camaraderie.

The one value Rzecki does not absorb from his master (and in fact must conceal from him) is his cult of Napoleon, inherited from his working-class father. The diligent clerk harbors a lifelong passion for the politics of revolutionary liberation and its embodiment in the Bonaparte dynasty; his father's portraits of the French emperor seem to taunt his aunt's more conventional pictures of the saints. Witnessing how his father easily trades a soldier's uniform for a doorman's, Rzecki sees no conflict between being a good clerk and worshiping Napoleon. Although the senior Mincel's unexpected hatred of Napoleon momentarily confounds him, the opposite enthusiasms of Mincel's nephew Jan and of Augustus Katz, another clerk, convince him to stay in service.

Indeed, far from imposing a bourgeois ethic on the quixotic young

Rzecki, the Mincel shop, divided into "two great factions," preserves and abets his political idiosyncrasies. Once Rzecki finally acts on his convictions and runs off to fight for the liberation of Hungary in 1848, he is joined by the taciturn Katz, who eventually commits suicide when the revolt fails. Rzecki's return to Poland, long prohibited by his revolutionary expedition, is subsidized by a sympathetic Jan Mincel. Readmitted into the Mincels' cozy family circle, Rzecki regales everyone with talk "about the yearnings of exile, the discomforts of a soldier's life, or of battles" and even the hausfrau grandmother, who lives only to provide the creature comforts of coffee and rolls, weeps repeatedly over his tale of Katz. Within the larger context of Poland's national repression, then, this shop of Polonized Germans represents a curious safe haven, a happy melting pot of bourgeois habits and romantic recollections.

Rzecki's duties as a clerk resemble more monastic (or revolutionary) service than white-collar job. His training involves serving and saving, not consuming. Old Mincel summarily discharged clerks who did not save some of their wages: "Not saving, or rather not putting away even a few groszy every day was as terrible a crime as stealing in the eyes of Mincel" (22). When Rzecki introduces himself to the reader as one of the few remaining "good clerks," he opines that a clerk should sell rather than wear fashionable collars, a remark that sums up his own self-effacing image. The manager of a haberdasher's shop, he seems willfully oblivious to fashion, dressed in laughably out-of-date clothes, inhabiting a spare cell of a room, wholly invested in serving the shop. In a curious reversal of Bela's church of conspicuous consumption, Rzecki transforms the shop into a sanctum and a cause, relinquishing its glories to a buying public and embracing the role of self-abnegating acolyte. Whereas Bela puts herself on display, Rzecki, keeping behind the scenes, dutifully takes responsibility for the display's arrangement and, somewhat like his altruistic employer, Wokulski, never presumes to buy for himself. His discomfort with his own consumption actually confines him to this shop-sanctum, for his dress makes him ridiculous elsewhere and the prospect of more sumptuous quarters only agitates him.[43] His limited forays into a consuming world simply extend or substitute for the "family ways" of the shop. Increasingly distant from his old friend, Wokulski, the clerk ventures out for food, drink, companionship, and talk. He apparently longs to recreate, by whatever means possible, that amalgam of comfort, intimacy, and divulged ideals he enjoyed at the Mincels' home.

It is no accident that Rzecki undertakes this quest as Wokulski retreats from his business and his very image as a businessman. For Wokulski, the Mincels' successor, had become Rzecki's intimate and idol, a man whose energy, drive, and vision earned him a Napoleonlike status in the old clerk's eyes. More attracted to individual role models than to political programs, Rzecki worships Wokulski as his post-1848 ideal, and he mulls over the significance of his every word and deed. As Wokulski makes one puzzling move after another in his pursuit of Łęcka, Rzecki refuses to accept a romantic explanation and instead pays his employer the ultimate compliment of reading his actions politically. All of the gambits prompted by Wokulski's love for Bela—his hands-on investment in the Russo-Turkish War, his flight to Paris, his hobnobbing with the aristocracy—Rzecki enthusiastically interprets as the covert campaign of a merchant-Napoleon; in his view, the shop is already a hallowed place and the exceptional person of its owner assures it some kind of grand, vaguely political destiny. Even when Wokulski sells the store and disappears, abandoning his business to the less enlightened supervision of the Jewish merchant Henry Szlangbaum, a dying Rzecki manages to find momentary inspiration in his absent friend Stas:

> A sharp pain in his chest reminded him he ought not to tire himself. Yet he felt tremendous energy within: "Stas has set to some great work," he thought, "Ochocki is going to join him, so I too must show what I can do.... Away with dreams.... The Napoleons aren't going to set the world to rights, nor will anyone, and we shall go on behaving like lunatics." (697)

Thus, although Rzecki's sentimental synthesis of clerking and revolutionary dreaming threatens to unravel with the depersonalization of his shop, he never suffers total disillusionment. His health fails and his loneliness leads to more late-night drinking with his friends, but he does not give up his dreams, and he leaves a far more affecting and personalized legacy *in writing* than Wokulski's monetary bequests. As silly and obsolete as Rzecki may have seemed in a post-1863 Poland, Prus privileges his cozy, small-scale, person-oriented idealism by granting him narrator status. Just as Rzecki entertains the Mincels with his tales of the military campaign, so he is allowed to engage the reader with his memoir's intimate recollections and ruminations. His blend of the material and the ideal is thereby rendered most sympathetic and most accessible, a source of psychological solace and comic relief, but definitely not a plan of action. Indeed, the only action Rzecki attempts involves maintaining the status quo. The two letters he pens just before dying propose opening yet another shop, building yet another refuge. Much like Stawska (the person he loves most after Wokulski), Rzecki proves the virtue of the good clerk and the human value of the doll, but he cannot realize any grander plans. His one convincing contribution to a better world remains his companionable talk of dreams.

The last idealist in *The Doll*, the young aristocrat and scientist Ochocki, is the least explored protagonist, hovering in the margins of cast and plot until he emerges as the surviving heir to a dead Rzecki and a vanished Wokulski. Ochocki represents an altogether different intersection of class and world view, one that at least augurs the brightest future. An aristocrat who circulates freely in Bela's world, Ochocki is at times caught up in courtship transactions, seduced into the cipher role of escort by Mrs. Wąsowska, and appraised as a potential suitor. But unlike Bela and Wokulski, Ochocki faces commodification as a temptation, not a necessity. He must struggle with ingrained habits rather than economic hardship. As he explains to Wokulski, he will not marry: "'I couldn't support a poor wife, a rich one would make a sybarite out of me, and either one would mean the end of my plans'" (666). Interestingly enough, his flight from high society is eventually underwritten by embittered suitors. Baron Dalski wants to divert his fortune from an errant wife and to place it in Ochocki's capable hands, and Wokulski settles the lion's share of his wealth on the young scientist. Possessed of financial independence, Ochocki realizes that he must leave Poland altogether to be free:

"Even putting aside the absence of a workshop, we don't have a scientific climate here. This is a city of careerists, among whom a real scholar passes for a boor or a madman.

"People here don't study for knowledge, but for a position; and they acquire a position and celebrity through social contacts, women, parties, goodness knows what else! I've bathed in that pond. I know genuine scholars, men of genius, suddenly brought to a halt in their development, who have taken to giving lessons or writing popular articles which no one reads or, if they do, they fail to understand." (649)

Exempted from clerking and freed from dollhood, Ochocki seems equipped to attempt great deeds. He has already proved his talents as an inventor and, for the most part, he demonstrates both psychological sensitivity and a social conscience. His appreciation of Wokulski as "a man of wide soul" reflects his perspicacity and elicits Rzecki's enthusiastic approval. Yet within the carefully limited purview of the novel, Ochocki is featured mainly as an articulate dreamer. We glimpse him as he muses over future inventions and yearns to devote himself to work in a better world beyond Poland. Ochocki is forever at the point of embarkation, forever expressing the sentiment encoded in his name. (*Ochota* can be translated as *readiness* or *desire*.) While his desires are clear of the pernicious romanticism that cripples Wokulski, this seems more the result of inexperience than voluntary triumph: Ochocki draws a naively materialist equation between the sufferings of failed love and the unanesthetized removal of a toenail (648). His dreams of a life devoted to science, a laboratory abroad (where a scientific climate is presumably possible), and a helpmate-wife may be at once less pedestrian than shopkeeping and more realizable than Wokulski's freighted love and Rzecki's Hungarian expedition, but, most important, these remain untried. We cannot know if he will succeed Wokulski as hero and better him in his achievements, because Ochocki has not lived enough to negotiate any plausible synthesis.

The New Merchant and Polishness

Individually, all the protagonists in *The Doll* demonstrate the possibilities and perplexities of survival in a commodified world, their responses ranging from a familial sanctification of trade to renunciation and retreat. On a larger thematic scale, the novel also calls into question whether Polish society can survive capitalism. Whereas the early Positivist novels offered pragmatic solutions and do-it-yourself heroic models, Prus's text features divided or ineffectual heroes and poses trenchant questions about the goodness and efficacy of capitalism and the capitalist. Writing in the late 1880s, Prus significantly chose to review the boom period that inspired earlier works.

In a brilliant and provocative article, Jan Kott argues that *The Doll* inscribes the characteristic progress of capital gain from patriarchal establishment to anonymous international cartel, yet the novel stops short of delivering a critique of capitalism, targeting instead a high-living and do-nothing aristocracy.[44] Markiewicz generally seconds this observation, noting that Prus reserves his main attack for an upper class that thwarted Positivist aspirations and insisted on its feudal privileges.[45] Yet another critic remarks that the aristocrats' bad example dominates Polish society in *The Doll* and infects the classes immediately below them; in other words, the upper class sets a kind of national standard of misbehavior that breaks down into the discrete flaws of immaturity, irresponsibility, elitism, idleness, and garrulousness.[46]

It is clear that Prus consistently satirizes his aristocratic characters. His narrator shrewdly dissects their parasitic function in a newly capitalist Poland, rendering them marvelous illustrations of Veblen's theories. As Bela's example indicates, the novel amply describes the ideology and practice of conspicuous consumption—the meritorious display of wealth and leisure, the careful masking of actual labor and production. The aristocrats' habits of consumption seem the more parasitic (or the more meritorious, depending on one's point of view) because they themselves almost never function as producers. They are mere investors, not industrialists or merchants, and they rely on intermediaries to conduct their business.

Yet it would be reductive to claim that the novel invokes the problems of capitalism for the sake of demonizing the Polish aristocracy and nationalizing its sins. Such characters as Rzecki and Stawska demonstrate that the novel delineates a wide variety of Polish attitudes toward labor and consumption. Indeed, its most favored Polish characters espouse the Positivist values of diligence and industry. Moreover, as if in defiance of a determinist capitalism, these good Positivists prove to be the least materialistic and the most compassionate figures. Wokulski, Rzecki, Stawska, Ochocki, even the carter Wysocki do not revolt against the capitalist system, whatever its injustices to them. They neither succumb to its blandishments nor enforce its Darwinian laws. Moreover, in *The Doll*'s scenario of a moderate, individualized revision of capitalism, Polish socialists are marginalized or disarmed, and the most nihilistic figures in the novel, the three students squatting in the Łęckis' old building, win clemency through their antics, not dogmatic agitation.[47] The anarchist spokesman for the trio delivers his pronouncements through Rzecki's narrative, and the old clerk labels him an "unusual young man" —an anarchist softened into a comic eccentric—and good-naturedly tolerates his financial irresponsibility.

Thus, the novel roughly divides its Polish characters into committed workers and committed, often aristocratic, consumers, and the contrast between the two camps conveys a quite relative critique of the selfish and exclusionary aspects of capitalism. Furthermore, one feature of the consuming aristocracy transcends their generally negative characterization: this might be described as their refined charm, their performed nobility or *szlachetność*. The "worker" Poles do not willingly emulate the aristocrats' extravagance and idleness, but they stand in awe of their social grace and occasionally "noble" gestures. The same Wokulski who scorns required table etiquette at the Łęckis' dinner party later acknowledges that "it is more agreeable to live with these gentlemen than with tradespeople. They really are beings made from a different clay" (196). Despite Rzecki's dismay over his friend's entanglements with the aristocrats, he admires the panache they flaunt in the face of adversity. Rzecki is very impressed by Tomasz Łęcki's august appearance while on the verge of bankruptcy and by Baron Krzeszowski's civility after Wokulski wounds him in a duel (210, 282). In fact, the figure of the baron epitomizes the devastating charm of the aristocracy. Somewhat like the antic students, the baron's comic figure tempers any ideological stereotype. He more than compensates for his prejudices, hot temper, and whopping debts with bravery and acts of public contrition. In addition, the irascible nobleman compares quite favorably with his long-suffering, but manipulative and middle-class wife. It is he who undoes much of the damage she perpetrates through her unscrupulous intermediary, the "fallen" aristocrat Marusiewicz.

Within the value system of the novel, the "positive" Pole in a capitalist

Poland emerges as neither wholly bourgeois nor anti-aristocratic. Rather, it seems desirable that the new merchant, the new power broker in Polish society, should evince the vague aura and signal gestures of *szlachetność*. The aristocrats, of course, discern such qualities in their chief business adviser, Wokulski, all the while assuring each other of his noble pedigree. At the other end of the spectrum, the unassuming clerk Rzecki celebrates Wokulski as a super-merchant, a man who magnifies his already worthy profession. Wokulski's clients and employees, in turn, attest to his nobility, compounded by compassion and conscientiousness, once he has passed from the scene. Through individual testimonials and hearsay, we learn that the soldiers in the Russo-Turkish War counted on the goodness of Wokulski's bread, that Wokulski managed his store with generosity and flair, that even the antiestablishment students judged him to be a good landlord.

Yet if Wokulski represents the new super-merchant and therefore the culmination of several decades of Polish merchant heroes, he also represents the new super-Pole, a man who, distressingly, would transcend his nationality. Through his constant metamorphosis and quest, this hero tries out various connections between national identity and capitalist success. Wokulski has been held up as the only Polish character in the novel to succeed as a shopkeeper (sandwiched between the German Mincel and the Jewish Szlangbaum), but his "wide-souled" nature already constitutes a hybrid of presumably national traits and international influences.[48] Wokulski first enters an interethnic alliance in the 1863 uprising, where he, an impoverished Polish gentleman, joins forces with assimilated Jews committed to a free Poland. His acquaintance with Dr. Szuman and Henryk Szlangbaum, his shop's subsequent owner, dates from this period, and he remains loyal to these comrades in the increasingly anti-Semitic climate of the late nineteenth century. His defense of the Jews distinguishes him from every other Polish character in *The Doll*, including the democracy-loving Rzecki.[49]

It is during this period, too, that Wokulski is befriended by the Russian merchant Suzin, a relationship he maintains regardless of his Polish patriotism and one that yields him his fortune. Wokulski's partnership with the hardheaded and big-hearted Russian testifies to his practicality and cosmopolitanism (requisites for financial success), but it also suggests a moral ambiguity his champions are anxious to dispel.[50] In the standard version of *The Doll,* which still bears the 1890 Russian censor's imprint, we see little of this partnership up close. One scene excised from this version, however, draws a convenient moral line between Suzin's jovial materialism (he advises Wokulski to "buy" Bela) and Wokulski's too sensitive Polish "heart." Chiding his friend for being "a mindless Polish noble," Suzin expostulates: "'This is what ruins all you Poles. You respond to everything—business, politics, women—with your heart. And in this lies your stupidity.'"[51]

In general, Wokulski must modulate his Polishness in order to do good business. We have considered the supposedly Polish trait of nobility that sanctions his trade in Polish eyes, yet, as the Polish characters are the first to admit, this trait alone cannot make him a financial success. As the prince enlists Wokulski to become the director of their cooperative, he admits that his peers cannot fill this position because, in spite of their "intelligence and noble hearts," they lack the necessary initiative (107). The prince's self-critique is constantly reiterated in *The Doll.* The other characters therefore herald Wokulski as a magnificent exception to his compatriots, different by virtue of his initiative, energy, pragmatism, and ability to act. Wokulski's aptitude seems to them positively un-Polish.

One might argue that Wokulski is following in industrious old Mincel's footsteps, schooled and enabled by other German tradesman to work hard and to prosper.[52] Yet given the novel's deliberately polyphonic structure, it is extraordinarily significant that the Jewish characters most vocally and repeatedly claim this aspect of Wokulski as their own. In direct contrast to the Poles who celebrate "nobility" as his saving grace, the Jews discover that his superb business skills redeem him from a Polish nobleman's usual ineptitude. Szlangbaum senior, Henryk's father, singles out Wokulski for special favors and, like Rzecki, refuses to criticize his imprudent actions, although he chooses to read them as sharp financial schemes rather than political conspiracy (191). In yet another demonstration of respect, the Jewish creditors besieging the Łęcki household desist once they receive Wokulski's word promising payment (315).

Wokulski is also echoed and analyzed through Jewish doubles. Dr. Szuman serves as the hero's keenest confidant (he analyzes whereas Rzecki nurtures) and his more cynical soulmate. The doctor has similarly experienced revolutionary fervor, romantic defeat (his love affair was destroyed by religious differences), suicidal despair, a deep commitment to science (he classifies types of human hair), and a passing attraction to business. Having suffered through a series of bitter disappointments, all exacerbated by anti-Semitism, Szuman seems well equipped to interpret a questing, suffering Wokulski. He divines the central paradox of the hero's personality—his Romantic and Positivist duality—and he waxes angrily eloquent over his friend's self-destructive love, blaming Wokulski's tragic waste on the Polish Romantic cult of woman and love (325–26). As a Jew "educated among you [Poles]," the doctor combines an insider's experience with the critical distance of the outsider in diagnosing Wokulski's peculiarly Polish pathology—his perversion of normal biological appetites with the illusory fruits of a "clergical-feudal-poetic theory of love" (327).

Although the financially independent doctor has long since abandoned his medical practice, he nevertheless takes it upon himself to cure his friend. This cure evolves in consequence of Szuman's changing attitudes toward his Jewishness. Repelled by the terminal disease of Polish civilization, the doctor at first articulates Jewish models as the antidote. He contrasts the wasteful extravagance of the Łęckis to the sensible money making of the Szlangbaums, and unions between frivolous Polish women and lovesick Polish men to prudent Jewish marriages in which husband and wife work together toward a common financial goal (562, 564). Yet when his new heroes, the Szlangbaums, attempt to cheat him, the doctor revises his program accordingly. As he keeps watch over Wokulski's recuperation from despair, he spells out his new perspective:

> "Just now the instincts of my forebears are beginning to awaken in me . . . a tendency to business. Oh, Nature! How I wish I had a million rubles, in order to make another million, and a third. . . . And become Rothschild's younger brother. Meanwhile, even Szlangbaum is deceiving me. I've moved for so long in your world that in the end I've lost the most valuable attributes of my own people. . . . But they're a great people; they will conquer the world, and not by common sense, but by cheating and boldness." (628)

Embracing the complex package of his Jewishness, Szuman nonetheless distinguishes between the "bad" Jews, who (in his words) are orthodox, reactionary, and particularist, and the university-trained, cosmopolitan "good" Jews with whom he allies himself. His cure for Wokulski, which prescribes an end to dreaming and the satisfaction of normal appetites (food, exercise, sex, intellectual stimulation), also includes an invitation to join the "good" Jews in business. Szuman perceives Wokulski's superior "Jewish" nature in his business acumen, his capacity for action, and, intriguingly, his persecution by other Poles: "'You only lived on equal footing with them, as it were, for a year—and what have they done to you?'" (629).

Whereas Szuman perceives Wokulski as a potential Jew who must be cured of his Polishness, Wokulski's other Jewish double, Henryk Szlangbaum, mistakes Wokulski as an already achieved Jewish role model. Szlangbaum, like Szuman, had at one time attempted assimilation, but changes course upon his return from Siberian exile. In *Poles and Jews: A Failed Brotherhood,* Magdalena Opalski and Israel Bartal posit that Szlangbaum's eventual reclamation of his Jewish identity reflects a general shift in the educated Jewish community as it barricaded itself against growing anti-Semitism after 1863.[53] Not only does Szlangbaum desire to replace Wokulski as store owner and director of the cooperative, but also he emulates the hero's cultivation of the Polish aristocracy—concluding, as he says, that "'a lot is done for the sake of social contacts'" (560). On all accounts, Szlangbaum's aping of the nobility is a misconceived and cheap imitation, the result of misapprehension or, perhaps, vindictiveness born of long persecution.

Both Szuman and Szlangbaum make an appeal for Wokulski's investment, whether financial or personal, after the hero has rejected Bela and is most disposed toward change. Yet Wokulski responds to both by withdrawing. In his relations with Szlangbaum, his withdrawal signifies resignation rather than endorsement; it is clear that he does not want to be associated with a "bad" Jew, although he allows one to buy him out. Dr. Szuman's cure, on the other hand, produces a more ambiguous effect, at once intellectually convincing and emotionally alienating:

> Szuman also claimed that the great majority of men are animals, but he neither believed in a better future, nor did he offer this consolation. For him, the human species was condemned to eternal animalism, in which only the Jews stood out like pike amidst minnows.
>
> "A fine philosophy, indeed," thought Wokulski. However, he felt

that Szuman's pessimism would soon flourish in his own wounded soul, as in a freshly ploughed field. He felt that love for Isabella was dying in him, and so was his anger. For if the whole world consisted of animals, there was no good reason to be insane about one of them, or to be angry because she was an animal, no better and certainly no worse than others. (636)

Despite its pragmatic appeal, Wokulski ultimately rejects Szuman's proposal to identify with the "good" Jews. Although he continues to defend the Jews' honor before charges of their "humbug, double-dealing, and trash" (Rzecki's words), he seems repelled by the prospect of conducting business for business's sake, and he sells off all the tokens of his merchant self.

In the terms of the novel, therefore, Wokulski renounces the distinctive features of both his native Polishness and his honorary Jewishness. In response to the prince, who urges him to remain "'a golden bridge between us and those who . . . are increasingly drawing apart from us,'" he declares that he "has been sawn away underneath" (639). Not only does his renunciation suggest the difficulties of being such a bridge, but also it implies a critique of both sides of the span. To be sure, the intermingling of these traits seemed to be the key to Wokulski's business success. Unlike his fellow Poles, Wokulski is able to amass and tend a fortune; unlike his Jewish peers, he earns a certain grudging admiration from the Poles and is granted conditional entry into aristocratic society.

But the value of his hard-earned success remains in question, and this question, in turn, applies to the various national role models depicted in *The Doll*. Wokulski finds no attractive ideal among the final options: the self-indulgent Bela, the self-sacrificing Stawska, the sentimental Rzecki, the university-trained and would-be businessman Szuman, the as-yet-unapplied scientist Ochocki. Although Wokulski's business sense and "nobility" accrued him a fortune, that fortune and his romantic dreaming yield no grander accomplishment and eventually plunge him into despair. In Prus's post-1880 fiction, financial gain and upward mobility do not translate into personal happiness or spiritual fulfillment; their value fades with the fading of the hero himself. The ascendancy of the likes of Szlangbaum and the dishonest character Marusiewicz in the final scene complete this devaluation, as a number of critics have remarked.[54]

More important, Wokulski's problematic cosmopolitanism prevents him from dedicating his fortune to a nationalist cause. Resisting Szuman's arguments for Jewish solidarity, he claims to "'despise the community, but sometimes respect individuals'" (630). He handily deflates the prince's pleas to support Polish industry with comments about the foreign financial backing of Polish businesses and the aristocracy's prejudice against merchants. Indeed, far from renewing his 1863 pledge to Poland, Wokulski faults his country for his own hard life and unhealthy mind-set. This judgment erupts during his visit to Paris. Overwhelmed by this center of European civilization, the Polish merchant hastily concludes that here he would find the meaning, approval, and support he had missed in a Polish "there":

> "Am I to go back there? What for? Here at least I have a nation living by all the talents which with man is endowed. Here the foremost places in society are not occupied by the mildew of dubious antiquity, but by essential forces that strive onwards—labor, intellect, will-power, creativity, knowledge, skill and beauty, and even sincere feelings. There, on the other hand, labor stands in the pillory, and depravity triumphs! He who makes a fortune is called a miser, a skinflint, a parvenu; he who wastes money is called generous, disinterested, open-handed. . . . There, simplicity is eccentric, economy is shameful, artistry symbolized by shabby elbows. There, in seeking to acquire the denomination of a man, one must either have a title derived from money, or a talent for squeezing into drawing rooms. Am I to go back there?" (407)

Normally an astute critic of class and ethnicity, Wokulski is so entranced by Paris that he can actually envision his happiness in a long-capitalized West. He muses that his country is too feudalistic, too parochial, too poor, and too melancholy to cultivate him, whereas "the eminent people I meet here don't have even half of my powers, yet they leave behind them machines, buildings, works of art, new ideas" (386). According to his example, the new Polish merchant may succeed initially in his own country because of his cosmopolitanism, yet may achieve great things only in an international (and preferably Western) context.

Returning once again to the question of Wokulski as a heroic model and that model's relationship to capitalism, we can see that while capitalist values restrict what Wokulski does and perceives he can do, these are not his only, and perhaps not even his main, stumbling blocks. For Wokulski, as for most of the other sympathetic characters in *The Doll*, doing good business is never an end in itself, but a means to a still unclear goal—whether that be technological progress or a cozy environment for a surrogate family or a base from which to perform good works. Wokulski, the character with the widest soul, is destined to discover this goal or die in the attempt. In a characteristic move for an nonideological individualist, he deludes himself for much of the novel with the personalized ideal of Bela—a goal apart from politics, high finance, art, or God. Yet, even in moments of disenchantment, he prays desperately for an alternative; after Bela is deposed, he shops once more for a motivating ideal. Indeed, Wokulski's agony over meaning and fulfillment, depicted extensively and with high seriousness in the text, links him most readily with the dramatically questing near-heroes of the great Russian realists—with the likes of Konstantin Levin in Tolstoy's *Anna Karenina* and Dostoevsky's Karamazov brothers. Wokulski graduates from the ranks of commendable nation-loving Positivist merchants to attain the grandeur of the tragic hero.

Yet, significantly, Wokulski's demons differ from the westernized devil that talks Ivan Karamazov into a brain fever. The West, rife with capitalist endeavor and the cult of reason, fills him with inspiration rather than corruption. In this pilgrim's eye, the horrors of capitalism, so vivid in Warsaw, are swept away by the cultivated, purposeful frenzy of the Parisian streets. It is his own underdeveloped, self-absorbed, dream-crazed nation that undoes Wokulski—at least for the moment. Capitalism produces terrible inequities and commodifies all meaning—flaws clearly evident to Wokulski—but what he particularly objects to is the current Polish incarnation of capitalism, an incarnation he also holds responsible for spawning the negative features of Jewish trade. His final act, whether it is obliterating suicide or definitive flight, confirms in either case his critique of his Polish context and context-determined identity.

In *The Doll*, therefore, the phenomenon that alternately allures and repels, dynamizing and problematizing the hero's progress, is neither capitalism nor the West, but a kind of national psychology sharpened by capitalism. It beckons in Rzecki's cozy chat and the surface charm of the upper class; it evokes disgust in the aristocrats' selfishness, Bela's narcissism, Wokulski's slavish devotion, and the Jewish characters' mercenary counter-response. On the basis of this interpretation, the novel's title figure can be read as a multivalent national image, a doll-Poland that elicits a tender, familial love as well as idol worship. Whether it inspires misguided dreams or affords addictive comfort, the doll-nation nonetheless remains a human counterfeit, unable to satisfy the needs of its doting and deluded "owners." It seems only fitting that the Jews, persecuted into a hard-nosed materialism, would move to commodify it. When Rzecki last plays with the shop's toys, this time lamenting their capacity to injure one another, Szlangbaum, through his stool pigeon Gutmorgen, significantly misinterprets the clerk's innocent play as possible theft. In the novel's judgment, a doll-nation that will not develop beyond its dollhood, that resists "living by all the talents which with man is endowed," is doomed to be a plaything, a product to be bought and sold. In the end, Poland's weary, would-be Pygmalions take flight, and the doll-nation reverts to its creditors.

"In Wokulski's Footsteps . . ."

In light of the complexity of his character and the exhaustiveness of his social critique in *The Doll*, it is altogether understandable that Wokulski produced no literary heirs. Certainly no other contemporary Polish writer matched Prus's achievement. Rather, as if acknowledging (and avoiding) Wokulski's unique status, the merchant heroes that appeared in his wake pursued the paths he deliberately rejected. The path of least resistance and most widespread appeal led directly to the patriotic merchant, and this was taken by the extraordinarily and astutely popular Henryk Sienkiewicz. After making his fame with historical fictions about a once glorious Poland, Sienkiewicz tried his hand at an uplifting saga about present-day capitalism in *The Połaniecki Family* (*Rodzina Połanieckich*, 1895). He designed the novel's businessman protagonist as a positive antipode to the "superfluous" antihero of his previous novel, *Without Dogma* (*Bez Dogmatu*, 1891).[55] His positive hero, concludes Markiewicz, is "an energetic speculator who makes enough money to buy back his wife's estate, returns to the ranks of the landed gentry, and rediscovers the meaning of life in family happiness."⁵⁶ *The Połaniecki Family* answers *The Doll's* incessant questions with easy platitudes about good works and the good life, and its untroubled protagonist "combines his financial skills with the conviction that he is serving both God and Country."⁵⁷ It is intriguing that Chekhov ridiculed this nationalist celebration of the merchant as covertly and cloyingly "bourgeois," a product contaminated by class bias rather than nationalism.⁵⁸

As I will show in chapter 4, the Połaniecki option was readily exercised and more simplistically interpreted by more popular (or, according to Polish terminology, "second-class") writers well into the twentieth century.⁵⁹ Yet even much less positive "serious" portraits continued this patriotic tradition, as is evident in the figure of Karol Borowiecki, the protagonist of Władysław Reymont's *The Promised Land* (*Ziemia obiecana*, 1899). A character who for all intents and purposes represents an overdetermined negative to Wokulski's open-ended positive, the aristocratic Borowiecki ruthlessly sacrifices class image, family feeling, a clean conscience, and a good Polish woman in order to stake out his own factory in the midst of Jewish- and German-owned plants in the great textile center of Łódź. Already a generation removed from Wokulski, Borowiecki has been schooled to be practical and for the most part abides by the self-evident premise that business success preempts romantic love and national allegiance.⁶⁰ Reversing Wokulski's pursuit of the beautiful Polish aristocrat as ideal, Borowiecki abandons his Polish fiancée for the comely daughter of a German factory owner and sells off his patriarchal estate without a shred of regret. But this dark portrait of an ambitious and unscrupulous industrialist does feature a silver lining in Borowiecki's superior business acumen, his commitment to high-quality goods (this in contrast to his non-Polish competitors), and his eventual pangs of conscience. Dissatisfied with mere financial gain, the weary Borowiecki is final-framed as an incipient national hero:

> Borowiecki had calmed down. He had found his future path and clearly saw his future goal. He broke with himself, fully rejecting his past and feeling himself to be a new man—a sad man, but strong and determined to fight.
>
> Very pale, he had aged noticeably over the course of that single night. A deep wrinkle was etched on his brow, as if a sign of determi-

nation, chiselled by painful realization, had settled and frozen upon his face.

"I've lost my own happiness, but I must make others happy," he whispered slowly, and his strong, manly gaze, like strong and resolute arms, embraced the sleeping town and those elusive spaces looming out of the night gloom.[61]

In this case, even the seriously compromised businessman is vouchsafed redemption and transcendence, made sympathetic as a Polish David among "foreign" Goliaths and projected as a hero in some indeterminate, but undeniably grand and presumably national cause. Although Reymont's ending sharply and perhaps unconvincingly reverses the relentless money making and mechanizing dynamic of the novel, this note of national promise is also accented by Borowiecki's last meeting with his jilted fiancée. The young woman who renounced her genteel way of life—her old Polishness—now devotes herself to the city's poor children, the nation's future.[62]

In a sense, Borowiecki demonstrates the necessary limitations and compromise that a post-1880 Wokulski would have had to endure and which Prus interestingly avoided. This hero's devotion to business results in a wholly anti-idealistic cosmpolitanism. The questions of siding with Pole versus Jew, or with "good" Jew versus "bad" Jew are immaterial and therefore moot; Borowiecki serves as a "bridge" because that is the only way for a Pole to do business in Łódź. As a matter of course, the novel focuses on the specific contexts and practices of prominent German and Jewish industrialists, highlighting, in turn, their very different social leap from lower to upper class. These merchant families resemble more the Russian merchant families found in the works of Chekhov and Gorky than the newly mercantilized gentry of Polish fiction.

In so doing, *The Promised Land*, like *The Doll*, registers the ethnic tensions of Polish capitalism without designating absolute scapegoats. Far more frequently, however, the figure of the patriotic Polish merchant prompted the demonization and, much later, the defensive valorization of his most expendable competitor, the Jewish merchant. As Opalski and Bartal observe, a host of Polish novels by such writers as Klemens Junosza-Szaniawski, Artur Gruszecki, and Teodor Jeske-Choiński cast the Jewish merchant as the "spider" who ensnares and destroys the poor Polish "fly."[63] These novels conveniently cleansed Poles of the sins of capitalism, ascribing these to the "unethical" and still unassimilated Jews. In tandem with the naturalists' pessimistic emphasis on biological determinism and the modernists' "fantasizing about the Jewish psyche and culture," their approach "reinforced the perception of the Jews as alien and threatening" in fin-de-siècle Polish literature.[64]

Contemporary Jewish writers and journalists quickly responded to these misrepresentations with their own patterns of idealization and demonization, exposing the latent anti-Semitism of the once progressive Pole and exploring the new possibilities of a Jewish nation independent of either the Russian empire or an oppositional Polish society.[65] Yet the major Jewish novels about fin-de-siècle Polish capitalism emerged only several decades later and in the United States—a continent away—as if they required a safe haven in time and space from which to deliver their critique. As exemplified by Israel Joshua Singer's *The Brothers Ashkenazi* (1936) and Isaac Bashevis Singer's *The Family Moskat* (1950), these works scouted yet another path not taken in *The Doll*, for they differently elaborated the perspectives expressed by the Szumans and the Szlangbaums. They mirrored and countered the Polish cultivation of the merchant-patriot with their own defensive ethnic self-absorption. These novels mainly differed from the Polish texts on account of the formative extremes of the Jews' persecution. Their organization by family implies that the family unit is the largest "community" the characters can hope for; their chronological purview seems set by a sense of impending or realized cataclysm (in Bashevis Singer's novel, the Holocaust); and their representation of Jewish capitalists, however negative, is tempered by an awareness of the Jews' excessively restricted condition.[66] Even Israel Singer's novel, *Brothers*, which echoes and amplifies *The Promised Land* with its cynical focus on Łódź and critical depiction of the different ethnic parties involved, articulates a convincing justification for Jewish economic progress. Observing the negative protagonist, Max Ashkenazy, in a rare moment of self-reflection after his brother's murder, the narrator quotes his rallying cry in full:

> The strength of Israel lay not in physical force, but in intellectual superiority, in reason. Since time immemorial, gentiles had persecuted, mocked, and oppressed the Jew, and he had been forced to keep silent because he was in exile, because he was a helpless minority, a lamb among wolves. Could the lamb then oppose the wolf? . . .

Had Jews adopted the gentile's ways, they would have already long since vanished from the face of the earth. But the Jews had perceived that theirs had to be a different course, and it was this perception that had lent them the moral strength to endure and to accumulate the only kind of force the gentiles respected—intellectual and economic power.

This was the strength of the Jew and his revenge against the gentile. Not with the sword, not with the gun, but with reason would the Jew overcome. It was written: "The voice is Jacob's voice, but the hands are the hands of Esau." The Jew lived by his reason; the gentile, by his fists. For hundreds of years Jews had danced to the gentiles' tune because they were too few to resist. In times of danger the Jew was obliged not to sacrifice his life, but to appease the wild beast in order to survive and persevere.[67]

While Max's brother Yakub had achieved comparable financial success with greater charm and "heart" (he is both a happy philanderer and a doting father), he perishes on account of his "gentile" sense of honor when he slaps a Polish officer who "would have the Jew dance." It is the outwardly compliant Max who escapes to reclaim his title as "king of Łódź." To a more desperate extent than the Polish Positivist, the Jewish character ghettoized in late nineteenth-century Polish society could rely only on the power of money. If Jews were not to be assimilated and/or destroyed, these novels implied, then they could not afford the luxury of Wokulski's isolation and divestment and vestigial "Polishness." Szuman's rather cynical philosophy of getting together and down to business remained the only viable mode of survival, although these retrospective novels forecast a final destruction in any case.

According to these examples, the ethnic tensions in Polish capitalism and the victimization felt by both Poles and Jews eventually resulted in the partisan development of the capitalist protagonist. Polish capitalists recaptured Polish glory or reenacted Polish martyrdom; Jewish capitalists persevered for separate survival. In the meantime, the capitalist per se was being targeted in Poland as well as in Russia as the perpetrator of the workers' misery, as a character corrupted by class rather than ennobled by nation. These various attempts to nationalize or class the capitalist effectively boxed in a hero with Wokulski's wide and uncommitted soul. Wokulski's paradoxical embrace of altruism and business acumen, *szlachetność* and a strong work ethic, a Polish "heart" and anti-Polishness, proved increasingly difficult to write.

It was also increasingly difficult to read. In the most bizarre twist of Wokulski's considerably twisted legacy, the Polish reading public transformed Prus's novel and its protagonists into national idols, public dolls. Various writers reductively celebrated Prus's complex work as a sentimental evocation of "old, middle- and lower-class Warsaw," a reading later resumed in the writing of émigrés uncritically cherishing the past.[68] In the period of independent Poland (1918–1939), a society that was struggling to empower its emerging bourgeoisie and improve its economy embraced Wokulski and Rzecki as cult heroes and real-life role models. Specifying this legacy, Stefan Godlewski, a frequent contributor to the *Warsaw Gazette (Gazeta Warszawska)*, penned a cycle of sonnets entitled "In Wokulski's Footsteps" ("Śladami Wokulskiego," 1937) and responded in essay form to readers' requests to locate the novel in present-day Warsaw.[69] In great part owing to Godlewski's initiative, two commemorative plaques honoring Wokulski and Rzecki (complete with Wokulski's date of birth and Rzecki's date of death) were affixed to their presumed places of residence in March 1937.[70] Commemoration proved to be concretely inspiring: in a speech delivered at the 1937 Great Congress of Christian Merchants, Andrzej Wierzbicki heralded Wokulski as a paradigm for the new Polish capitalist, a man who combines "a strong character, a pioneering initiative, the blazing of new trails, and the creation of beautiful and permanent things on a grand scale."[71] Wierzbicki's response to this literary figure is particularly interesting, for although he misses the crucial ambiguities in Wokulski's character, he ascribes to Wokulski the same accomplishments Wokulski ascribes to the French. Wierzbicki either overlooks or disregards Wokulski's Polish complex. The hero's tragedy lies not in his nationality, he implies, but in the fact that other Poles do not yet realize the Wokulski in their national heritage.

In this fashion, Wokulski's footsteps came to trace a self-regarding circle rather than a path forward, and Prus's masterpiece succumbed, at least for a time, to the phenomenon it so richly evoked. Whereas the texts of the Polish Romantics, written in the painful aftermath of war and national dissolution, were divined as a call to arms, Prus's work, produced in an era of long-term foreign occupation and commercialization, was embraced as yet another beloved doll by readers who cherished and showcased every token of their national greatness before and after the granting of Polish independence. In comparison with the ambiguous and sometimes sympathetic merchants found in fin-de-siècle Russian litera- ture, the figure of the Polish merchant, even in its "serious" incarnations, was irresistibly filtered through this doll legacy, at rare moments achiev- ing complexity and high tragedy, but almost always inscribed or endowed with a "Polish heart" and assured of the reader's sentimental engagement.

four

The Birth of the Middlebrow?
Russian and Polish Romances

As CHAPTERS 2 AND 3 ILLUSTRATE, by the end of the nineteenth century "serious" literature had become a more market-driven, professionalized, and inclusive enterprise, recruiting and reflecting the talents of a wide array of authors. In Russia the former street urchin Maxim Gorky spectacularly crashed the gate of "serious" literature and exhorted others to follow him through the breach. In the Kingdom of Poland, the esteemed writer Bolesław Prus coped with the vagaries of professional writing, maintaining himself through his journalism, expanding his creative work to sell journal issues, and explicitly commenting on the Polish writer's hard lot. Chapters 5 and 6 will show how the audience for "serious" works was also growing and diversifying as the mass-circulation press targeted and engaged new sets of readers.

Parallelling the transformation of "serious" literature was the burgeoning production of popular works throughout the tsarist empire in the latter half of the nineteenth century. Other scholars have copiously documented this phenomenon, listing the contributing factors outlined in chapter 1: emancipation of the serfs, industrialization, urbanization, greater class mobility, rising literacy rates, improved printing technologies, expanded transport systems, and the emergence of new commercial publishers either from abroad or from the same lower classes addressed by the market.[1] It is significant, too, that the intelligentsia in both Russia and Poland ventured to take charge of this kind of literary production in order to supplement (and conceivably replace) its harmful diet of commercial formulas with the "good spiritual food" of "good" literature.[2] This they attempted by specially composing works for the "folk" or by issuing popular editions of the "classics."[3] Indeed, Markiewicz cedes almost total control to a literary elite: "With few exceptions, [popular-folk prose] was the work of the intelligentsia [in all the partitioned sections of Poland]."[4] Whatever the extent of their involvement, their participation indicated, on the one hand, the similarly inclusive nature of popular literary production and, on the other, the intelligentsia's presumption of its necessary authority.

As these different producing groups overlapped, more and more hybrid works appeared that variously combined "serious" and "popular" forms and functions and hence did not quite fit at either end of the literary spectrum. As Polish literary historian Janusz Dunin observes, such works "had nothing in common with the gutter press," comprising instead a form of "literature *sensu stricto*."[5] Some of these texts were conceded to be "serious" works of "second rank"; such, for example, was the general critical opinion of the novels of Maria Rodziewiczówna, a prolific Polish author.[6] Others, like the novels of the Russian Anastasiia Verbitskaia, achieved a "best-seller" popularity (a new phenomenon in that part of the world) that overwhelmed the issue of their critical ranking, much to the dismay of "serious" critics who wrote harsh reviews to limit their currency and expose their corrupting influence. The problem of categorizing these texts raises larger questions about our understanding of the relations between literature and the market in fin-de-siècle Russia and the Kingdom of Poland. How did these hybrid texts express and assess the capitalist culture to which they explicitly owed their existence? Did that culture at last produce in them a positive mirror? Can we announce them as the birth of the middlebrow in Russian and Polish literatures?

The Middle and the Middlebrow

To begin to answer these questions, we need first to consider the audience for such texts, to determine whether they were addressed to or, in the classic consumer dynamic, demanded by a middle-class readership. After all, the concept of the middlebrow, coined in the United States in the 1920s, supposedly took shape in response to the needs and desires of middle-class readers. The very creation of the middlebrow presumed the existence of an audience willing to acknowledge its middle-class status and to consume a literature that purveyed certain desirable class-specific characters, images, and plots. Was there a middle to be marketed to in these societies?

In the Russian case, it appears that the answer is a qualified no. Resisting the temptation to impose Western conceptual grids on scattered Russian data, Western scholars in particular deny the existence of a coherent middle class in late imperial Russia. They point to the deep ethnic, religious, regional, and economic divisions that prevented the middle social groups from coalescing into a single class; the clear separation of professionals from entrepreneurs in this professionalizing society; and the cross-class condemnation of the bourgeoisie as a composite of selfishness, coldness, and greed attributable to non-Russian ethnic groups, such as the Germans, the Jews, and (interestingly enough) the Poles.[7] As Samuel Kassow, James West, and Edith Clowes aptly observe, such new social groups as professionals, industrialists, and artists "were defined by what they were not: They were not gentry, not *chinovniki* (bureaucrats), not peasants."[8] Although these groups adopted much of the intelligentsia's mind-set—its social conscience and vaunting of education and culture—they differed markedly over such issues as individual self-interest and a need for a private life.[9] Rather than fashioning a positive image of themselves as "middle," many of these disparate groups tended to conceive of themselves as segments of the intelligentsia "with a difference."

Notwithstanding their "bourgeois" reputation among Russians, the middle groups in the Kingdom of Poland faced a similar identity crisis plagued by even deeper ethnic divisions.[10] The mass exodus of Jews from the countryside earlier in the century (1827–1865) produced a sizable growth in the Jewish populations in major cities and the emergence of a distinctly Jewish "middle."[11] As *The Doll* showed on the most developed economic map of Warsaw, an incipient Polish "middle" necessarily competed with Jews, Germans, and Russians for financial prowess in the latter half of the century, and this sense of international competition somewhat lightened the stigma of being perceived as bourgeois. At the same time, this loosely constituted middle echelon was flooded with bankrupt nobility and impoverished members of the intelligentsia in the aftermath of 1863, and the influence of these articulate writers, critics, artists, and students effectively prevented the development of a positive bourgeois self-image. Like their Russian counterparts, the Poles in the middle of the social spectrum were ill-defined and, what is more important, displeased by currently available middle-class labels. If anything, they were more vehement in distinguishing themselves from the "bourgeois" Germans, the "mercenary" Jews, and the "rapacious" Russians. They, too, aspired to some upper-class or beyond-class identity more along the lines of the intelligentsia or even the aristocracy than those of a bourgeoisie.[12]

In both contexts, therefore, the middle did not cohere into a recognizable middle-class market ripe for middlebrow products. There seemed to be no programmatic need for a middlebrow culture, or at least the sort of middlebrow culture shrewdly designed and marketed in the United States some decades later. Although the American middlebrow was redefined pejoratively by the likes of Virginia Woolf and Dwight Macdonald, it was put forth originally as a positive concept, and its literature was to bridge the gap between precious genteel art and vulgar mass-produced culture, furnishing "a genial middle ground."[13] The American middlebrow was to engage the vast numbers of "fairly civilized, fairly literate" men and women who eschewed crass commercial fiction, yet also felt alienated by a too rarefied highbrow literature. While it clearly developed under the influence of the market, it also implied a moral critique of a highbrow art that failed to address basic human concerns or to make that address accessible to a general readership.

In the main, readers in imperial Russia and the Kingdom of Poland could not level such a charge against their "serious" literary works, for both literatures were traditionally freighted with pressing moral and philosophical questions. In fact, until the advent of modernism at the turn of the century, "serious" writers in both the Russian realist and Polish Positivist traditions were virtually obsessed with the accessibility, relevance, and ethical impact of their books. In these contexts, a middlebrow literature could not possibly improve on "serious" literature's noble intentions. The hybrid texts could do no better than aspire to "serious" status, and many of these were duly packed with the philosophical discussions and the implicit or explicit moral messages that flagged them as "serious" for the reading public.

Nonetheless, certain aspects of "serious" Russian and Polish literatures apparently dissatisfied these inchoate, non–middle-class middles, problems which, judging by their extreme popularity, the hybrid texts seemed to redress. These works do overlap with Western middlebrow writing in their explicit anticipation of reader desire and their aspiration to respectability. They self-assuredly vaulted the divide between what the elite prescribed for the literate public and the cheap, derivative, popular material that the public clearly preferred to consume.[14] Fin-de-siècle writers were not the first to attempt this, but a flourishing publishing industry enabled them to do so on a mass scale and a dramatically commercializing society approved their self-indulgent visions.[15]

For, like the middlebrow literature of twentieth-century America, these texts were overtly connected with the market, displaying and endorsing all kinds of consumption. Rather than skirt material temptations and ennoble self-sacrifice—common thematic turns in Russian realist and Polish Positivist novels, as we have seen—these texts presented consumption as a notable and worthwhile activity. This is not to say that they made heroes of gluttons and sybarites, but that they recognized the appeal and symbolism of material pleasures for a wide range of readers—extending from those weary of the intelligentsia's sermon of self-renunciation down the socioeconomic ladder to those who could only just afford such goods. These texts also resembled American middlebrow literature in intimating that proper consumption was a kind of education, a justifiable means of buying one's way to a more cultivated and experienced self. Many of these narratives laid out a rather simplistic, conveniently pragmatic path to true cultivation that never fully dispensed with the notion of innate goodness of character but emphasized the incredible results obtained from special schools and select acquisitions and tours.[16]

Just as these texts sanctioned the private material indulgences afforded by a new commodity culture, long criticized in "serious" literature and generally desired in fin-de-siècle Russian and Polish society, so they voiced new notions of the self partly abetted by consumer dynamics. In this way, too, they predicted certain developments that would take place in the American middlebrow. Their characters embodied the contemporary fascination with "personality" that spotlighted the newsworthy and sensational individual in preference to the model citizen or, more specifically, the positive heroes proposed by "serious" writers. This cult of personality, a popular phenomenon entirely different from the later legislated Stalinist "cult," neatly dovetailed with the emergence of unprecedented assertions of individualism in Russian and Polish culture at this time.[17]

The new modernist movements in literature and the fine arts also championed the artist's subjective expression as a growing commodity market sought to elevate and exploit the consumer as an infinitely desirous, infinitely needy individual. The hero or heroine with "personality" thus came to function as an exclusive product that combined personal distinction (both physical and temperamental), extraordinary charisma, and high emotions for the reader's unique enjoyment. The last feature was very important, for the cult of personality placed a special premium on emotional indulgence and emotional release. Such characters were to feel as well as think for the reader. The "personality" in the text also figured as a model consumer, a character who knew what and how to buy to attract attention and admiration, and how to inspire the reader to do the same. These functions frequently applied to the author as well, for many of these best-selling writers cultivated a real-life celebrity and maintained a loyal readership through their public gestures and flamboyant life style.[18]

Reading the Russian and Polish Romance

Do these points of consonance mean, therefore, that the Russian and Polish texts constituted a de facto middlebrow, a literature that anticipated and catered to a potential bourgeoisie, yet, like that undeclared "middle," insisted on its highbrow status? Or did these works effectively subvert middle-class values and middle-class scripts?

The extraordinary variety of these texts precludes a categorical answer, and I propose instead a closer comparative evaluation of two "block-busters" of this period—the six-volume *Keys to Happiness* (*Kliuchi schast'ia: Roman daidzhest,* 1908–1913) by Anastasiia Verbitskaia and the slightly less voluminous novel by Helena Mniszek, *The Leper* (*Trędowata,* 1909).[19] These works—Russian and Polish, respectively—qualify as representative hybrid texts not only because of their incredible popularity, but also because they constitute variations on the popular romance, a genre that over the last two centuries has become steeped in Western middle-class virtues and desires. Indeed, with its evolving focus on the marital fortunes of the middle-class woman, the popular romance neatly registered the growing dominance of the middle class in Western societies and the concomitant twin phenomena of more leisure time for women and more women authors finding a ready livelihood by writing for a female or female-inclusive audience.[20] Throughout its post-Renaissance evolution, the popular romance recreated a context in which the middle-class heroine attracts a wealthy, upper-class, gift-giving admirer whom she eventually domesticates for marriage and family life. Tania Modleski thus summarizes its script:

> In the classic formula, the heroine, who is often of lower social status than the hero, holds out against his attacks on her "virtue" until he sees no other recourse than to marry her. Of course, by this time he wants to marry her, having become smitten by her sheer "goodness."[21]

Like all good middle-class women, the popular romance heroine consumes to submit and submits to consume some more, all the while teaching her lover to respect her (i.e., to propose marriage) for doing so. Her lessons extend to her readers: Western feminist scholarship contends that late twentieth-century popular romance explicitly caters to a middle-class female readership with its promises of escape from household drudgery ("a disappearing act") and its visions of a fulfilled female self nurtured by a man "of almost feminine sensibility."[22] Whatever its common attractions, the popular romance flourishes today as one of the most wildly successful commodities of late capitalist culture—written to order, sold in supermarkets, and consumed by millions of readers.[23]

Both Verbitskaia and Mniszek were primed to realize this success by their particular situations and economic contexts. Both came to writing through the professionalization of the upper classes in their respective societies. A daughter of a nobleman, Verbitskaia worked as a governess, teacher, proofreader, and journalist before she could earn a living by writing fiction. The noble-born Mniszek, twice widowed and the mother of four daughters, did not look to writing for her livelihood and never sacrificed creature comforts for a "writing life," but she found inspiration in contemporary women writers and psychological refuge from domestic tedium in her quite astonishing graphomania.[24] Despite their mass production of texts, both conceived of themselves as "serious" writers, and both benefited to a surprising degree from a rapidly growing "in-between" literary market.[25] Jeffrey Brooks credits Verbitskaia with the innovation of the best-seller in Russia, her popularity attesting to the broad attraction of her work.[26] Mniszek's first novel truly took the market by surprise, confounding the critics who had already dismissed it as a derivative failure.[27]

In adapting this genre to their own contexts, Verbitskaia and Mniszek borrowed and embellished on some of its key features.[28] In addition to starring a nonaristocratic heroine and her rich, upper-class lover, their novels assiduously display the fancy goods, estates, and tourist sites designed to tantalize the reader with opulent living and armchair travels. True to middlebrow purposes, consumption in these texts serves at once to gratify and to educate. In her analysis of *Keys to Happiness,* Laura Engelstein notes the "endless excursions through museums, antique ruins, and moldy palaces" dutifully interjected into the life story of the heroine, the barefoot dancer à la Isadora Duncan, Manya El'tsova.[29] *The Leper* lavishes attention on the sumptuous surroundings and elaborate ceremonies of the well-to-do, thereby initiating uncultured and deprived readers and conveying what Teresa Walas calls the "form and order of love."[30]

Both texts also showcase a charismatic heroine—a protagonist with "personality" whose features I will analyze in the following section. But, above all, these texts' imported focus on the romance of the romance— on drawn-out courtship and sensual thrills—makes them unusual within their respective national traditions and asserts their anticipation of the middlebrow. In *Keys to Happiness* as well as in her other novels, Verbitskaia was one of the first and most remarked-upon writers to foreground women's sexual desire, a topic doubly proscribed in nineteenth-century Russian literature with its constant critique of fleshly appetites and its general privileging of a male perspective.[31] While Mniszek did not venture the same sort of focus in *The Leper,* she deviated from national tradition in attempting the romance genre, for in a Polish literature burdened with national fulfillment and social service, "the theme of love had dwindled to the sensible level of emotional motif, a support for the plot and a concession."[32] If Verbitskaia had to smuggle in sex, then Mniszek had to smuggle in a full-blown love story, and both gambled heavily on their characters' emotional appeal to make them acceptable.

Such signs of an incipient middlebrow literature alarmed the "serious" critics, who intriguingly echoed (or presaged, as the case may be) other highbrow critics in ascribing a vulgar materialism and immoral emotionalism to female authors. Russian and Polish critics reiterated a general European tendency to link women readers and writers with a "mass culture" of "serialized feuilleton novels, popular and family magazines, the stuff of lending libraries, fictional bestsellers and the like," in tawdry contrast to "genuine" folk culture or the masterpieces of fine art.[33] Yet, whatever their critical disrepute, Verbitskaia's and Mniszek's novels did not simply import Western models. Both writers relied on native traditions to establish important themes and suggest contextual relevance. Given the absence of a self-declared middle class and their awareness of an unsatisfactory status quo (definitely not a staple of the Western popular romance), both writers had to adapt the genre's characters, plots, and conclusions to their own purposes. As a result, they produced quite different versions of consuming heroine, providing hero, facilitating context, and illustrative plot; they rewrote the popular romance as a different sort of product for Russian and Polish readers.

What Class Heroine?

As in most popular romances, the plots of *Keys to Happiness* and *The Leper* hinge on the heroine's nature and her progress. Readers are to identify with a sympathetic and attractive female protagonist and to experience her courtship, conquest, and domestic success vicariously.[34] In

Western romances, the middle-class heroine provided those points of access. Rarely a stunning beauty, she was sure to be courted for her nature rather than for her looks or her money. Unaccustomed to luxury, she proved to be a quick student (and implicit teacher) of conspicuous consumption, even as she retained the superior traits of middle-class modesty, kindness, and virtue. Her final reward combined the moral satisfactions of the middle class (the constitution of marriage and home) with the physical satisfactions of the aristocracy (a luxurious life style, a sexual partnership with a handsome and experienced man).

Verbitskaia and Mniszek also opted for an attractive, other-than-upper-class heroine, but they had to improvise her accessibility, with intriguing consequences. Like so many romance heroines, Verbitskaia's Manya El'tsova extensively samples the life of the affluent without being "to the manor born." Yet a review of her family, class, and nature reveals an unusually complex profile of a heroine divided and conflicted. Manya is born into an impoverished gentry family and is both stigmatized and favored because she is illegitimate—the product of an illicit affair. Her long-suffering half brother and half sister carefully screen her from their mother's mental illness (there is definitely a madwoman in Manya's attic), and lovingly indulge her ambitions and whims, sending her to an exclusive boarding school in Switzerland, allowing her to vacation with her wealthy friend Sonia, and ultimately helping her to embark on an unorthodox dancing career. Striking, but not unequivocally beautiful, passionate in spirit, and driven by an insatiable hunger for beauty, Manya takes heedless advantage of her siblings' sacrifice. She clearly thrives on lovely surroundings and lovely things, whether created by nature or furnished by the tasteful rich.

Her appreciation, however, is not covetous. As her devoted teacher, Frau Kessler, explains at the beginning of the novel, Manya is impetuously attracted to things, but they "have no hold over her soul." In the habit of borrowing beautiful jewelry and forgetting to return it, Manya simply behaves "like a princess."[35] Manya later confirms this judgment by labeling herself "a gypsy and a terrible egoist" (1:123). Her princess-cum-gypsy nature, which conveniently identifies her with two charismatic extremes against the middle, also harbors the virtues of devotion, self-sacrifice, and a capacity for "noble" suffering.[36]

Manya emerges, therefore, as an absorbingly paradoxical "personality," as a poor bastard and a coddled princess, an incipient madwoman and a child of nature, an altruist and a hedonist. The same dichotomy marks her sexual behavior. Although Manya displays great sexual appetite and almost no prudery, she plays the part of victimized virgin and tender mother figure with the man she loves most, despite the fact that he rapes and impregnates her. In much the same way, she alternates between a delectating cosmopolitanism and a heartfelt nationalism. Entranced by the beauties and opportunities of Europe, yet drawn to the landscapes of home and concerned about the plight of the Russian poor, Manya appeals to her readers as a woman poised between royal affluence and bohemian poverty, sexual prowess and sexual subjugation, flesh and spirit, nation and world. She enacts an important resistance to the roles and conventions that very nearly entrap her—those of mother and wife, self-sacrificing nurse (her siblings' example), and, curiously enough, financially successful artist. The character of Manya thus presents the reader with a wide spectrum of vicarious experience and experimental role playing. In her breadth, ambiguity, and philosophical seeking, she also suggests an important resemblance to the familiar heroes of her national literature. Manya could be read as yet another incarnation of the hard-living, ever-questing Russian realist hero who hails from the margins of society (the "underground") or the nongentry *(raznochinets)*, scorns social conventions, flirts with the West, and tries out various answers to the "cursed questions" of life.

Stefcia Rudecka, *The Leper*'s protagonist, more closely approximates the middle-class romance heroine in terms of class and family, yet she also demonstrates an exceptional capaciousness. In the Polish class hierarchy, her comfortable gentry family occupies a rank below the great magnates, the "first families" of the land, and her family's homey tenderness and unaffected life style recall the oft-pitched virtues of the middle class in Western romances. In addition, the novel voices an intermittent critique of the Polish aristocracy's usual sins of self-indulgence, self-absorption, ineffectualness, and an uncritical mania for all things Western. But the Rudeckis' example and the novel's critique are actually devoted to constructing a better aristocracy, not its displacement by a new bourgeoisie. The *szlachetność* that glimmered in *The Doll* absolutely bedazzles in *The Leper* and easily outshines middle-class virtue and sentiment. Mniszek's portrayal of the Rudeckis—particularly Stefcia and her father—concentrates on their ability to "pass" for aristocrats and, in Stefcia's case, to improve on the aristocratic model. Whereas Manya attracts notice by living between estates and beyond conventions, Stefcia distinguishes herself by her mastery of the highest estate and its most refined gestures. Stefcia invariably impresses a chorus of onlooking aristocrats as she excels in the pastimes of the rich, playing tennis, riding horseback, and dancing at balls. Her beauty, grace, and even choice of clothing qualify her as an innate, if not hereditary, aristocrat who bests her female "superiors."[37]

But if Stefcia adapts so ably to her lavish surroundings, she, like Manya, shows no inclination toward ownership and control.[38] In contrast to her chief rival and foil, the wicked brunette Countess Barska, Stefcia does not scheme to possess the magnificent estate of her beloved, Lord Waldemar Michorowski. Rather, the opulence of Głębowicze, declared to be a Polish Versailles, either delights or frightens her.[39] Stefcia seeks most to maintain a sense of freedom *(swoboda)* among the aristocrats, a feeling she truly achieves only in nature. The novel begins by establishing nature as Stefcia's true home, the touchstone for her beauty and grace, as the narrator's eye traces her passage through a mansion into an even more sumptuously arrayed park:

> She tiptoed through several richly and tastefully furnished rooms. In the great entrance hall of the palace she had to pause before the heavy locked glass doors.
>
> She was helped by a servant who was just walking up the stairs with a brush in his hand. Seeing her, he opened his sleepy eyes wide, but politely hurried to undo the lock.
>
> In a moment she ran into the park.
>
> Walking along the paths, she tore off white willowy narcissus. Swaying, fragrant, lily-white lilacs fell from the bushes in luxuriant sprays. The transparently white sweet-smelling calyxes of the narcissus were filled with cold dew; red-lashed, the yellow eyes of the flowers looked as if they had been crying.
>
> The girl touched her lips to the white goblets and drank in their tears with a playful smile. (1:6–7)

This passage initiates a detailed focus on the "riches" of flowers, a leit-motif that naturally involves Stefcia's characterization as a cornflower, a blossom of the Polish fields, and her contrast with the hothouse (that is, unnatural and imported) blooms of aristocratic beauties. Elsewhere, Stefcia is also characterized as a natural and nationalized aristocrat, untainted by foreign influence and uncorrupted by privilege and pampering. The reader is thereby encouraged to connect with the heroine through ethnicity and patriotic feeling and to aspire to her model as a convincingly "self-made" aristocrat.

Love and Money

The romance heroine's plot charts the progress of her love, lingering longest on the drama of courtship and the mystery of her lover. As Modleski observes, fathoming the hero constitutes one of the chief goals of the romance, perhaps reflecting women's real-life dilemmas as they attempt to understand the men to whom they have entrusted their persons and their fortunes.[40] We might also read this act as part of a flesh-and-spirit exchange: while the hero constantly assesses the heroine for public suitability and aims to possess her physically and provide for her materially, the heroine tries to divine the inner qualities of a frequently opaque hero in order to "save" and keep his soul. The usual course of the romance heroine's plot describes a kind of tug of war between flesh and spirit; the two lovers initially clash because of erotic tension as the hero toys with the idea of physical seduction, and then the heroine tempers him into truly loving and respectful husband material.

Although both *Keys to Happiness* and *The Leper* retain the convention of the initially enigmatic, high-born male lover, Verbitskaia and Mniszek customize their male protagonists much as they improvised their heroines, and the characters' changed profiles spark rather different love affairs from those found in the usual romance plot. As might be expected, Manya's love plot is the more convoluted. In an interesting reversal of traditional male-female relations in Russian literature, whereby women come to symbolize different aspects of the hero's psychology, Manya's duality in *Keys to Happiness* is intricately embodied in her two chief lovers, a reactionary Russian nobleman, Nikolai Nelidov, and a radical Jewish tycoon and art patron, Mark Steinbach. Both men appeal to her because of their good looks and mysterious air, but she does not retrace the romance heroine's course of antagonism, near seduction, and true love with either one. Her relationship with Nelidov, which promises to follow the familiar scenario of rakish nobleman courting a simple maiden, almost immediately erupts in rape and burdens her with pregnancy. Nelidov's sexual brutality is no passing phase, but of a piece with his political views and class behavior, for he runs his estate with an iron hand, believes in maintaining a "pure" Russian race (avoiding the taint of foreign blood or physical and mental defects), and stands poised to repress any peasant uprising. Manya must love Nelidov, then, with full knowledge of his ambiguous character; her brutal lover is never transformed into the benevolent prince. Manya's story further strays from the Western model in her rebellion against contemporary conventions that demanded women's premarital virginity and promised the reward of marital bliss.[41] She refuses Nelidov's proposal, his one attempt at recompense for his actions, and exerts no tempering, "domesticating" influence on him or any other man.

Manya's relationship with Steinbach represents a different sort of variation on the popular romance plot. She is at first awed by the handsome, remote tycoon, but her feelings for Steinbach evolve into a strong friendship between art lovers and fellow rebels against a money-grubbing world. Manya is a woman who resists commodification as wife or mistress to pursue an artistic calling; Steinbach is a wealthy Jew who attempts to divest himself of his fortune by supporting the unprofitable causes of both art and revolution. Although Steinbach falls deeply in love with Manya, his marriage and her own occasional outbursts of anti-Semitism hobble the development of any grand passion. While he cannot offer her his hand until his wife's demise, she never can offer him her whole heart. In lieu of a full-fledged love affair, the two characters settle for a loving business relationship, with Steinbach financing Manya's general education and dancing career, and Manya accepting his encouragement and advice (and piano accompaniment), but denying herself his proffered luxuries. Even saddled with a child and a nanny, Manya insists on paying her own way and scorns the commercial aspects of promoting a career, leaving such details to Steinbach and her worldly dance teacher. As she expostulates to her faithful "manager": "I don't want to think about money. I want to earn enough for what is most necessary. And I want to dream, dream! And cherish my dreams like flowers" (1:472).

Interestingly enough, Steinbach reads their relationship as a reversal of gender roles. "In our love," he declares, "you are the man and I am the woman. You give orders and I obey" (2:260). Manya thus plays the "husband" immersed in his art and pursuing other love affairs, whereas Steinbach accepts the part of the devoted "wife" who takes care of the minutiae of daily life and waits faithfully to be summoned. This gender-reversed reading also transposes the Western middle-class roles of the hardworking provider-husband and the bored, leisured wife who dabbles in art and romance. Here the male "wife" facilitates while the female "husband" concentrates. Examined in either comparison, Steinbach's theory (very probably derived from the contemporary philosopher Otto Weininger's definitions of masculine and feminine behaviors) assures the reader of Manya's commitment to art and her disdain for worldly goods and rewards.[42] Indeed, whenever commercial success or domestic bliss looms on the horizon, Manya begins to fret and to search elsewhere for the keys to happiness, sampling the various unsatisfactory panaceas of post-1905 Russian society—art, sex, politics.[43]

Stefcia Rudecka also attracts several lovers, but in succession; and again her attractions prove her true aristocratic worth. Her first love affair, which occurs before the novel opens, exposes her to the ignoble noble Edmund Prątnicki, who decides against marriage because her dowry is too small. Stefcia's instantaneous revulsion toward Prątnicki doubles as revulsion toward his mercenary nature; she cannot love a man who so loves money. In an intriguing variation on the governess heroine in romances and gothic fiction, Stefcia accepts a teaching post with an aristocratic family not because she needs the money, but in order to flee the scene of her disillusionment, to recover from the revelation of aristocratic pettiness and her own gullibility. In consequence, an experienced but still unsullied Stefcia finds herself adopted by a family of (largely) good aristocrats—cherished by its patriarch, Pan Maciej; beloved of her charge, Lucia; and eventually wooed by the heir apparent, Michorowski. Her inclusion directly demotes Prątnicki, who is inferior in class rank to this magnate family and who is actually fired from his position as its steward on Stefcia's account.

Once the scene has been set for Stefcia to meet her noble intended, her love affair does follow the formulaic pattern. Hero and heroine spar, much to Stefcia's bewilderment; the hero toys with the idea of seduction; and finally the heroine's resistance and her goodness refine his lust into love. As I have mentioned, Mniszek's lengthy dalliance with this plot distinguishes *The Leper* from other Polish novels and links it to the tradition of Western romance. What differentiates *The Leper* most from Western models, on the other hand, is its presentation of the lovers as national heroes in a forward-looking, industrializing, and moderately democratizing Poland—in short, Mniszek's successful investment of the romance with a Positivist mind-set and plot. Walas readily identifies its Positivist trappings:

> Mniszek's novel fit perfectly into the general schema of the Positivist and post-Positivist novel, and although that narrative tradition was not dominant when *The Leper* appeared, it was most widely known and generally accepted as valuable. . . . The misalliance that is so essential to Mniszek's plot and so appealing to her reader was one of the staple thematic elements in Polish literature in the second half of the nineteenth century. Positivist literature used this element eagerly and often as a way of exploring class prejudice and its harmful consequences: A successful misalliance was most often a symbol of the triumph of progressive social forces, a sign of national unity, and an image of harmony and a redemptive, reciprocal mingling of estates.[44]

Yet in lieu of the Positivist tendency to pit parasitic aristocrats against "progressive social forces" and "national unity," in *The Leper* Mniszek takes great pains to redeem the aristocracy through the figures of the self-made noble heroine and the hereditary noble hero.[45] Michorowski is equipped to manage this redemption singlehandedly. He articulates much of the critique of his class, decrying its piggishness and insularity, and he exemplifies its salvation and that of the nation as the energetic, effective, and appropriately philanthropic tycoon. The novel lavishes at least as much attention on Michorowski's patriotism, industry, and good works as it devotes to the "proof" of Stefcia's nobility. Most important, the energetic hero overcomes class prejudice and weakness by proposing to Stefcia and winning his family's blessing for their marriage. A generation before, the otherwise impressive Pan Maciej, betrothed to Stefcia's grandmother, had caved in to family pressure, broken the engagement, and sacrificed a lifetime of happiness to gain financial security and class approval. Michorowski represents the new aristocrat-redeemer, the drastic reduction and solution of Wokulski's dilemma.

So the novel exhibits Stefcia, the Polish miss who outclassed her aristocratic rivals, and Waldemar, the aristocrat who would renationalize his class, as the first couple of the land, the charismatic industrialist-benefactors of a developing nation. The narrative intones a litany of Michorowski's glorious goods and works—his restored and superbly governed estate, his successful ventures into farming and industry, his model provisions for the sick and destitute, his efficient and adoring staff. Carefully locating the hero in the commodity culture of the period, Mniszek sets off his achievements and expertise at a national exhibition, where Lord Michorowski grandly escorts Stefcia, her charge, Lucia, and the lovely "amazon," Miss Rita:[46]

> Miss Rita, Stefcia, and Lucia carried bouquets which the lord had purchased for them in the flower section. Stefcia held a bunch of golden daisies.
>
> They entered a pavilion and stopped awestruck by its display of power. Huge locomobiles and motors riveted the eye. Everything was in motion, and although the machines worked quickly, their silence attested to their superior construction. Stefcia and Rita walked slowly under the whirring belts; both enjoyed this kind of craftsmanship and were filled with a sense of its strength. The machines seemed to them like live beings. Waldemar explained their workings. He spoke well, with precision and a specialist's knowledge. . . . He showed them what sorts of systems he had in place at Głębowicze. Stefcia was enthralled, but Lucia began to get bored. (1:253)

This scene shows the couple to every possible advantage: Michorowski serves as gallant aristocratic host and self-taught industrial expert, while Stefcia, bearing wildflowers and "enthralled" by machines, emblematizes the beautiful wedding of nature and industry. The two are posed to preside as king and queen over a microcosm of a modernized Poland.

When Stefcia finally consents to be mistress of Michorowski's progressive estate, she along with her admiring father effectively confirm Michorowski's patriotic and Positivist credentials. For once, the lesser Polish gentry recognizes a hardworking, nation-loving aristocrat. Although Michorowski, like Nelidov and unlike Wokulski, mixes nationalism with anti-Semitism, this flaw is little remarked and wholly unjudged in the novel, eclipsed by the repeated observation that the "people" (the Polish peasants) naturally love Michorowski and bow before Stefcia's innate nobility.[47] Any competition for economic power has simply disappeared. In *The Leper* "socially progressive forces" remain comfortably ensconced and unquestioned in their castle. Waldemar and Stefcia are poised to realize the nation's happy capitalist development as enlightened, ethnically homogeneous, and utterly charming feudalism.

It is significant, however, that this powerful, beautiful, talented couple still depend so heavily on family approval. In contrast to the wild child Manya, who flouts conventions and a doomed heredity, both Waldemar and Stefcia are deeply conservative in their regard for family feelings and rituals. Their attitude partially reinforces the novel's theme of an ascendant aristocracy, a class that defines itself by bloodline and ceremony. Yet particularly Stefcia's concern for family acceptance also conveys a highly sentimental world view. Despite her spirited nature and quick tongue, the heroine cannot bear the thought of defying the family's wishes, of living outside its blessed circle. She will not marry Waldemar until he has secured his grandmother's blessing, and a good portion of the novel describes grandmother-grandson negotiations to this end. Stefcia desires to be both the wife and the granddaughter of aristocrats, to sit contentedly beside her husband as he talks good business for the nation, or at her "grandfather's" feet as he relates stories of Poland's glorious and tragic past.[48] The romance of Stefcia and Waldemar therefore resonates with the sentimentalized nationalism we have already seen represented in and evoked by such "serious" Polish works as *The Doll*.

Unhappy Endings

Whereas Western romances and their late twentieth-century derivatives commonly feature a happy ending, the romances of both Verbitskaia and Mniszek close with the heroine's death. Such an ending would be cataclysmic in the middle-class romance, for the whole aim of its plot is to make a home for the heroine—to provide for her possession by the hero and her possession of his estate. Yet while both Verbitskaia's and Mniszek's novels foreclosed on that possibility, both turned out to be tremendously popular. Clearly their readers did not feel cheated by an unhappy ending.[49] Although we cannot conduct retroactive "market studies" of these audiences, one may conclude that a protagonist's death was an acceptable and even satisfying formula in these cultures, perhaps a clever final diversion into the no less popular genre of melodrama.[50]

In both *Keys to Happiness* and *The Leper*, then, the death of the heroine prevents her enfranchisement and domestication, and functions unambiguously as an unhappy ending. Yet, to paraphrase Tolstoy, all unhappy endings are unhappy in their own way, and their differences deserve careful analysis. If both conclusions preclude the possibility of the heroine settling down in marriage, home, and wealth, the particulars in each case not only reveal different reasons why a happy ending is impossible, but also separately critique or reject the value of a happy ending.

In *Keys to Happiness*, Manya's voluntary death comes exactly at the point of her settling down. Having established her career, married Steinbach, and returned to Russia, the heroine seems to have achieved a delicate balance between vocation and family, self-assertion and sexual involvement, only to be thrown off kilter by the reappearance of Nelidov. Their old passion ignites and overwhelms them both, while their respective obligations, Nelidov's jealousy, and Manya's continuing rejection of conventional wifehood deny them a future of domestic happiness. The heroine's love for the hero, made the more compelling by its forbidden and "poetic" nature, eclipses and displaces the more prosaic joys of career, motherhood, a "free" marriage, and an affluent life style. When Manya's aristocratic lover kills himself in despair, unable to reconcile his love for her with his reactionary beliefs and conservative mores, Manya can only follow suit.

Manya's suicide has been interpreted as the failure of the "new woman" who abandons the many options open to her for a self-destructive love; her final submission to Nelidov does refute the "lordly" maleness that Steinbach ascribes to her and that Otto Weininger deemed superior to femininity.[51] Yet Manya's and Nelidov's joint suicide also suggests a unisexing of despair, as neither woman nor man can bear to live without true love. Read within Russian literary tradition, it also strongly implies the heroine's superiority—even in death. Committing suicide after she has explored the options open to the "new woman"—which amount to the usual male protagonist's options of sexual adventure, pursuit of career, and family life—Manya completes the requirements for becoming a serious (male) character in Russian literature. She may not have attained the keys to happiness—the heights of emotional control and creative commitment demonstrated by the novel's other "great" artist, the poet Harold—but she, a mere woman, has acquitted herself admirably and exhaustively as intellectual and artist. To a large extent, it seems that she and the narrative have simply run out of ideas. Manya is no "poor Liza" who drowns herself after her first rejection, no Anna Karenina who lives and dies by the traditional plot lines that cornered women. This heroine eventually succumbs to and is ennobled by the same crisis of belief, the same general question of how one should live, that dogged nineteenth-century realist heroes and engulfed the Russian intelligentsia at the beginning of the twentieth century. In Verbitskaia's romance, a thoroughly experienced heroine destroys and transcends the very body she has so indulged and controlled. She self-destructs to quit a life of unsatisfying consumption and mundane experience.[52]

In *The Leper*, on the other hand, Stefcia's epitaph renders her a pure victim: "She died prematurely, poisoned by the fanaticism of certain members of her fiancé's sphere" (2:304). The iron-willed Michorowski wins her acceptance from his immediate family, but he and Stefcia's equally protective father cannot shield her fully from the hostility of other aristocrats, including the spurned Countess Barska. Very much unlike the rebellious Manya, Stefcia is slain by rejection, appropriately delivered in the form of personal letters that convey anonymous warnings and attacks. These ill wishes provoke a fatal onset of brain fever, and Stefcia takes leave of a strife-torn world on her wedding day to the tender accompaniment of nightingales. Stefcia's sentimental world view is therefore disordered and destroyed by a class divided against itself, by those few bad apples that spoil the nation (symbolized by Stefcia) and the nation's prospects (symbolized by her marriage). These spoilers curse the healthy, pure heroine as a leper, the stigmatizing, murdering word of the title. They blight a sentimental nationalism, a nationalism of familial harmony, with a pathological classism.

I also submit that Stefcia's symbolically timed death conveys a deep ambivalence about her passage from "natural" aristocrat to well-heeled lady of the manor, from free agent to possession and co-proprietor. The heroine is literally shaken by bad premonitions as she views the Michorowski jewels, for these worldly riches, set in opposition to her trademark flowers, seem to crystallize and bestow the family's sorrow.[53] She is felled by brain fever as she dons her gorgeous wedding dress, her first and last costume as Waldemar's wife. In place of a problematic worldly transformation, Stefcia is transfigured (much as Bela might have wished) into various works of art and, in consequence, she not only transcends the material trappings of her married life, but also forever "spiritualizes" her fiancé and his grand estate.[54] Denied her actual body, Michorowski commissions both a statue and a portrait to preserve her image. The statue is erected at her gravesite, and the portrait is hung in the Michorowski family portrait gallery among the very pictures that at one time appeared to reject her. Stefcia is vouchsafed a sentimentalized afterlife, existing as two monuments on the national landscape—as a permanent landmark in nature and an eternal member of Poland's first family.

According to these unhappy endings, both Manya and Stefcia cease to be consuming heroines and are themselves unnaturally consumed because of an unsatisfactory context which they, as sensitive and exceptional beings, have taken too much to heart. The status quo in Russia and Poland does not afford them the domestic and social haven that Western romance heroines typically find in their own environments. The material well-being that each stands to gain as a wife guarantees neither the spiritual sustenance nor the loving solidarity they desire. Rather, their deaths symbolically reflect national dilemmas that overshadow individual and even class prosperity, cementing their stories in native traditions obsessed with national character and national destiny. In a sense, a happy ending in either case would have denied the nation its due. Only a suicidal Manya bound to a despotic aristocrat could adequately express the Russian empire's crisis of belief and direction, and its enduring feudal roots. Only Stefcia as victimized virgin could embody an idyllic "untried" Poland alternately beloved and rejected by its aristocracy. In terms of the heroine's identity and plot, the concept of *nation* proves to be a

more compelling influence than that of class or gender or even successful Western models.

Thus, while Russian and Polish readers surely sampled some of the
pleasures associated with the middlebrow in *Keys to Happiness* and *The
Leper*, they also were compelled by a familiar, powerful, and uplifting
national message, a popularly packaged "seriousness." These two novels
flaunted the accoutrements of the rich, conveniently relayed information
about cultured habits and tastes, and prompted tears and emotional titil-
lation with their detailed description of the heroines' love affairs. Both
novels, too, featured the types of empathetic heroine and charismatic,
providing hero that continue to appeal to romance readers in the West.
But these romance-tragedies also innovated very distinctive attractions for
Russian and Polish readers: (1) a highly accessible, personalized presentation of the big ideas and issues that ennobled their "serious" literature; (2)
an emotionally unabashed plot designed to vent popular frustration and
despair over a shared tragic context (a politically and ideologically stag-
nant Russia, a class-obsessed and class-martyred Poland); (3) a narcissis-
tic savoring of national heroes and heroines asserted to be different from
and superior to Western models; and (4) a final tragedy that redeems
both heroine and reader from charges of indulgence.[55] Both Verbitskaia
and Mniszek achieved the commodification of high meaningfulness,
rewriting the romance heroine as a most affective national martyr. Instead of pitching readers gilded dreams of middle-class happiness, their
well-loved, well-dressed, and well-tried heroines succeeded in fleshing
out readers' conceptions of an exalting national melodrama.

II

THE MARKET ON LITERATURE

five

The Icon and the Ad
The Marketing of Russian Literature

BY THE TURN OF THE TWENTIETH CENTURY, the mass-circulation press had overrun Europe and the United States, heralding important common developments for readers everywhere. Through its varied format, contents, tone, and pretensions, the press expressly catered to a growing and diverse audience, registering and exploiting differences in class, gender, profession, and taste. Underlying these variations was the presumption of universal access to the word: mass circulation presupposed that anyone could and should be a reader. Yet however commendable the explicit pluralism and implicit egalitarianism of this new kind of literature, these characteristics stemmed in large part from its most provocative attribute—its pervasive commercialism. The mass-circulation press openly linked the word and the market, the privilege and accomplishment of reading with the venality of consumption.

Scholars have shown that the enormous volume and scope of the mass-circulation press prompted quite radical changes in Western literary relations between author and reader.[1] In the United States, for example, the new press's emphasis on speed, efficiency, and good business practices threatened to render obsolete the tradition of the gentleman "editor-toastmaster" and Victorian habits of leisure reading.[2] Yet in the West the trademark trinity of pluralism, egalitarianism, and commercialism that characterized the mass-circulation press recombined and intensified social, political, and economic trends long present in Western societies. In imperial Russia, such a combination was potentially revolutionary, not evolutionary. Here the pluralism and egalitarianism of the mass-distributed press at once reflected and facilitated a new social order that challenged the oddly twinned hegemony of the aristocracy and the intelligentsia by giving voice to newly emerging middle groups. The press was the first Russian institution to attempt popular representation and to heed the different interests, tastes, and ideological stances of a recently constituted "public" unused to notions of consumer rights and customer satisfaction.[3] Above all, the press's overt commercialism introduced a new phenomenon into Russian book culture. Its acknowledgment of the market unsettled Russians' traditional reverence toward the written word, audaciously attaching monetary value to what had been perceived as a spiritual or moral transaction between writer and reader and reshaping the mentoring bond into the more pragmatic menage à trois of *publisher-writer-reader*.[4] Before its readers' very eyes, the mass-circulation press blatantly transubstantiated the printed word from semisacred text into a made and paid-for product accessible to anyone.

What interests me most is how the Russian press controlled and represented this radical transformation, how it mediated the market's seemingly fundamental revaluation of the writer and the writer's work. Chapters 2–4 explored how various literary works describe and assess capitalist culture and the capitalist in the Russian and Polish contexts. Chapter 5 begins the inverse examination of how the market-making press defined and valued the general phenomenon of *literature* and how it trained readers to be consumers. My analysis of the Russian case focuses on *Vol'f Bookstore News (Izvestiia knizhnykh magazinov tovarishchestva M. O. Vol'f)*, an influential and virtually encyclopedic journal-cum-catalogue issued by one of the largest publishers and booksellers in late imperial Russia, M. O. Vol'f. The Vol'f firm explicitly developed this publication to "cover all literary phenomena—both Russian and foreign" and to satisfy "the reading public's need to know" about new books and important new articles.[5] With a self-declared and diligently pursued mandate to package the entire book world for the Russian reader, *Vol'f Bookstore News* affords a kind of concentrated documentation of how the Russian press constructed and moved the literary market.[6]

Tailor-making the Marketplace

The extraordinary service of *Vol'f Bookstore News* evolved from the lifelong enterprise of its founder. M. O. Vol'f (1825–1883) was one of those immigrant publishers who experimented with the customs of "serious" Russian book publishing. A Polish émigré, Vol'f learned the book trade in Paris and Leipzig, opened his first bookstore in Saint Petersburg in 1853, and came to dominate the Russian market by the 1870s, boasting yearly profits of over one million rubles.[7] Vol'f's business success was built in part on conservative strategies, for he preferred to publish "works by the classics" or writers with an established reputation, and his editions were renowned for "the high quality of their binding, paper, and print, and their sumptuous production."[8] But Vol'f also trailblazed innovative modes of marketing. He conducted consumer surveys in his stores and regularly consulted with his far-flung trade representatives about sales. Vol'f trained his clerks in marketing as well, advising them that "it's not enough for a bookseller to hand the customer the book he wants. One should know how to interest the customer in other books that might be to his taste."[9]

Vol'f Bookstore News, which began to appear in 1897, shrewdly expanded on this practice, assuming the role of obliging bookseller to the entire empire. It comprised a mail-order marketplace, a giant bookstore with the print equivalents of knowledgeable and persuasive clerks. (See figure 1.) Indeed, the pages of *Vol'f Bookstore News* projected a marketplace far superior to a physical store, because its cleverly segmented print format fostered the illusion of offering, on the one hand, disinterested and high-minded commentary (contained initially in the prefatory "News" section) and, on the other, a catalogue for perusing and buying books. Feeling its way in the new Russian literary market, the Vol'f firm seemed more intent on cultivating the journal's authority rather than its sales lists. In 1905 Vol'f ceremoniously expanded the editorial content of the

FIGURE 1. *Vol'f Bookstore News* occasionally enticed its readers with product displays. Here potential book buyers are shown an exhibit of Vol'f publications mounted for the general "Children's World" exhibit in Saint Petersburg. *Vol'f Bookstore News* 7 (March 1904): 34.

News by adding the "Literary Herald" ("Vestnik literatury"), a segment with "serious" critical pretensions and made weighty with "critical analyses, detailed histories of belles lettres, history, philosophy, and other branches of general and specialized literature, articles and correspondence on literary questions, sketches about the life and activity of writers as a collective and as individuals, biocritical sketches, literary reminiscences and annals, reviews of new books and journal articles, and so on and so forth."[10]

Similar structural and narrative strategies for uplifting or otherwise distracting the reader from the book's obvious commodification were at play in the commercial components of the *News*. The publisher prefaced and then bordered the catalogue with an ever-increasing number of "news" subsections—a general "Chronicle of Books and Literature" and

нія и класса. Городской голова П. А. Зеленый, высказавъ полное сочувствіе этому благому дѣлу, предложилъ присутствовавшимъ тутъ-же присоединиться къ предложенію В. В. Навроцкаго своими посильными пожертвованіями, и самъ первый подписалъ 300 руб. на этотъ призывъ откликнулись многіе изъ присутствовавшихъ. Затѣмъ, въ слѣдующіе дни продолжали поступать новыя пожертвованія, и по 9 января с. г. поступило уже на убѣжище для инвалидовъ печатнаго дѣла въ Одессѣ 9.598 р.45к. Дальнѣйшія пожертвованія продолжаютъ поступать.

✳ 10 января исполнилось сорокалѣтіе литературной дѣятельности Николая Александровича Чаева, драматурга, беллетриста, археолога и ученаго. Н. А. родился въ Костромской губерніи, Нерехтскаго уѣзда, въ 1824 году.

ВѢСТИ ИЗЪ ФРАНЦІИ *)

✳ Французскимъ министромъ народнаго просвѣщенія сдѣлано распоряженіе о помѣщеніи портрета Верлена въ одной изъ залъ люксенбургскаго музея. Портретъ исполненъ художникомъ Шанталя и поднесенъ въ даръ государству той группою поэтовъ и писателей, въ которую вошли Анатоль Франсъ, Сюлли Прюдомъ, Эредіа, Пуанкаре и Морисъ Форъ.

✳ Монтіоновскія преміи присуждены французскою академіею въ н. г. слѣдующимъ писателямъ: G. Goyon —2,000 fr. за „L'Allemagne religieuse"; G. Pariset—1,000 fr. за „L'Etat et les Eglises en Prusse sous Frédéric-Guillaume I (1713—1740)"; Théodor de Wyzewa (Вижевскому) 2,000 fr. за „Ecrivains étrangers"; Legros—1,000 fr. за „Henri Heine poète"; Ernest Seillière 1,000 fr. за „Etudes sur Ferdinand de Lassalle". Такъ-называемая „литературная премія" присуждена деканъ факультета въ Бордо, Полю Статреру, за сочиненіе о Боссюэтѣ и Адольфѣ Мано. Премію книгопродавца Кальмана Леви въ 3,000 получилъ Жюль Казъ за „La Vassale". Жюдитъ Готье получила 5,000 фр. (премію Нée) за свои повѣсти, проф. же Брюнъ 3,000 фр. за сочиненіе объ исторіи Мишле.

✳ Вышло составленное Обаноелемъ описаніе путешествія президента французской республики въ Россію и. з. „Une page d'histoire". Изданіе украшено иллюстраціями, сдѣланными по фотографіямъ съ натуры.

✳ Въ серединѣ января выйдетъ въ свѣтъ новый романъ моднаго теперь беллетриста Поля Адама „La Force".
✳ Эмиля Зола „La Fête à Coqueville"

*) Сообщенныя нашимъ корреспондентомъ въ Парижѣ.

БИБЛІОГРАФІЯ

ПЕРЕЧЕНЬ

НОВѢЙШИХЪ КНИГЪ.

Цѣны книгамъ, какъ русскимъ, такъ и иностраннымъ, отмѣчены въ рубляхъ и копѣйкахъ.

БЕЛЛЕТРИСТИКА И ПОЭЗІЯ

Аверкіевъ, Д. Повѣсти изъ современнаго быта. Т. I. Исторія блѣднаго молодого человѣка. Спб. 1898. 2 —
Т. II. Новая барышня. Лавры и терніи. Ученый сонъ. Исторія трехъ невѣрныхъ мужей. Спб. 1898. 1 50
Т. III. Художникъ Безналовъ и нотаріусъ Подлещиковъ. Комическій романъ. Спб. 1898. 2 —
Авенаріусъ, В. Школа жизни великаго юмориста. Третья повѣсть изъ біографической трилогіи „Ученическіе годы Гоголя". Спб. 1899. Ц. 1 р. 75 к., въ переплетѣ 2 50
Авсѣенко, В. Новые разсказы. Т. I. Спб. 1899. 1 —
Allegro. Стихотворенія. Съ виньетками автора. Спб. 1899. 1 —
Астаховъ, И. Романъ въ тюрьмѣ. Разсказы. М. 1899. 1 —
Ауэрбахъ, Б. Три единственныя дочери. Повѣсть. Перев. съ нѣм. Е. Б. М. 1898. 1 —
Баранцевичъ, К. Чудныя ночи. Рождественскіе и пасхальные разсказы и очерки. М. 1899. — 45
Берховецъ, Я. Д. Незабвенное прошлое. Спб. 1899. Ц. 25 к., на лучш. бум. — 35
Бурже, Поль. Голубая герцогиня (актриса). (La duchesse bleue). Пер. съ франц. И. И. Перелыгина. М. 1899. 1 25
Вербицкая, А. Сны жизни. Разсказы. М. 1899. 1 —
Гауптманъ, Гергардъ. Одинокіе люди. Драма въ 5-ти дѣйствіяхъ. Пер. съ нѣм. О. Н. Поповой. Спб. 1899. 1 —
Германъ, Ф. Къ исторіи моего диспута (Отвѣтъ моимъ оппонентамъ). Харьковъ. 1898. — 30
Господинъ Топотунъ. Переводъ съ французскаго. Спб. 1899. 1 —
Гофманъ. Щелкунчикъ и мышиный царь. Съ рисунками худ. Ю. Я. Кремеръ. М. 1898. — 75
Гранстремъ, М. Варееоломеевская ночь. Историческ. романъ. Съ англійск. 99 рис. Спб. 1899. 2 —
Григоровичъ, Дм. Бѣдный мальчикъ. Повѣсть. Съ рис. художн. С. С. Соломко. Ц. въ роскошномъ переплетѣ 2 —
Додэ, Альфонсъ. Прекрасная Нивернеза. Пер. съ франц. С. Круковской. Съ 45 рис. Спб. 1899. — 30
Животовъ, Н. Н. Разрытая могила. Романъ. Спб. 1899. 1 25
Жизнь, какъ она есть. Повѣсть въ 3-хъ частяхъ. Т. I. ч. 1—II (гл. I—XVI). М. 1898. 2 50
Жиркевичъ, А. В. Друзьямъ. Стихотворенія. Спб. 1899. — 40
Жуковскій, В. А. Рустемъ и Зорабъ. Повѣсть. Спб. 1899. — 40
Калимахъ. Избранные гимны и эпиграммы. Съ греч. перев. В. Алексѣевъ. Съ введеніемъ и примѣчаніями. Спб. 1899. — 30
Кардо-Сысоева, Н. Е. Три разсказа для дѣтей. М. 1899. — 85
Лаврентьева, С. И. Новый сборникъ театральныхъ пьесъ для дѣтей и юношества. Спб. 1899. 2 —
Лейкинъ, Н. А. Въ деревнѣ и въ городѣ. Спб. 1899. 1 —
Лухманова, Н. А. Въ волшебной странѣ пѣсенъ и нищеты. Спб. 1899. 1 —
Мало, Гекторъ. Приключенія Ромена Кальбри. Пер. съ франц. Спб. 1899. 1 50
Маминъ-Сибирякъ, Д. Н. Свѣтлячки. Сказки. М. 1899. 1 —
— Святочные разсказы. Спб. 1898. 1 —
— Уральскіе разсказы. Т. I. Изд. 3-е. Спб. 1899. 1 —

FIGURE 2. An example of the *News* catalogue: Here "News from France" borders the "List of Latest Books." Catalogue prices for both Russian and foreign books are noted in rubles and kopecks. *Vol'f Bookstore News* 2 (January 1899): 66.

more specialized headers such as "News from France," "Rossica," and "Pushkiniana." (See figure 2.) The editors thereby modeled this segment into a kind of newspaper about books, making the catalogue not a mere advertisement but another important source of information. Juxtaposing its sales lists against news about the global book market, Vol'f pitched them as reports on a vital and global commodity, much like stock exchange columns. Although *Vol'f Bookstore News* displayed plenty of advertisements, it presented its voluminous catalogue as a "helpful guide to streamline one's search for a particular book."[11] Its advertisements, in turn, were tempered by such uplifting devices as official endorsements (written by tsarist ministers, for example), blurbs quoting positive reviews, and special listings that grouped together identifiable classics with new best-sellers.[12]

Vol'f Bookstore News thus constructed a constantly expanding and extremely decorous marketplace, conducting the reader, as it were, on a lengthy tour of the museum of literature and then inviting participation in an auction of fine art next door. It encouraged the reader to revere, to study, and then to acquire. The journal chose to emphasize both the "cultured" nature of this transaction and its tangible appeal. The catalogue approximated the physical experience of browsing by including pertinent data on a given book's "price, format, length, and number of volumes." Even the ostensibly serious "Literary Herald" fired the reader's interest and desire with portraits of the artist, illustrations, and reproduced autographs. These pictures sooner resembled museum displays than shop windows, but they enhanced the reader's sense of the materiality of the book and its production.

Market Value

As this tailor-made marketplace attests, Vol'f handled the hot potato of market value—the force that threatened to *de*value the revered Russian book—with great caution and no little ingenuity. Whereas its catalogue and advertisements pioneered highbrow marketing through graphics and layout, the *News* conducted more conventional forms of reader education on the market value of books and authors in its "serious" verbal segments. Signed feature articles and authoritative "reports" subtly turned the reader's attention to the producing and consuming aspects of writing and reading.

Rather than depict the book's descent into a commodity, these texts carefully elevated the book as an object of desire and devotion. If a book's monetary value was mentioned at all, it was likely to be an impressively astronomical sum (the book as collector's item) or an equally impressive low price set to make it accessible to the culture-starved masses.[13] While the *News* advertised books as gifts (especially during the Christmas and Easter seasons), it haughtily distinguished these from other, "lesser" commodities. A characteristic report appearing in the November–December 1904 issue protests the displacement of books as gifts by the vogue for statuettes and bric-a-brac. These admittedly pretty "dead things" could not compare with the "living" and "eternally replenishing" gift of a book.[14] The journal insistently purveyed the book as an altogether different order of acquisition.

In keeping with this approach, the *News* proffered features on bibliophiles and book collecting—that is, on the refined and impassioned pursuit of books. (See figure 3.) A September 1898 article chronicles the notable bibliomania of the entire family of Count Dmitrii Nikolaevich Bludov, who was a champion of the sentimental writer Nikolai Karamzin and a founder of the literary circle Arzamas that launched the great Russian poet Aleksandr Pushkin.[15] F. Lopukhin's essay of October 1900 baldly pronounces book collecting to be a passion—"an extremely curious and interesting phenomenon"—and develops a typology of bibliomaniacs. Although he portrays such characters as eccentrics, their quoted beliefs articulate an extraordinary defense of the power of a mere "possession." Lopukhin sees fit to insert a lengthy encomium that French writer Jules Janin ascribed to a "lover of books":

> Do you want to experience every possible human misery? Then sell your books! God, to sell your books! They are my strength and my glory! They put me on a par with the wealthiest, and draw me close to the poorest. Books are my constant companion in my talk and ambitions. I think of them while I am awake and I see them in my dreams. When I go away, I weep over them, and I greet them upon my return! They are my friends, my cohort, my retinue! They are

my chosen children, my holidays, my savings and my true love! My dear books! If I sell them, then what else can I possibly sell, and who will know when I die?[16]

To underscore its special quality as a commodity, the *News* intermittently published articles about the book's maintenance and use. An opening article in the March 1903 issue explicitly anthropomorphizes the book by naming its "enemies," cataloguing its "sicknesses," and describing its "cures" in pragmatic detail. Dust stains, for example, "can be removed with the middle of a piece of white bread or a soft eraser"; wet stains "can be cured . . . with a cold or hot bath" and the emergency addition of a few drops of bleach; mold, however, "dooms a book to certain death."[17] Curiously enough, although the author packs his instructions with do-it-yourself remedies and book housekeeping hints culled from a variety of Western sources, he (along with his sources) presents book maintenance as an exclusively male occupation, a task altogether nobler than ordinary housekeeping and hence incomprehensible to women. In fact, he lists *women* (after dust, insects, vermin, direct sunlight, candle wax, bookbinders, et cetera) as one of the book's chief enemies:

> And those dear housekeepers who grab up "old books" and the "dreadful papers" lying in the attic as they search for jam jar labels!
>
> And those generous mamas who keep their children happy (or quiet) by giving them books to decorate—that is, old books with wood engravings!

What the author particularly objects to in these imagined "housekeepers" and "mamas" is their crudely utilitarian attitude toward the book. To the "materialistic" sex, this wondrous object is only raw material, a source of paper and pretty pictures.

Just as there exists a "hygiene of book maintenance," so the *News* insists on both a proper "hygiene" and "art" of reading. One *News* commentator even argues that *how* is more important than *what* one reads.[18] Other articles progressively define reading as a total engagement of body and spirit. The pseudonymous N. P-v dwells on the physical activity of reading, dictating requirements of clear and uniform print and page whiteness (not brightness) to publishers, and prescribing that readers read in good light, with eyes 30–40 centimeters from the page, and preferably

FIGURE 3. The *News* often featured photographs of impressive libraries, including this private library of the famous Moscow collector, Aleksei Petrovich Bakhrushin. *Vol'f Bookstore News* 4 (April–May 1901): 83.

not while lying down or traveling in a railway coach.[19] At the other end of the spectrum, Mariia Gertsfel'd concentrates on the aesthetic and, in a sense, moral duties of the reader. Although she readily admits that the successful "art of reading" depends in part on an individual's temperament and education, she exhorts all readers to take to their books with selfless and patient devotion:

> To put aside your self-consciousness, to forget yourself, to experience another's suffering and joy—how this cultivates your sensitivity to the life of a universe in which great minds interweave with a larger whole, how this tutors you in self-abnegation, in that almost religious sensation of erasing the difference between "I" and "thou." . . . And how our soul expands and strengthens when we fully live out a thousand lives in fantasy! . . . Of course, you cannot attain this by reading out of hasty curiosity, wanting to shorten the tedious hours and seeking only the hottest topics and sensational effects.[20]

Gertsfel'd's pitch of reading as spiritual training concludes by promising readers co-creative status as they learn to reconstruct for themselves a book's inner world. A *News* subscriber thus was conditioned to value reading as a different order of consumption, as an activity requiring certain "medical" precautions, demanding a kind of religious commitment and concentration, and bestowing life-transforming aesthetic and spiritual riches.[21]

Aside from earnest admonitions and prescriptions, the *News* reinforced these notions about the book and its consumption in a playfully negative way. A remarkably prescient essay entitled "The End of the Book" envisions future technologies that would dispense with the printed page completely, replacing it with audio and video recordings.[22] Authors would seek out actors and singers to record their works; phonographs would be installed in restaurants, buses, doctors' waiting rooms, and Pullman cars; newspaper subscribers would receive their news by "cylinder" (the contemporary form of sound recording) or by telephone; and the kinescope ("Thomas Edison's new invention") would be synchronized to project book illustrations for those many "big children" who demand pictures. If authors opted for self-publishing, "they would walk the streets with a machine strapped across their shoulder like medieval troubadours; on demand, they would point the machine's pipes toward the open windows of their buyers, who would hear all manner of artistic works just as we hear a barrel-organ today."[23] This fanciful sketch, replete with illustrations uncannily suggesting today's Walkman and VCR, defines the issue of the book's commodification from the safe distance of a dystopian parody. (See figure 4.) The tongue-in-cheek narrator celebrates the fact that "listeners" would not have to waste time in concentrated reading. They could lie on a sofa (the hygiene of reading would no longer apply) and indulge themselves in the hedonistic comfort of listening. Although this sketch is probably the work of a British writer (the listed author is one Octave Iuzan and the text features such characters as a Mr. Blakecross and a Mr. Poole), its inclusion in the *News* suggests that publication's increasing self-assurance about the "higher" market value of the book, a value that could sustain a little futuristic ridicule.

In the parody summarized above, authors figure as little more than glorified organ-grinders, hawking their "sound" on the street. Within

FIGURE 4. One of the illustrations for the serialized article, "The End of the Book," here depicts "Phonographic Literature for Strolling." *Vol'f Bookstore News* 3 (November 1899): 27.

the journal's purview, this image serves only as a playful foil, for elsewhere the *News* attempts the same sort of respectful, highly qualified materialization of the artist it assayed in representing the book. The author is not traduced into becoming a tradesman or street vendor, but is portrayed as a professional who must cope with such quotidian matters as honoraria and royalties.

Not even the classics were exempt from this sensible approach. When the *News* joined in the 1899 commemoration of Pushkin's centenary, it volunteered, in addition to the usual tributes, an article on the great poet's earnings. Opening with a quote from Pushkin's famous art-versus-commerce poem, "Conversation Between a Bookseller and a Poet," the author Viktor Rusakov (a Vol'f regular) assigns this work to the poet's carefree early period and points to Pushkin's later need to make a living from his writing. Rusakov states his thesis defensively but insistently: "Be that as it may, [Pushkin's] literary earnings played an extremely important role in his life and literary activity . . . and these have essential significance for his creative biography."[24] Throughout this lengthy article, Rusakov tactfully lays bare Pushkin's "business"—quoting the prices paid for his works, chronicling his various ill-fated endeavors to make more money, and, perhaps most interesting, foregrounding the achievement of Pushkin's chief financial intermediary, the critic, biographer, and eventual editor, P. A. Pletnev. Pletnev emerges as a helper-hero in Rusakov's pragmatic biography, which largely reviews the Pushkin-Pletnev correspondence and the deals they clinched:

> According to Grot [an eminent Pushkin scholar], Pletnev was the "recipient" of most of Pushkin's work, managed his affairs and dealt with the typographers and booksellers, and either sent Pushkin his earnings or kept them for him, according to the poet's wishes. As is apparent from his correspondence, Pletnev exhorted Pushkin to write, reminding him what would bring him good profits at a given moment and proposing lucrative projects, etc.[25]

Yet as Rusakov acknowledges market value with his focus on the writer's material conditions and material helper, he takes exceptional care to assert Pushkin's primary commitment to art: "But Pushkin was no 'merchant,' and the manuscripts left after his death eloquently attest to the fact that the poet did not write for *the sake of honoraria*."[26] These assertions function as an essential safeguard, reassuring readers long used to the pure image of their national bard that Pushkin's publications could be bought, but his *creation* could not. His necessary commercial transactions neither lessened his artistry nor cheapened his image as artist. Instead, Rusakov revalues Pushkin's person and work as positive and necessary blends of genius and professional, invaluable masterpiece and valuable product.

Reporting on the writer's business became standard practice in the *News;* if the great Pushkin was fair game, then all writers could withstand this sort of scrutiny.[27] More generally, the *News* encouraged the reader's progressive understanding of the *business* of literature. It assiduously reported on such issues as authors' rights and literary property laws, often comparing the Russian case unfavorably with established codes in Western Europe and the United States. It also championed the relationship between writer and publisher over the writer's previous dependence on a patron. In an article on the earnings of French writers, N. Chernov claims, "Thanks to the honorarium, writers do much less groveling before their benefactors."[28] A supposed "letter to the editor" goes so far as to declare the publisher "the author's first and immediate benefactor" and applauds the publisher's role in producing books and spreading enlightenment.[29] Through such roundabout self-promotions, the *News* bestowed on the publisher—the ultimate materializer of the text—some of the writer's "noble" luster and "pure" commitment.

Most intriguingly, the materialization of the writer also entailed the materialization of his or her person and things, a process the *News* openly abetted, inscribing the market value of both literary product and literature producer. Again, Vol'f's publication managed this ticklish revaluation with a large dose of decorum. It mainly and predictably followed the high road of scholarly and institutional materialization, reporting on the formation of writers' archives and the founding of writers' museums. The writer's museum or monument recurs as an almost standard subject in the *News*, as the late nineteenth-century vogue for the museum rapidly took root in Russia. A sample article on the Dostoevsky museum conscientiously lists its inventory (manuscripts, books, book illustrations, letters, autographs, diplomas, portraits, busts, furniture) and features photographs of its studiously arranged "corners."[30] It bears noting that the same "still life" pictorial strategies obtain in the journal's other biocritical sketches, evincing the same "respectable" impulse to portray the creative writer as a collection of telltale artifacts displayed for "scientific" quantification. (See figure 5.)

In addition, as I have argued elsewhere, the *News* catered to contemporary consumption of the writer's "celebrity personality."[31] The news columns prefacing its catalogue burgeoned with tidbits ranging from publication announcements to the "latest" about an author's health, travels, or marital status. Sketches and advertisements for forthcoming publications increasingly attended to how a writer lived and worked.[32] Articles and photos cast beyond the figure of the artist as artist to recover an intimate portrait, embellished by images of family members and loved ones.[33] Information about and emblems of the writer's daily life appeared to be important selling points. Although *News* readers were not advised to buy such outright kitsch as a perfume bottle doubling as a Pushkin bust, they might have purchased one of the decorative portraits of the artist featured in a Vol'f advertisement, and their *News* subscription got them the inside story on the writer's life and work.[34] In these in-

тели и критики искренно уважаютъ меня, пусть разъ навсегда откажутся отъ термина являться признаки приближающагося припадка, я не нашелъ возможнымъ больше

домъ, бывшій гр. а. п. толстого (нынѣ н. а. шереметьевой), въ москвѣ, гдѣ жилъ и умеръ гоголь.

«преемникъ Гоголя». У Гоголя нѣтъ и не можетъ быть преемниковъ...»

Такъ какъ мой собесѣдникъ началъ сильно волноваться и у него замѣтно стали по-

утруждать его и раскланялся, обѣщавъ сообщить результатъ моей бесѣды въ печати. Это обѣщаніе я и исполняю.

МЕМУАРИСТЫ ПОСЛѢДНЕЙ ВОЙНЫ.
Очеркъ М. К. СОКОЛОВСКАГО.

Среди матеріаловъ, которые могутъ освѣтить во всей полнотѣ такое крупное явленіе, какъ война, мемуары занимаютъ весьма видное мѣсто. Пополняя офиціальные документы, реляціи, донесенія, предписанія, отчеты и придавая этимъ бюрократическимъ

дѣтищамъ, такъ сказать, жизненную окраску, мемуары, не только заставляютъ пульсировать сухіе, офиціальные документы, но и возсоздаютъ всю ту дѣйствительную обстановку войны, которую никакъ не можетъ передать языкъ реляцій.

Однако мемуары никогда не могутъ быть положены въ основу сужденія о событіи. Ихъ нужно просѣять сквозь сито критики, сито анализа. Мемуаристъ далеко не безгрѣшенъ;

FIGURE 5. A typical material tribute to the dead writer: the Moscow house in which Nikolai Gogol' died and a sketch of his death mask. This issue commemorated the centenary of Gogol's birth. *Vol'f Bookstore News* 12 (March 1909): 70.

stances, the materialization of the writer brought readers enhanced social cachet, the privileged information that made them feel, at least, *au courant* and cultured.[35]

The Vol'f firm considerably anticipated and thus determined their readers' respectful consumption of celebrity. It developed new products directly from the advertised portraits and biocritical sketches appearing in the *News*. These are epitomized by Vol'f's packaging of Tolstoy, certainly the most revered and best known living writer in fin-de-siècle Russia and the best candidate for celebrity exploitation. In what proves to be an extended advertisement in the October 1903 issue, the ubiquitous Rusakov opens with a review essay that claims for Tolstoy world celebrity:

> One can state boldly that no Russian or foreign writer awakens such interest *as a personality* as Count Tolstoy. The pettiest details about the life of the famous author of *War and Peace,* information about how he lives and works, about the circles he frequents, about the works of art he especially prefers, about the thinkers and writers he favors—all of this is read with voracious interest by millions of intelligent readers throughout the cultured world and serves as a subject of conversations, debates, and discussions not only among the great writer's admirers, but also among his sworn enemies and ill-wishers, whom Tolstoy, like all great writers, has in abundance. Since the world began, since the beginning of human consciousness, there has not been such a phenomenon as this all-encompassing interest in this writer's *personality*.[36]

Of particular significance here is Rusakov's unabashed jumbling of vocabularies signaling culturedness ("intelligent readers," "cultured world," "great writer") and consumer desire ("personality," "voracious interest"). As he mounts a spectacular sales pitch, inflated by the impression of an unprecedented and worldwide "phenomenon," he also systematically reassures readers that their curiosity is respectable and cosmopolitan.

The product Rusakov pitches is deliberately designed to satisfy what he calls "the intelligent public." It comprises a kind of high-quality scrapbook on Tolstoy, helpfully elaborated in its title: "Count L. N. Tolstoy, the great writer of the Russian land, his wife, family, friends, critics, and

interpreters in portraits, engravings, medallions, paintings, sculptures, caricatures, etc."[37] (See figure 6.) This album performs a fascinating metamorphosis, materializing the person of the writer into a commercially viable, but nonetheless respectable book, and rendering the writer himself into a collectible of a higher order. In lieu of buying a Tolstoy statuette (recall the stigma the *News* attached to such "dead things"), a reader in good conscience could purchase a printed collection of such statuettes, for their transformation into printed matter, complete with edifying explanations, sanctioned them as evidence, knowledge, the acceptable imprint rather than the idolization of a revered subject. As the album's editor makes plain to an intelligent yet presumably unconvinced audience, the totality and clarity of this sort of printed collection (the assumption here is that the visual is clearer than the verbal) qualify it as an important biography and a national treasure. Consumption of the Tolstoy album (priced at thirty kopecks, unless one splurged for the sixty-kopeck vellum paper edition) not only sated readers' "voracious interest" in the writer's personality, but also forever impressed on them and their descendants a "canonical" rendition of the writer's life. Thus, in its *News* representation, even a glorified picture book inextricably joined market value with cultural value.

Market Access

When the *News* considers the contemporaneous publication of *The Golden Fleece (Zolotoe runo)*, one of several magnificent turn-of-the-century art journals financed by wealthy industrialists (in this case, Nikolai Riabushinskii), one might expect approval for such an extraordinary instance of the Russian market subsidizing Russian culture.[38] The reviewer, M. Vasil'evskii, does credit the exemplary production standards and cultural import of such publications as *The Golden Fleece* and *The World of Art,* but he mainly criticizes their real costs and limited currency. *The Golden Fleece* operated at an annual loss of 71,818 rubles and attracted only 638 subscribers; its predecessor, *The World of Art,* folded for much the same reason. Rather than applaud the millionaire backers who financed such ephemeral beauty, Vasil'evskii deprecates

французскому, почти повсемѣстно послѣ беллетристики интересуется, какъ показываютъ отчеты, популярно-научными книгами по всѣмъ отраслямъ знанія, и вовсе не беретъ книгъ по музыкѣ и искусству, тогда какъ у французскаго читателя научнымъ книгамъ отводится всего лишь четвертое мѣсто.

Л. ЛЬВОВСКІЙ.

жизни знаменитаго автора «Войны и мира», свѣдѣнія о томъ, какъ онъ живетъ и работаетъ

ОБЛОЖКА АЛЬБОМА «ГР. Л. Н. ТОЛСТОЙ».

ЖИВАЯ БІОГРАФІЯ ГР. Л. Н. ТОЛСТОГО. — КРИТИЧЕСКАЯ ЗАМѢТКА ВИКТОРА РУСАКОВА.

Можно смѣло утверждать, что ни одинъ писатель—не только изъ русскихъ, но и иностранныхъ—какъ личность

въ какомъ кругу вращается, какія произведенія искусства особенно почитаетъ, какіе мыслители и писатели пользуются его расположеніемъ и т. д. и т. д.—все это читается милліонами интеллигентныхъ читателей во всемъ культурномъ мірѣ, читается со захватывающимъ интересомъ, служитъ предметомъ разговоровъ, споровъ, разсужденій и пр. — и притомъ не только въ средѣ усердныхъ поклонниковъ великаго писателя, но даже и среди его прямыхъ враговъ и недоброжелателей, какихъ у Л. Н. Толстого, какъ у каждаго великаго человѣка, найдется не малое количество. Положеніе Л. Н. Толстого, какъ писателя, совершенно исключительное. Съ тѣхъ поръ, какъ существуетъ міръ, съ тѣхъ поръ, какъ помнитъ себя

ТИТУЛЪ АЛЬБОМА «ГР. Л. Н. ТОЛСТОЙ».

не возбуждалъ такого интереса, какъ графъ Л. Н. Толстой. Мельчайшія подробности изъ

человѣкъ, не было въ исторіи явленія, подобнаго положенію этого писателя въ

FIGURE 6. Rusakov's article on the Tolstoy album, complete with pictures of the cover and title page. Note that the cover photo includes a Tolstoy statuette. *Vol'f Bookstore News* 6 (October 1903): 101.

them as capricious and inferior to the "professional publishers" who must weigh "the benefit of each publication for the broad masses." His comparison reinforces the notion of the publisher's superiority to the patron. What is mainly wrong with these journals, he submits, is their exclusivity: "It seems to us that there would be greater benefit if that sum of 71,818 rubles were spent not on spoiled art-lovers (who, as they say, cannot be impressed), but on inculcating good taste among the masses."

In this shrewd review of the "competition," Vasil'evskii highlights yet another recurring theme in *Vol'f Bookstore News*—the importance of market access. He implies that the mere production or reproduction of high culture cannot constitute "benefit." Like food, culture should be prepared for and given to the hungry, not the gourmands. The *News* belabored this thesis from various angles, with articles lamenting the paucity of books in the provinces, commending publishers on cheap editions of good contemporary works, and agitating for school editions of the classics. Perhaps more important, it also put this thesis into practice with the catalogue and services it offered subscribers. A deprived schoolchild or provincial reader could order a needed volume at a reasonable price from Vol'f's huge stores. If readers could not afford many such purchases, they were advised to form a "union of readers," which could pool its resources for subscriptions.[39] Clearly the firm paid more than lip service to concerns for a book's availability and affordability.

Vasil'evskii's critique implies yet another, subtler notion of market access developed in the *News*, one that challenges critical rather than financial and physical exclusivity. Although the journal readily coopted book endorsements by high-culture critics, in most instances it countered their attempts to establish an exclusive canon of "beneficial" books. Writers for the *News* presumed their own authority to review and recommend, and they cleared their path to power by deploring the injustices perpetrated by past critics and dismissing the present scene as "critical hard times" *(kriticheskoe bezvremen'e)*. Adrift in the current critical inane, the *News* critics intimated that they were above the partisanship of their politicized predecessors and fashionmongering peers. They implied that their criticism was the more sound because they often let the "amateur" public guide them to good writers. An early *News* article about the "meaning, use, and inadequacies of the periodical press" hints at this credo when it asserts that "the public, of course, is the best judge" of a writer's merits (in this case, a writer for the journal itself).[40] *News* critics monitored, publicized, and usually approved what was already popular.[41] They credited the sensitive reader with greater perspicacity than that of recognized critics.[42] And they were quick to point out when the reading public outstripped the critics in discovering a writer.[43]

While writers for the *News* did not relinquish their role as critics, they masked the arrogance of their authority with just such ingratiating deference, and their projected "alliance" with readers furnished them with a convenient mandate for revaluating Russian literature both diachronically and synchronically. Their basic criterion for judgment was what they deemed to be real talent—some essential and conveniently elusive quality that cut through politics and fashion. As they reviewed the past achievements of Russian writers (and not so coincidentally found in them new publishing opportunities), they portrayed themselves as recovering "classics" from undeserved oblivion or opprobrium. In one particularly pathos-ridden example, the critic Pavel Rossiev mourns the unsung reputation of the "novelist-ethnographer" Pavel Mel'nikov, who had "the great misfortune" to live and die in an era bereft of great critics.[44] (Rossiev here coins the term "critical hard times.") To dramatize this point, Rossiev recounts his pilgrimage to Mel'nikov's forgotten grave and reconsiders the writer's epitaph: "I think that both P. I. Mel'nikov and 'Andrei Pecherskii' await a more nonpartisan assessment than that given them by critics of a certain renowned persuasion. I firmly believe that there will come a time when this gifted writer and leading expert on Russian life and the Russian folk spirit will be rewarded according to his deserts." After escorting readers through the vicinity that Mel'nikov made famous and in which he is still "beloved and understood," Rossiev metaphorically leaves them—enlightened and indignant—at the writer's shabby graveside.

Whereas Rossiev opts for rank sentimentalism, local support, and broad accusatory strokes, A. Nalimov, in reviewing the work of the poet and prose writer Evdokiia Rostopchina, performs a kind of critical dance —sometimes endorsing and sometimes cautiously sidestepping established critics. This approach may stem from his doubly difficult subject, a woman writer firmly allied with conservative aristocratic circles. Nalimov admits as much halfway through the piece, probably by way of deflecting predictable attacks. But there is no doubt that he seeks to rehabilitate Rostopchina's reputation, as shown in his star-studded second paragraph:

> Rostopchina's fiftieth anniversary is almost upon us (December 3). Will our literary circles remember her? Will they remember an authoress whose name resounded in her time—one whom Viazemskii pronounced the "Moscow Sappho," one to whom Senkovskii, Pletnev, and Shevyrev gave enthusiastic reviews, and one whom even Belinskii credited with "poetic inspiration"?[45]

Although Nalimov subsequently admits that the critic Dobroliubov ridiculed his subject and the aforementioned Belinskii damned her with faint praise, he nonetheless persists in finding "something promising" in Rostopchina's dated work. In this period of increased female authorship and readership, Nalimov partly exonerates Rostopchina's suspect classism with evidence of her incipient feminism. A protofeminist message, he implies, lends her work both social relevance and market appeal.

The two examples of Mel'nikov-Pecherskii and Rostopchina demonstrate the wide range of works that *News* writers aimed to make critically palatable for their readers. In both instances, the reviewers sought to convince their audience that these authors were worth reading, despite their previous critical devaluation. Of course, the *News* reader had to rely on the reviewer's critical word, but this dependency was usually finessed by the critic's magnanimous or conciliatory persona and careful identification with the reader's "best interests." In an ingenious strategy, *News* critics created the illusion of sharing their authority with reader-consumers. They enjoined readers to right past critical wrongs, to trust their own critical judgment, and to make their own stars.

Rusakov worked this strategy most ambitiously in his review article on the novelist Nikolai Leskov. His piece hooks the reader at the outset with a variation on the graveside scene. He actually reports on the funeral procession, with its plain wooden coffin and handful of mourners. The plank coffin was Leskov's own idea, Rusakov explains, but he attributes the poor attendance to the fact that

Leskov was not one of those writers who kept to a dominant party line and deftly cultivated his popularity among the youth. On the contrary, Leskov always had a lot of enemies and ill-wishers who did not understand him and considered him retrograde, an enemy of progress and youthful impulses and ambitions, almost a literary informer on young people, who tried to destroy the dreams of the 1860s progressive circles.[46]

To dispel this critical storm cloud, Rusakov ushers his readers behind the scenes into a tête-à-tête with a distraught Leskov still fending off "unjust" attacks in the 1880s. Rusakov boldly pitches his infamous subject to the reader as a worthy celebrity. His title promises to divulge "How the Author of *The Cathedral Folk* Lived and Worked." His sketch dwells on the peculiarities of Leskov's home and writing habits, and one of his telling conclusions is that "Leskov's personality is far from being properly appreciated." He not only lobbies for the writer's critical rehabilitation, but also musters all the ingredients for celebrity consumption—to the point of remarking on Leskov's reader-mirroring passion for collecting.[47] (See figure 7.)

Rusakov is also quite dogged in asserting Leskov's talent, testifying to his perfectionism, his love of language, and his excellence as a raconteur. He uses the odd measure of the paucity of his works to prove Leskov's quality, surmising that the writer would have produced four to five times more if he had not been so painstaking in his revisions. Most significantly, Rusakov finally invokes the reader as judge: "The indisputable popularity of Leskov's works shows that our public does not always blindly follow the directions of the critics." With this closing compliment, Rusakov sets Leskov's rehabilitation in motion from the bottom up.

The synchronic process of reviewing the hordes of contemporary writers, by contrast, entailed more evident discrimination from *News* critics. To a certain degree, they had to reverse their inclusive course so as not to seem too facile in their enthusiasms, no matter how much those enthusiasms reflected the "reading public's" buying patterns. One strategy cast the *News* critic in the part of concerned cultural and moral guardian, as the situation demanded, although such guardianship was assumed in overt service to rather than in defiance of the public. Rusakov illustrates this tactic, for instance, as he ponders the "pornographic trend" in recent writing. Again, the reader finds him on the scene, in conversation with a

FIGURE 7. A strategic picture of Leskov at his desk, surrounded by his collected clocks, "little pictures," and "ivory statuettes." *Vol'f Bookstore News* 3
(March 1900): 82.

"serious" journal's publisher (interestingly enough, a woman), who de-
plores the many pornographic submissions she receives from her journal's established writers. A kind of Socratic dialogue ensues in which
Rusakov attempts to rebut the publisher's objections with the old maxim
that literature must mirror life, but after several months of reading and
deliberation, he echoes her shock and dismay. His recapitulation of the
"pornographic acts" that occur in works by Lidiia Zinov'eva-Annibal,
Mikhail Kuzmin, Mikhail Artsybashev, and others is designed to shock
and dismay the reader as well. The ever-politic Rusakov refrains from
directly blaming either Russian society or its writer-reflectors, yet he interjects his own "aesthetically discriminating" moralizing:

> But a sense of fine art, a sense of beauty should suggest to the artist
> when he must stop in representing real life and where the boundary
> of art lies. The depiction of the pathological aspects of a perverted
> sex drive, like other processes of human life, does not belong in good
> literature. And the sprinkling of erotomania in literature is an action

which, despite freedom of speech, is subject to legal punishment, like any ordinary crime against morality.[48]

Rusakov returns to this thorny question in the following issue of the *News*, only this time he converses with a "famous scholar" who more or less convinces him that some of these producers of "pornography" are mentally ill.[49] This conclusion conveniently permits him to dissociate the pitiable person of the author from the condemned work. What is most significant, however, is that the critic maintains the impression of being morally sound in a conventional sense without being censorious. Rusakov manages to express the general reader's concerns and discomfort without demonizing any one author or representing himself as an undiscriminating philistine. (As his scholar-interlocutor remarks, the mentally ill do have their "bright moments.")

Yet this tactic was frequently and expediently reversed. Even Rusakov's mild-mannered protest against "pornographic" works by such writers as Kuzmin and Artsybashev was not binding in the *News*. In a number of illustrative cases, the critic's guardianship is offset by a different sort of critical discrimination—really, a kind of second-glance redemption. Exactly a year after Rusakov vented his dismay about pornography in Russian literature, the *News* reconsiders the chief architect and blueprint of this trend—Artsybashev and his scandalous novel, *Sanin*. A lead arti- . cle by Vsevolod Borisov treats the reader to a visit with the much-visited author, who, simply dressed and earnest in his manner, shows no inclination to talk about sex or to indulge in vulgarity: "As a man [he] is many times more moral than most of his contemporary writers—and undeniably more moral than many of his heroes."[50] As it happens, the sincere Artsybashev prefers to characterize his main hero as "sincere" rather than "amoral," vehemently objecting when a visitor attempts to banalize Sanin as a deceiver. Other reported virtues further enhance the author's image—his aid to struggling writers, his neglect of his own poor health to nurse his ailing wife. Upon closer acquaintance, the mad pornographer appears to be quite sane and decent.

Borisov's revelation is immediately followed by Rusakov's review of *Sanin*, a piece that at first largely seems to reiterate and elaborate the critic's prior complaints. Rusakov's plot summary disapprovingly recounts the heroes' sexual obsessions and conquests and the heroines' "easy" capitulation; his critical gaze singles out the "simply vulgar" depiction of several erotic scenes and the author's apparent fixation on breasts. Yet his final paragraph enacts a remarkable about-face:

> Despite all of this, *Sanin* is indisputably a talented work, a highly talented work that is worth reading, that should be read. It is written with such elan, such fire, and it is saturated with such "dark, voluptuous trembling" that only a reader with a completely shrivelled heart, a person with no drop of feeling could read this amazing book indifferently and dispassionately. . . . And *Sanin* doubtless will have a lasting place in contemporary belles lettres. Right now it is only a *succès de scandale.* But time will pass, and the real virtues of *Sanin* will be recognized apart from those pornographic scenes, words, and phrases that shock so many readers.[51]

With somewhat suspect generalizations and in a suddenly fervent tone, Rusakov concludes by attributing "real talent" to Artsybashev's pornography. Here he accentuates his critical authority, penetrating through the scandalous success of the novel to its "real virtues" and "lasting place." Whatever Rusakov's motive for doing so—whether he actually discerned these qualities or was obligated to capitalize on the book's success—it is significant that he resorts here to the old role of "discriminating critic," that he redeems a contemporary work as a literary expert flaunting his perspicacity, eloquence, and capacity for feeling. Whereas the critic recovering a past work manipulated an alliance with the "general reader," affirming popular taste in the face of past critical condemnation, the critic redeeming a contemporary work from charges of shameless trendiness did so by pulling critical rank, discovering real merit in the text *in spite of* its popularity. Not surprisingly, both tactics had the same practical consequence: readers felt that their choices and purchases were culturally and even morally vindicated, and they were encouraged to buy more and more widely.

News critics truly tested their capacity to redeem in reviewing the works of popular women writers. As I suggest in chapter 4, these products epitomized the exploration, if not the establishment, of a new "middle" literary stratum and hence were special highbrow targets. An early reaction to the first volume of Verbitskaia's *Keys to Happiness,* for example, attempts to overwhelm the reader with enthusiastic and emotional praise. It lauds the book's "spirit" rather than its contents, transcribes that spirit through extensive quotation of the ecstatic monologues in the novel, and anthropomorphizes it as "the youngest book of the year."[52] Although there is plenty of potential pornography in *Keys to Happiness* (admittedly, more in later volumes), this reviewer persists in generalizing it as a "hymn of a girlish heart." The fact of Manya's passionate girlishness (and the reviewer's echoing style) succeeds in expiating and ennobling the book, as the review firmly concludes:

> Even if these words have already been uttered, then they have never before resonated so beautifully and nobly, and it is this that distinguishes the works of the author of *Keys to Happiness* from those vulgar or pornographic hymns to "free love" shown from a different angle of vision that unnecessarily repel and lack the poetry that makes life worthwhile.

It is intriguing that the reviewers of both *Keys to Happiness* and *Sanin* base their critical redemption on the work's emotional power. They seem to be discriminating according to criteria quite different from those of their highbrow predecessors and peers, as if they are anticipating a middlebrow aesthetic with its valorization of high emotion and strong personality.[53]

Yet in some reviews even the resourceful *News* critics threw up their hands. Such was the case with Evdokiia Nagrodskaia's *Wrath of Dionysus,* another scandalous best-seller published in 1911. The *News* reviewed the novel twice, its second attempt clearly making amends for its first negative reaction. (The phenomenal sales of Nagrodskaia's novel, the work of a relative unknown, took many naysayers by surprise, including the critic at the *News*.)[54] Much of this second review recapitulates the novel's extraordinary popularity and controversial critical reception, thereby deferring its own moment of judgment to the final paragraph. When that moment arrives, the reviewer beats a shrewd diplomatic retreat:

> They [female fans] say that *Wrath of Dionysus* is written clearly and richly, in an exemplary, light, and expressive language, and that it thrills them with its psychological insight. But there are no small number of novels that possess the same qualities and yet go unno-

ticed. This means that there is something else in *Wrath of Dionysus* that elicits and continues to elicit interest, something that the critics cannot discern and that even its most ardent fans—more likely, female fans—are unable to account for.

Can no one explain the success of Mme. Nagrodskaia's novel?[55]

Rather than offend Nagrodskaia's many "ardent fans," the reviewer not only cedes them the floor ("they say"), but also concedes his own critical limitations. Although he cannot find a familiar aesthetic reason for the novel's success and so cannot play the role of comforting authority, he takes care not to dismiss the reader's judgment. Perhaps more than any other reviewer in *Vol'f Bookstore News*, he acts on the implicit principle that "the buying reader is always right." He conveys the reader's taste as another form of discrimination, as the sensing of an unknown aesthetic, not vulgar enjoyment. As this odd example reaffirms, the Vol'f critics stood ready to validate and explicate every reader choice—whether that choice was Tolstoy or Leskov, Gorky or Nagrodskaia. If a reader sought help in choosing, the Vol'f critics approved and proffered as many different works as space and time permitted. Through such customized "service," the *News* facilitated market access without appearing to compromise on quality.

Market and Empire

The very existence of the Vol'f firm demonstrated how imperial Russia's admission of the market opened wide relations between Russian culture and the rest of the world. A non-Russian businessman such as Vol'f had succeeded in applying his knowledge of the Western book market to the Russian scene. His stores purveyed a supposedly global sampler to the Russian reader and his tastefully commercialized journal initiated the Russian reader into the ways of Western book culture. The latter operation was the more delicate, for it involved ranking Russia in an ambiguous European world.

The *News* conducted this operation with an unfailing patriotism founded on the premise of Russian culture's equal place among the great European cultures of the period. Like other Russian publications, it touted culture as the tsarist empire's most glorious and least sullied export.[56] In fact, the *News* occasionally dared to intimate the superiority of Russian culture to that of the West—particularly on account of its lesser commercialization. A representative article on "advertising in literature" quite pointedly contrasts Tolstoy's decency with the publicity-stirring misconduct of one of his American publishers; all of its other references to "advertising" are taken from French literature.[57]

Always implying Russia's grand national endowment, Vol'f's gentle lessons in book culture constituted not so much a catch-up education as a necessary turn to secular matters. The how-to of book collection and maintenance served as complementary Martha to the Mary of the Russian reader's spiritual concerns.[58] Such a "corrective" also implied, quite flatteringly, that the Russians thought too much about the soul and not enough about the flesh. In "On the Book and Its Exterior" (May–June 1904), Dmitrii Filosofov, a critic for the *World of Art,* offers *News* readers this penetrating analysis of their national book complex:

> Russians love to read; they value books. The gray dreariness of provincial life and a thirst for education and enlightenment force our intelligentsia and semi-intelligentsia to devour one useful book after another, especially if that book augurs a solution of "the cursed questions." We produce more "serious" (thick) journals than any other country in the world, and their widespread circulation attests to our intelligentsia's great need to read.
>
> Parallelling this special, youthfully exalted love for the book as a source of knowledge is an astonishing indifference to its *exterior,* its physiognomy. It seems, rather, that the grayer and uglier the book, the more appeal and assurance it holds for the Russian reader. A Russian reader is convinced that a beautiful book cannot be useful and serious. All beauty is harmful luxury. Of course, not everyone consciously persecutes the aesthetic. Many simply unconsciously fear beauty out of inherited habit, and they have become so inured to the ugliness around them that they don't notice it and don't suffer from an unaesthetic external culture.
>
> There are very serious and profound reasons for this. Russian culture has gained every step forward with such difficulty and suffering that it is simply not up to luxury and beauty.[59]

Filosofov defines the Russian complex as a kind of puritanism, a religious asceticism that curiously reverses the Russian Orthodox emphasis on external show. He imputes the Russian disregard for decoration to an excess rather than an absence of reverence. Yet Filosofov also implies, in the most sympathetic possible terms, an underdevelopment in this attitude. The Russians with their "youthfully exalted love" simply have not yet graduated to an appreciation for beauty. Russia's lack of a material book culture is not just a matter of religious habit, but also a sign of historical hardship and cultural immaturity.

This mixed message obtained in other discussions of book culture, as *News* critics issued a muted appeal for the next "step forward" in national progress. They implied that Russian publishers, writers, and readers needed to secularize their approach for their own international good. For example, Rusakov's promotion of the Tolstoy album slyly interjects that this sort of product may be completely new in Russia, but it is commonly published "abroad." With one deft aside, he goads the proud Russian reader into a worldwide competition. Another article on book decoration identifies the gap more plainly. While French, German, English, and Swedish publishers have moved forward in such matters, the anonymous author writes, "we Russians still lag behind this pan-European trend in book decoration, although we demonstrate an ever-growing taste for such things."[60] *News* critics insinuated that material investment would manifest innate national worth, that the development of book culture would identify imperial Russia as an explicitly enlightened and technologically advanced European empire. The concerns of the market, refined into the concerns of book culture, were invoked to measure Russia's imperial greatness, even as their "newness" underscored Russia's peculiar spiritual superiority.

If the market so clearly affected attempts by the *News* to advance the Russian empire in the world, how did it influence its readings of the empire from within, of Russian imperial *subjects*? Did the *News* present a united imperial front or vent the diversity and competing visions of its readership? Did market value outweigh internal political concerns? The journal's coverage of Polish literature serves as the best illustrated and certainly most appropriate case for my purpose. Such a westward-looking publication as the *News* singled out the Kingdom of Poland for special treatment because, of all Russia's subject nations, this would-be nation enjoyed the highest reputation in Europe.

A perusal of the *News* catalogue and its advertisements shows that the market did dictate one sort of equality for the Poles. Russian translations of Orzeszkowa's and Sienkiewicz's novels regularly appear in catalogue listings that include the translated texts of William Shakespeare, Jean-Jacques Rousseau, and Mark Twain, as well as new editions of Pushkin's and Tolstoy's works. Polish periodicals, like their Western European counterparts, merit an entirely separate catalogue section. An advertisement for the third part of Sienkiewicz's novel, *The Crusaders*, shares column space with an advertisement for the works of Victor Hugo.[61] And Adam Mickiewicz's various works, collected and individual, are granted an exceptional three-quarters of an advertising page, mammoth script, and the distinction of named translators and illustrators.[62]

Nor did the *News* skimp on its narrative tribute, although their representation was judiciously "rationed"; the journal was more likely to focus on a few select Poles who garnered the greatest critical reputation and/or the greatest sales. Therefore Orzeszkowa earns a lavish obituary in which she is called a "great heart" and recognized as a writer for all humanity.[63] Ever attuned to the market, the *News* devotes a lead essay to Sienkiewicz's success and elsewhere mimics the Polish press in citing the "great writer's" opinions about literature.[64] In relating politically problematic episodes in these writers' biographies, the *News* observes a magnanimous neutrality, replacing government censure with artistic appreciation or indirect report. A sketch of Mickiewicz's life scrupulously glosses over his anti-tsarist involvements and ponders from a high-minded distance how his patriotism fueled his artistry.[65] Indeed, the biographer V. V. Chuiko ascribes the nationalist polemics between Mickiewicz and Pushkin to "poetic questions" (the Pole's anti-tsarist poems provoked the Russian's most patriotic verse), and he assures the reader that this "temporary disagreement" would have passed if Pushkin had lived a few more years.[66] Chuiko effects a quite amazing sleight-of-view in summing up Mickiewicz's significance, inducing the reader to forget that the tsarist empire was responsible for the Polish poet's tragedy: "He is a tragic poet in the highest sense of the word—like Dante, who also devoted his genius to the political and social unification and restoration of Italy and who, like Mickiewicz, wandered in exile and died in poverty."

Chuiko heaps honors on the Pole by comparing him to great European poets (the list includes Goethe, Hugo, and Byron, as well as Dante), and he eschews a simpleminded chauvinism that would condemn Mickiewicz's rebelliousness and dismiss his work as seditious. But his magnanimity also harbors condescension. *News* critics implied their position to be "above" politics and oriented to the "high" questions of art, yet they almost invariably played the role of imperial arbiters who presumed to see farther and to judge better than their subject brother Slavs. Chuiko opens his essay with a generous (and ultimately self-serving) vision of Mickiewicz among the Europeans, and then he whisks the Pole off for Russian consumption and influence: "In Russia his name is more popular than that of any other foreign poet, and it is the more dear because it is closely tied with the name of Pushkin." Admittedly, Chuiko is writing for a Russian audience, but his comment serves to remind the Russian reader that Russians, among all Europeans, best appreciate and connect with the Poles.[67]

Moreover, as at least half of this article spells out, Russian culture (embodied here in the example of Pushkin) is shown to exert a most salutary influence on the inherently limited Poles. During the five years of Mickiewicz's Russian exile, Chuiko claims that the poet "discarded his provincialism and became a man of the world. Much that had been dark and unclear in him became conscious; he became less one-sided, his conceptions broadened, and his intellectual horizon expanded." Once in Russia, it would seem, a Pole can at last become a man of the world, and consequently a great poet. Although Mickiewicz produced his most vehemently anti-tsarist work during and after this exile, Chuiko highlights instead the mutual admiration of Mickiewicz and Pushkin, two great Slavic poets. On the one hand, as I have pointed out, this focus undermines a narrowly nationalist bias; on the other, it specifically plays down *Polish* dissent, the unfortunate stumbling block in what otherwise would have been a beautiful friendship. Because Chuiko does not admit Russia's imperializing role, he defuses Mickiewicz's political charge by deeming him vaguely tragic and a man who "could not not submit" to the ultra-determining, yet expediently generalized "influence of his time."[68]

As Chuiko's understated essay shows, there is probably no more effective way to maintain imperial authority than by exercising an enlightened condescension. A similar tactic is at work in Glovskii's obituary piece on Orzeszkowa in which the critic hastens to defend the writer from a narrowly Polish reputation: "But although she only knew and loved her own people well, anguishing over them and suffering together with them, at the same time she managed through the strength of her talent to bring her people closer to all humanity, to make them comprehensible to others." Such mediating authority presumed a global reach: the magnanimous Russian critic demonstrated his "superior" knowledge of the European scene and intervened on the lucky Pole's behalf. Rusakov delivers a characteristically shrewd performance of this role in his essay on Sienkiewicz's success "in Russia and abroad." At the outset, he stages an "us-versus-them" scenario that conveniently assigns to Poles co-star status:

> Before our very eyes something truly extraordinary is taking place.
> The European West, that proud West which teems with famous
> writers, which never before allowed that there could be great writers
> from Slavic countries and neglected Slavic literature, suddenly,
> over the last five or six years, has completely changed its mind.
> The foreign-sounding names of Tolstoy, Dostoevsky, Turgenev,
> Orzeszkowa, Sienkiewicz, and Prus have become familiar and even
> familial in the West. Those works written in a "barbaric" language by
> authors from nations the West recently deemed "half-cultured" are
> being read intensively, translated, published in dozens of editions,
> commented on, discussed, debated, and imitated. A truly extra-
> ordinary fact![69]

This opening paragraph establishes the Russians' credentials as Polish interpreters, for both groups have shared an undifferentiated neglect and reaped an undifferentiated glory. Rusakov's frontispiece also happens to steal some of Sienkiewicz's thunder in an essay ostensibly devoted to his triumph. When he begins to chart the Polish writer's rise to success, he toys with the spotlight once again, recording the Poles' instantaneous recognition of native genius and then ventriloquizing for a skeptical West: "'We all know how the Poles exaggerate the importance and talent of their native sons; Sienkiewicz is probably one of those propped-up celebrities whose glory subsists on Polish patriotism alone.'"[70] Casting Westerners as imperialist snobs, Rusakov paves the way for the generous, perspicacious Russians, whose "critics and reading intelligentsia" recognized Sienkiewicz's merits as quickly as his Polish compatriots. In fact, given the Polish writer's phenomenal popularity in Russia, Rusakov argues that "Sienkiewicz's glory reached the West *through Russia*"—more specifically, through the superior offices of Russian critics and readers.

As it turns out, Rusakov is simply the latest in an illustrious line of facilitating Russians, and it is his specific task to discover which works of the Polish author especially attracted the Western public. The Russian reader, he quickly notes, feels spiritually close to most of Sienkiewicz's novels, "despite their specifically Polish character." Yet it was the un-Polish *Quo Vadis* that won the heart of the West, eclipsing even the "enormous popularity" of Tolstoy's *Resurrection* and surprising even experienced Western booksellers who thought they knew their clientele. When pressed to account for the appeal of *Quo Vadis,* Rusakov falls back on the nebulous "something" that served Nagrodskaia's reviewer so well. In covering a Polish success story, he focuses on its international implications rather than its literary merits, thereby claiming that success as a partisan victory for "our" pan-Slavic side and representing the Russian cultural establishment as the true international handler of Polish culture.

Such coverage suggests that while the market dictated some deference to the tsarist empire's best-selling subjects, critics for the *News* devised quite effective ways of retaining imperial primacy and control. Unlike the spokesmen for Western European empires, who presumed to impose their "civilizing" stamp on "savage" places of conquest, the Russian writers for the *News* dealt with their already "civilized" subjects as level-headed referees. In the examples cited above, they subtly conveyed Polish provincialism and chauvinism, stepping forward to "serve" their co-regionalists as more worldly partners, interpreters, and benefactors. Packaging the Polish context, they euphemistically cast imperial repression as generic tragedy, erased the empire as an occupying force and Poland as a policed state, and rewrote Russia as a sophisticated, enlightened, and powerful cultural establishment that spearheaded Slavic opposition to Western hegemony. At least in the pages of the *News*, the market transformed the empire into a more civilized, but no less authoritative entity.[71]

Over the two decades of its existence (it ceased publication after the 1917 October Revolution), *Vol'f Bookstore News* industriously carried out its mandate to "cover literary phenomena" of every sort, and it expanded and diversified in response to its perceptions of its audience. We can only guess at its impact through its constant self-study and self-renewal. Vol'f's advanced marketing techniques do suggest, however, that the journal closely monitored and likely satisfied its subscribers.

What we can trace is how the *News* redefined and revaluated the book market for a Russian clientele, how it managed a finely calibrated infusion into that market of traditional Russian attitudes toward reading and books. The commercialization that threatened to profane the book and to prostitute the author—to demote the word from scripture to product—was tastefully diluted by assertions of the book's higher worth and reading's higher purpose; the transformation of the author into a legally entitled professional, a scholarly subject, and a refined collectible; the declassing, depoliticizing, and consumerist orientation of the critical establishment; the consequent expansion of a recommended canon; and the adoption of a material book culture as a means to imperial greatness and a sign of imperial prowess. In essence, *Vol'f Bookstore News* projected a "serious" Russian soul in a Western body, grounding and extending the intelligentsia's spiritual quest amid the material concerns and relations of a Western-style consumerism. In its innovative and tempered representation, the Russian book market remained a most "serious" business, and the Russian reader, still honored as a seeker, was further cultivated as collector, cultural arbiter, and enlightened despot.

six

Patronized Saints
Polonizing the Literary Market

Marketplace and Nation Space

THE LATE NINETEENTH-CENTURY Polish press also tended to integrate the literary market temperately and decorously, standing watch over the high reputation of "serious" Polish literature and on guard against a wholesale "bourgeoisification" of Polish culture. As in the Russian case, the many merchants who ventured into the publishing business in this period did so for profit, but their product rarely displayed a crass commercialism.[1] Whatever the publishers' views, the staff of the press—largely drawn from a dispossessed intelligentsia driven into the work force after 1863—ensured its generally moderate tone and steady maintenance of high-culture values.

Moreover, the commercialization of the Polish press did not represent the same precipitous descent from "sacred to secular" so cautiously navigated by the Russian press. Not only were Polish publishers and writers traditionally more attuned to Western models than their Russian counterparts, they also had had previous recourse to these models in coping with imperial interference. In her essays on Warsaw journalists, Alina

Słomkowska notes this expedient tailoring of national mission to Western forms in the post-1831 Polish émigré press and the Warsaw press of the 1850s. Denied political commentary and derived more from Paris and London prototypes than were Russian publications, the Polish press aspired to keep its far-flung readers informed and educated by whatever means available.[2] In his influential *Daily Gazette* (*Gazeta Codzienna*, later *Gazeta Polska*), Józef Kraszewski, one of the most respected pioneers of the Polish press, had approved the images of commerce and industry as early as 1861. Although Kraszewski initially disdained the West's "worship of Mammon," his disillusionment with the Polish aristocracy goaded him toward Positivist beliefs and practices *avant la lettre*.[3]

As such precedents indicate, the commercialization of the post-1863 Polish press yielded more national opportunities than dangers—especially in terms of circulation. A commercial venture could cross the boundaries of a partitioned Poland; a commercial publication presumably exploited rather than conspired with its Polish clientele.[4] The safe passage guaranteed by commerce served as a means to unification, a frequent and regular exchange in which Poles from each occupied territory shared their local news and immersed themselves in an otherwise outlawed or dispersed Polishness. Thus, concludes Słomkowska, the post-1863 journalists carried on the vital fusing and focusing efforts of their similarly besieged predecessors, who "defended the Polish language and culture, countering the fashion for foreignness that reigned in aristocratic salons. They labored to maintain national consciousness and unity in the era of the partitions. Despite their loss of independence, Poles could read and think in national terms, not submitting to germanification or russification or other attempts at deracination."[5] Polish publishers and journalists essentially transformed the marketplace of the press into a surrogate nation-space, reconstituting and considerably enhancing the nation on paper.

The fin-de-siècle Polish press also reiterated the general Western pattern of dynamic growth and reader-specific diversification. In the Kingdom of Poland, which housed the most influential, far-reaching, and standard-setting Polish publications, the press burgeoned from 20 to 140 titles in the period 1864–1905, split into a wide variety of formats (dailies, weeklies, biweeklies, monthlies), and addressed a host of special interests ranging from medical advice and child rearing to world culture.

Of particular importance and prestige among these diverse publications was the illustrated magazine, which combined "articles on Polish history, profiles of those accomplished in culture and science, descriptions of monuments, correspondents' reports, and coverage of current affairs."[6] The illustrated journal comprised a sort of compendium of what the "new" press had to offer Polish readers. It embraced traditional talking points and new technologies; it contained "serious" essays, news reports, chatty feuilletons, and advertising supplements; it was verbally engaging and visually attractive, illustrated with artistic reproductions and photographs. Much like the hybrid *Vol'f Bookstore News,* the illustrated magazine approximated a museum-marketplace with its displays and solicitations.[7]

A number of illustrated magazines vied for the attention of readers in this period, including *The Literary Repast (Biesiada Literacka)* for "poorer" members of the intelligentsia; *Ivy (Bluszcz)* for women; and the ambitious *World (Świat),* which promised up-to-the-minute narrative and photographic coverage of current cultural and political events.[8] Edited by the gifted journalist Stefan Krzywoszewski, *World* gathered a large readership and exerted much influence over the Polish publishing scene. But it shared that influence with the true standard-bearer for Polish illustrated journals, *The Illustrated Weekly (Tygodnik Ilustrowany).* This long-lived publication reigned as the period's "most serious sociocultural periodical covering all of Poland."[9]

Founded in 1859, *The Illustrated Weekly,* based in Warsaw, was not strictly a fin-de-siècle product, but its purchase in 1882 by the prestigious and powerful firm of Gebethner and Wolff, and the consequent installation of Józef Wolff as its innovative editor-in-chief, markedly increased its popularity and ensured its highly respected position by the end of the century.[10] Circulation figures leaped from 7,000 in 1898 to 20,000 in 1909; both coverage by and subscription to this Warsaw-based publication extended to all three partitions. The Gebethner and Wolff connection guaranteed that it would publish virtually all the most famous Polish writers.[11] *The Illustrated Weekly* proudly featured installments of such major works as *The Teutonic Knights* by Henryk Sienkiewicz, *The Peasants* by Władysław Reymont, and *Ashes* by Stefan Żeromski. The journal also attracted the essay-writing talents of Ignacy Matuszewski and

Bolesław Prus; beginning in 1886, Matuszewski served as its literary editor, and Prus helped to set the journal's basically Positivist tone with his "Weekly Chronicles."[12]

A sample listing of the journal's contents, indexed every six months, itemizes its attractions:

I. Biographical articles
II. Novels, novellas, and short stories
III. Poetry
IV. Historical studies, literary reviews, and serialized articles
V. Articles about painting, sculpture, and architecture
VI. Theater and music reviews
VII. Correspondence
VIII. Miscellaneous articles
IX. "Week by Week" (*"Z tygodnia na tydzień"*)
X. Reviews of new books
XI. "Chronicle of Current Events" (*"Kronika powszechna,"* a general news column)
XII. "From the Editor"
XIII. Graphology and financial news

The journal's prose contents ranged freely from creative fiction and "serious" studies to the informal "Week by Week"—a kind of "Talk of the Town" containing news tidbits, editorials, and advice. As its own advertisement boasts, *The Illustrated Weekly* succeeded in being at once an illustrated journal, cultural periodical, source of news, and family magazine.[13] A separate listing of illustrations reveals much the same sort of diversity in type and seriousness:

I. Portraits
II. Images of churches, important buildings, historical sites and monuments
III. Reproductions of art works and original drawings
IV. Miscellaneous drawings
V. Drawings for "Chronicle of Current Events"
VI. Humorous drawings

The subjects of the journal's reproductions also varied, encompassing realistic historical murals, art nouveau experiments, and sentimental portraits of children, animals, and peasants. But all were invariably printed using the latest technology. *The Illustrated Weekly* was one of the first periodicals to include color reproductions and was particularly extravagant in its use of photographs.[14]

Well stocked and diversified, this "marketplace" never strayed far from the main subject of Poland. Indeed, the journal is credited with "the significant popularization of Polish history and Polish intellectual and artistic achievements."[15] Although *The Illustrated Weekly* was produced in the Kingdom of Poland and such features as "Week by Week" were steeped in Warsaw life, the magazine aimed to cover all of Poland for all of Poland. It regularly featured reports by special correspondents to the Austrian and Prussian partitions as well as to certain sites in the Polish diaspora. Like other publications self-consciously serving as nation-space, it frequently tested its national reach by sponsoring all-Poland contests in writing, drawing, and even photography. It systematized this special focus with issues devoted to a single Polish image, oeuvre, trend, monument, or artist.[16] *The Illustrated Weekly* also negotiated coverage of such rallying events as the Battle of Grunwald (1410) and the participation of the Polish legions in the Napoleonic wars.[17] Despite tsarist censorship, the journal lavished ample resources on these patriotic episodes, reprinting relevant memoirs and reproducing mammoth two-page battle scenes.

The Illustrated Weekly's national focus, however, remained primarily cultural. Although tsarist governance allowed the journal to print a sometimes vehement critique of the Prussian authorities for their injustices against the Poles, the publication had to mask its anti-tsarist and pro-independence bias until after the 1905 revolution had liberalized censorship policies.[18] Operating under these restrictions and in accord with the lingering Positivist credo of industry, moderation, and realpolitik, *The Illustrated Weekly* eschewed an explicit political stance. The nationalism it purveyed was thereby generalized, depoliticized, and presented as cultural property to be inventoried and financed.

Poland in the World

In manipulating the market to serve national ends, *The Illustrated Weekly* adopted a tone somewhat different from the teacherly address of *Vol'f Bookstore News*. Like their Russian colleagues, Polish critics acknowledged the underdevelopment of their national book culture vis-à-vis Western models, but they did so with the urbane air of an initiate. These writers comported themselves as cultural authorities familiar with both the achievements and failings of the European market and self-assured enough to indulge in a kind of charming self-criticism against this background. Typical Polish sins, in their words, were dilettantism and egotism. Poles, for example, were neither as diligent nor as pedestrian as Germans in their cultural production, and they were too self-interested to embrace some common cultural cause.[19] Such facile worldliness conveyed both superiority and a sense of detachment. In contrast to Rusakov's bristling at European condescension, these critics understood and accepted the fickleness of European fashion. When Slavic writers triumph on the European scene, one commentator ascribes their victory to trendiness: "It has gotten to the point that Slavic literature has become a much desired and profitable 'commodity' on the world book market." He glibly adds that the vogue for Slavic literature has replaced the vogue for Scandinavian works.[20]

Writers for *The Illustrated Weekly* employed this kind of cosmopolitan market-wise persona to project the autonomy of Polish culture on the world scene. With their assured tone and "fashion sense," they implied that Polish artists could hobnob with their Western European counterparts and stood equal, if not superior, to any Russians. The *Weekly*'s writers tacitly resisted Russian intercession with their personae as long-time citizens of Europe. Whereas Vol'f's Russian commentators conveniently overlooked their nation's imperialism, the *Weekly*'s critics conveniently overlooked the fact of their nation's subjugation. The Russians played helpful big brother to the Poles on the grounds of a shared Slavic experience, while the Poles hinted at a very different kind of brotherhood with such oppressed nationalities as the Czechs or the Hungarians.

Cleverly articulating the illusion of Polish independence, the staff of

The Illustrated Weekly exploited new means of national self-assertion afforded by the market and the press. Sales figures gave them surprising leverage. Implying that imperial pressure could not dictate purchase, they were pleased to note the irony of Prus's and Sienkiewicz's popularity in Germany, the empire most cited (at least in the pages of *The Illustrated Weekly*) for its mistreatment of Poles.[21] Understandably more circumspect with the Russian authorities, an entry in the "Chronicle of Current Events" in 1906 issues a rather smug apology to the Moscow Art Theater for poor attendance at performances during its recent tour of Poland. Although the troupe meant well, "it came too soon," during a turbulent period when Poles were more concerned about obtaining their national rights than patronizing Russian theater.[22]

Just as consumer choice was reported to thwart imperial prowess, so press coverage managed to circumvent imperial dictation. The Russo-Japanese War proved to be a most interesting test case for *The Illustrated Weekly*. In lieu of a pro-tsarist slant, the journal paid much nonpartisan attention to the war, scrupulously balancing its investigation of the Russian and Japanese forces and supplementing news reports with the sophisticated travel notes of W. Sieroszewski, a leading Polish essayist on the Far East.[23] As a February 1904 article blandly states: "The differences between Russia and Japan are so great that this conflict must arouse the greatest interest."[24]

Covering other "imperial" subjects, *The Illustrated Weekly* does a little imperializing of its own, imposing a Polish model or endorsing a Polish world standard. In intriguing contrast to the Mickiewicz portrait in *Vol'f Bookstore News,* a portrait of Pushkin in *The Illustrated Weekly* recasts the Russian as a Polish Romantic poet, exaggerating his ties to Byron and accentuating his anti-tsarism and turbulent love life:

> Entering the poetic stage as a romantic, a bard *[wieszcz]* of a new
> rousing movement, Pushkin found a strong source of inspiration in
> the Napoleonic wars. He strongly expressed his heartfelt feelings in
> patriotic songs stylized on the verse of Zhukovskii, a poet who had
> been strongly influenced by the aggressive patriotism of contempo-
> rary German poetry. On the other hand, Pushkin was taken with
> the liberal spirit of the times and wrote poetry and epigrams of a so-
> ciopolitical nature, copies of which increased his popularity as well as
> the suspicions of Arakcheev [the tsar's minister of the interior].[25]

A bolder post-1905 essay, comparing Russian and Polish writers, dispenses with Pushkin altogether, declaring the archetypal Polish Romantic Mickiewicz to be "the true humanist."[26] Rewritten in *The Illustrated Weekly*, Russia's great poet turns out to be a somewhat paler Mickiewicz clone, and the parochial, "overly determined" Mickiewicz, as invoked in *Vol'f Bookstore News*, flamboyantly upstages all Russian rivals.

The Illustrated Weekly conveyed Polish autonomy most ingeniously by validating the material presence of Poland in the world. In aiming to cover all of Poland for all of Poland, the journal assayed a kind of physical coverage as well. Its correspondents not only transmitted reports about special events in the different occupied territories, but also described and photographed Polish colonies around the globe. Readers could learn about the bookstores, churches, associations, and daily lives of compatriots who had settled deep in enemy territory (that is, the Russian interior), retrace the difficult journey of Polish emigrants to South America, and scrutinize the photographs of Polish cathedrals erected in the United States.[27] Eventually (after 1905) they could obtain coveted information about Polish political exiles in Siberia. The journal conscientiously archived all evidence of Polish existence, recollecting the nation through words and pictures. (See figure 8.)

The Illustrated Weekly's emphasis on the Poles' "being in the world" was especially concentrated in the materialization of the artist. As noted in chapter 5, this materialization was widespread in the European press and reflected the joint influence of literary science (quantification of the artist) and the market (the celebrity made into a collectible). Yet in the Polish case, the artist's materialization also extended a national tradition and performed a vital national service. Since the failed 1831 uprising, the Polish artist—specifically, the Polish Romantic bard or *wieszcz*—had become the symbolic substitute for an absent political leadership.[28] Although the commercial press could not spell out this political-cultural analogy, its figuring of the artist stood in for Poland itself on the world scene. The materialized artist therefore distilled a materialized Poland and refracted an otherwise eclipsed national glory. (See figure 9.) Sienkiewicz's jubilee committee expressed this notion with typical extravagance: "Great writers are like a sun that is ignited by Providence and illuminates and warms its people. Their talent pours out the radiance of glory and a source of health and life."[29]

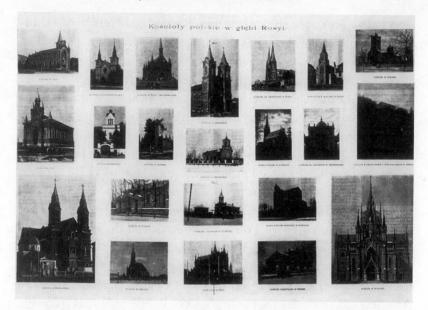

FIGURE 8. A particularly trenchant example of Polish presence in *The Illustrated Weekly*—a two-page photo spread for an article, "Polish Churches in the Russian Interior." *The Illustrated Weekly*, no. 40, 1906, 778–79.

Because they compensated for the deficiencies of a subjugated and seemingly second-rate European nation, it was imperative that Polish artists should "prove" equal to other European "greats." In one such series about the relative ranking of Mickiewicz, the prototype of the *wieszcz*, Matuszewski conducts a rather desultory survey of the "geniuses" of the world before he reaches the foregone conclusion that Mickiewicz "has the right to the title of world poet, whether or not he is known and understood beyond the Slavic countries."[30] An international frame of reference seemed essential for buttressing Poland's high pedestals. The Romantic poet Juliusz Słowacki is compared with Shakespeare (this on account of his delayed, but considerable influence), and the "complementary" geniuses of Sienkiewicz and Stanisław Wyspiański are likened to Michelangelo and Leonardo da Vinci.[31] The ritual proclamation of Poland's greatness was almost always uttered with a Bakhtinian "sideward glance" at the "world" culture of Western Europe, anticipating objections or calls for proof.[32]

Through the artist-surrogate, *The Illustrated Weekly* not only put Poland on the map, as it were, but also rendered it tangible and desirable

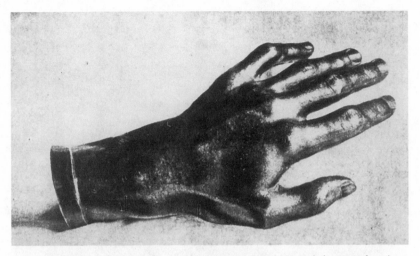

FIGURE 9. Some materializations of the artist inclined toward the sacred, as in this photograph of a bronze cast of Chopin's hand. In this case, the physical imprint of the artist is displayed as a kind of relic. *The Illustrated Weekly,* no. 42, 1899, 819.

to readers. This surrogate greatness was realized, in large part, by skillful and insistent articulation. (See figure 10.) Review articles and editorials cited examples of Polish greatness in the authoritative tones of the cosmopolitan and judicious critic. The "Chronicle of Current Events" reported it as fact, noting the number of translations and the popularity of Polish works abroad. The chatty "Week by Week" confidentially shared Polish triumphs and high-minded self-criticism with an exclusive club of readers.[33] In fact, the narrative voices of *The Illustrated Weekly* successfully mimicked, on a broad scale, the discourse of the salons and cafe society that served as de facto nationalist gatherings in the late nineteenth century.[34] They, too, featured pundits and gossips, talked incessantly about the nation, discussed the latest exhibits and publications, and fostered a sense of privileged responsibility and camaraderie among their club of readers. Readers were encouraged to conceive of themselves as educated and refined patriots who at once revered and were on familiar terms with their national geniuses. For narrator and reader, the great Polish artist became no distant deity, but an exceptional and indulged member of the family. Even reports on the artist's success read more than a little like hometown success stories.[35]

This multilayered connection of world genius with local readership

FIGURE 10. On occasion, *The Illustrated Weekly* indulged in kitschy murals that spelled out the artist's greatness, as in this rendering of Słowacki's moment of inspiration (conveyed by sunset, urn-topped monument, shining icon, and praying child) as he composed his famous "Hymn." *The Illustrated Weekly,* no. 38, 1899, 746–77.

was essential to national survival. The materialization of the "world-class" Polish artist required grounding in Polish customs, landscapes, and family ties. According to one writer's formulation, genius definitely belonged in the family:

> Descendants try to discern in the darkness of the ages that point in space and time from which emanates, like a tiny stream, the family that gave its people a great man, and the radiance of this famous name falls on the modest figures of his ancestors, who otherwise recede into the past.[36]

Predictably, Mickiewicz's family ties were traced and retraced with particular zeal. In its efforts to claim the poet as "one of us," *The Illustrated Weekly* sought out eyewitness accounts that attested to the poet's love of children and homely comforts and spawned articles on his lineage and hunting skills—popular preoccupations of the Polish gentry (and would-be gentry).[37] Readers were therefore encouraged to compare pedigrees and perhaps discover ancestral connections with their *wieszcz*, to hail him as boon companion, and to picture him relaxing in his dressing gown and frolicking with his children.

Recurring patterns of cooption underscored the artist's human relations with family, lovers, and, in some cases, the long-suffering "folk." A March 1899 article examined the role of Słowacki's mother as his protector and archivist.[38] The editors of *The Illustrated Weekly* explicitly thanked Chopin's nephew, Antoni Jędrzejewicz, for allowing them to peruse the composer's few remaining artifacts which, significantly enough, document the expatriate Chopin's Polish boyhood.[39] As was evident in its Pushkin portrait, *The Illustrated Weekly*'s biographical sketches tended to highlight the artist's love affairs as a formative influence, frequently reinforcing the Polish Romantic equation of tragic love with national heroism. Mickiewicz's ill-fated but artistically productive relationship with Maryla Wereszczakówna was the subject of much scrutiny and speculation. A lengthy series of articles closely followed the poet Zygmunt Krasiński's romance with Countess Delfina Potocka. The journal published their correspondence by way of fathoming the poet "as a man and a lover in the beautiful and ideal sense of the word, and even as a scholar."[40] With much the same emphasis on "national character," *The Illustrated Weekly* likewise explored the artist's love affair with the Polish people, describing variations on the popular scenario of the benevolent aristocrat earning the love of the peasants. So one critic unearthed evidence of Mickiewicz's appreciation of "folk culture," and another observed firsthand the respect paid by local peasants to the famous pianist Ignacy Paderewski when he was visiting his Kąśnia estate.[41]

The Illustrated Weekly most surely asserted the material link of genius to nation by touring physical landmarks, a tactic that reinforced, in turn, the journal's general recommendation for local travel. An ongoing series instructed readers "How to Visit [Their] Native Land." A more specialized version of the prescriptive travelogue appeared in Napoleon Rouba's "In the Footsteps of the Wieszcz" ("Śladami wieszcza"), articles that offered a kind of spatial biography of Mickiewicz by revisiting, in chronological order, his Polish places of residence. Rouba surveyed the many different permutations of the artist's relationship with his surroundings, in at least one instance crediting native genius with the revaluation of a poor landscape: "One would have to be Mickiewicz, with his largesse of sincere feeling, fantasy, and fame, to create two such beautiful ballads here on the shores of Świteź, culling motifs from this modest locality and filling in the rest with the creative sweep of one's poetic pen."[42] Whatever his verdicts about Polish nature, however, Rouba's travelogue, voiced in a tour director's *we* ("Let us cast our eyes once more . . .") and replete with authenticating photographs, confirmed both the reality and native provenance of the artist.

As a verbal commemoration, Rouba's travelogue represented a first step in placing the artist in a native landscape, matching person and site exclusively for *The Illustrated Weekly*'s readers. Concomitantly, the journal's reporters and essayists were quick to record and promote the further steps of *physical* commemoration. At this moment in Polish history, volunteer committees were eagerly producing material equivalents to Rouba's travelogue, erecting plaques and statues to mark the sites of a given artist's daily life. In this way, an emblem of the artist's greatness became part of the landscape—indeed, served to *distinguish* the landscape. This same act of commemoration applied to grave sites and the increasingly popular practice of reinterment, suggesting the artist's physical conflation with his or her native land. The "Chronicle" and special feature articles kept readers informed about these new landmarks, which (significantly) moved beyond Polish borders into the diaspora and constituted yet another means of placing Poland in the world.[43] A characteristic note about the grave of a Polish artist in Rome made this connection explicit: "This monument on foreign soil will bear eternal witness to the common thread between our community and our art, as will the name of the artist who glorified his people with his far-flung works."[44]

The trend of erecting monuments in this period, extensively documented by *The Illustrated Weekly*, often expanded the material connection between artist and site into a grander symbolic materialism.[45] Monuments to great artists, especially to Mickiewicz, appeared in virtually all the major cities of Poland at the turn of the century, and while these objects featured the subject's likeness (with varying degrees of success), they effectively transformed the artist's person into a symbolic figure which, wherever it was placed, was meant to connect with and signify the totality of Poland. As Matuszewski surmises in an 1898 article:

"A monument is a symbol, in the broadest sense, of powerful intellectual, social, religious, national, sovereign or general humanitarian aspirations," "a most laconic synthesis in tangible form."[46] Reporting on these projects, *The Illustrated Weekly* emphasized at once their *thingness* (what materials were used, the cost, and how construction was progressing—see figure 11) and their spiritual impact (the preliminary tributes, the doffing of hats, the ecstatic cries and spontaneous applause upon their unveiling). Thus, the journal presented the symbolic, yet material tribute to the great artist as one in a series of superhuman monuments—castles, churches, even the wonders of the national landscape. It also demonstrated how the very process of erecting a monument consecrated the surroundings and ennobled participants in the event. A typical report on the 1898 festivities for the new Mickiewicz monument in Kraków describes a city transformed:

> The magnificent procession went down Floriańska street, circled the Market, and entered Grodzka. All the windows and buildings were adorned with banners, tapestries, and busts of Mickiewicz. Every window along the entire route was filled with onlookers, thousands of whom also lined the sidewalks. Shouts greeting the huge procession resounded from the windows. All the stores in the city were closed.[47]

The erection of a single monument thus preempts "business as usual" and turns an entire city into monument consumers and, tacitly, nation builders. Every resident is to show off his or her purchased piece of Mickiewicz, thereby extending the metaphor and metonymy of nation.[48]

Patronized Saints: Homage and Patronage

As I have indicated, *The Illustrated Weekly*'s representation of the "great" sentimentalized them, romanticized them, and at the same time made them familiar, even familial. To a large extent, this sort of packaging evolved from the journal's variegated format and broad reach. Addressed to an ever increasing public, *The Illustrated Weekly* presented a rivetingly wide angle of vision on the artist, encompassing the intimate, neighborly, romantic, and mythical. This medium also facilitated the respectful com-

FIGURE 11. This characteristic photograph documents the process of installing Cypryan Godebski's monument of Mickiewicz in Warsaw. *The Illustrated Weekly,* no. 52, 1898, 1019.

modification of the artist's person, life style, and work. Especially in a journal like *The Illustrated Weekly,* whose appeal was predicated on its representation of the highest achievements in literature and the arts, the artist figured as the ultimate purchase.

In *The Illustrated Weekly* we see a fascinating exaggeration of the spiritual and commercial approaches to the artist manipulated in *Vol'f*

Bookstore News. On the one hand, as revealed by its attention to the artist's monument, *The Illustrated Weekly* maintained the long-standing Polish practice of paying homage to the great, idolizing them as the repository of world genius and national glory. On the other hand, this homage, with its absolute assertion of the artist's spiritual ascendancy, was to be underwritten by the readers themselves, what might be construed as their ministrations to the material being of the deity. It is this ingenious admixture of homage and patronage that transformed the image of the artist in *The Illustrated Weekly* from transcendent *wieszcz* into what I term the patronized saint.

Patronage of the artist clearly stemmed from the general commercial nature of the press and directly addressed the exigencies of the press's own artists. Like all writers in late nineteenth-century Poland, contributors to *The Illustrated Weekly* relied on the mass-circulation press for an extremely modest livelihood. They were personally and painfully aware of the writer's hard lot in Polish society and pragmatic about self-promotion. Moreover, since a number of the most famous Polish writers and painters also had their works published or reproduced in *The Illustrated Weekly* and, not coincidentally, issued in book or album form by the parent company of Gebethner and Wolff, it was in their best interest to encourage reader patronage of contemporary "greats."

Just as homage to the artist was shrewdly underpinned by concrete sales, so reader patronage was skillfully rendered a respectable and even noble act. *The Illustrated Weekly* aimed for a seamless blend of "serious" reverence with more or less tasteful advertising. To be sure, the journal's supplements displayed an unrefined hodgepodge of goods and services, juxtaposing publishers' lists with ads for perfume, cacao, soap, dry goods, and liquor, and occasionally hawking such crude commodifications of the artist as cufflinks and tiepins embossed with portraits of Mickiewicz, Słowacki, Krasiński, Sienkiewicz, and Prus.[49] Yet one could argue that the entire journal functioned as a subtle sales pitch. "Week by Week" amiably recommended authors to be sampled and artists to be seen and included occasional notes about subscriptions to *The Illustrated Weekly*. The "New Books" section in the end pages provided more formal "review" recommendations of the latest publications, many of them by Gebethner and Wolff. In its summary of the news, the "Chronicle" often as not reprinted rave reviews of "in-house" artists or otherwise trumpeted their commercial success around the globe.[50] Feature articles, in turn, focused more substantively on recent books and "important" artists, in quite a few instances praising the book that eventually emerged from installments published in the journal. Some issues of *The Illustrated Weekly* were devoted in part or in full to a particular artist or work and integrated their coverage, showcasing installments of works of fiction or art reproductions with accompanying biographies, critical sketches, extra illustrations, and perhaps a discreet ad on the journal's back page.[51]

In fact, the joint packaging of fiction installments and art reproductions functioned as a kind of marketing ploy, especially when illustrations were matched with texts excerpted from a forthcoming book. An illustrated edition of Sienkiewicz's phenomenally successful *Quo Vadis?* serves as a case in point. The illustrator, Piotr Stachiewicz, was accorded a full-page accolade for his "real art" (as opposed to the "rebus sketches" of most illustrators) and one entire issue features his art work along with Sienkiewicz's canonized novel, much as a church might display biblical pictures, with each scene underscored by an appropriate quotation from Sienkiewiczian "scripture."[52]

The Illustrated Weekly also cultivated the reader's art-owning proclivities with special premiums. It catered to the desire for collectibles and interior decoration with a yearly series of "fine art" reproductions. It capitalized on the popularity of such writers as Sienkiewicz by offering subscribers, over time, a free set of the author's collected works printed "on good paper and in clear type."[53] In contrast to the utilitarian premiums (clothing, tools, machines) offered by other magazines, *The Illustrated Weekly* distinguished its subscribers as the discerning patrons of a writer "who has become the pride of his nation and has earned international popularity."[54]

Enjoined to assess and consume art works in these ways, subscribers to *The Illustrated Weekly* learned to view consumption of the arts as an investment in the potential nation of Poland and as a means to social, cultural, moral, and even national betterment. In Western theories of consumer culture, consumer goods are said to substitute for external reality; yet the select artistic goods purveyed in *The Illustrated Weekly* transformed a nonreality into something real and purchaseable, into a gift-boxed Poland.[55] In contrast to the essential passivity of the consumer posited in Western theories, the "refined" consumer culture practiced by *The Illustrated Weekly* rendered art consumption one of the few forms of activism available to Poles, a spectacular variant on the Positivist imperative of self-improvement.[56]

Indeed, as *The Illustrated Weekly* represents it, investment in the arts naturally resulted in a more altruistic investment in public commemoration of the artist, in a special kind of spectacle. I have already noted the journal's emphasis on the *thingness* of the artist's monument. Reports on a monument's cost or costliness frequently named its underwriters and sometimes issued public appeals for funds. *The Illustrated Weekly*'s coverage of the Mickiewicz monument raised in Warsaw even included a photo display of the monument's sponsoring committee and a public announcement of thanks to all the participants in the affair.[57] Readers were similarly informed about and invited to participate in jubilee festivities for the living and reinterment for the dead. The pages of *The Illustrated Weekly* were dotted with announcements about fundraising for this or that jubilee and more bizarre items about "local youth" collecting money to repatriate the remains of a great national figure.[58] Such invitations to contribute and participate virtually erased the line between consumer and patron, subscriber and patriot.

The Sienkiewicz Jubilee

An examination of one such jubilee highlights the intricacies and deft management of the journal's homage-patronage approach. The year 1900 marked the twenty-fifth anniversary of Sienkiewicz's debut as a writer, and this occasion prompted a massive commemoration in public and in the pages of *The Illustrated Weekly*. Of all his peers, Sienkiewicz most handily fulfilled the role of contemporary *wieszcz* on account of his artistic preoccupation with Poland's "glorious" past and his enormous popularity both at home and abroad.[59] Sienkiewicz had already been exploited, to great effect, as a symbolic figure at the unveiling of monuments to Mickiewicz and Słowacki.[60] (See figure 12.) When the spotlight at last

FIGURE 12. *The Illustrated Weekly* snapped Sienkiewicz in the act of consecrating this Słowacki monument in Milosławie. *The Illustrated Weekly,* no. 40, 1899, 780.

turned fully on him, it was altogether predictable that the public and ever obliging mass media would make grand plans for *his* jubilee.

The Illustrated Weekly paced its coverage very cleverly, with a preview in March trained exclusively on the writer and late December issues chronicling the actual jubilee festivities. Cover photo-portraits of the artist signal this special topic in the tenth and fifty-first issues; in the tenth issue, the portrait is captioned with a formal dedication to Sienkiewicz. That inaugural issue is also grandly framed by an opening editorial, "World Renown," in which, without specifically naming either Sienkiewicz or Poland, Matuszewski argues for the national importance of worshiping and exporting one's native geniuses:

> The noblest and most suitable weapon in the fight for equal citizenship in the world is, on the one hand, the production of the greatest number of spiritual goods and, on the other, taking care that such goods are made available to the common market of civilization, not only as anonymous products, but as works bearing the clear imprint of their origins, as testimonials to the vitality of the people who brought them forth.[61]

Underscoring the morality and nobility of such exports, Matuszewski declares that each nation "has the right and the duty" to record the international renown of its geniuses—indeed, that a nation is judged by the tributes it bestows. At the same time, the nation must be discerning in what (or whom) it chooses to export, for "world renown has significance only when it affirms the creative power of the nation's spirit and its moral vitality." In his final observation, Matuszewski neatly summarizes the very strategy of "realizing" Poland through national genius by embellishing on the Cartesian formula, *Cogito, ergo sum:* "I think, I create, therefore I am."

Stamped with this authoritative and enlightened license for promotion, the issue outlines its agenda on the following page. In lieu of focusing on the writer's work and significance for his own nation ("matters already much discussed by [our] finest critics and literary historians"), this issue means to shed light on Sienkiewicz's person and international currency, those intimate details and outside endorsements that will "sell" him to the broadest possible audience. These rather calculated acts of homage culminate in a bid for concrete patronage. The editors of *The Illustrated Weekly* here remind their readers that the "committee for funding the jubilee gift" has authorized them to serve as a collection point; a footnote helpfully notes that their office is accepting contributions on weekdays from nine to three. The issue further includes (1) a succinct biographical and bibliographical overview of the writer; (2) a leisurely visit to Sienkiewicz's main haunts, illustrated by exterior shots of his places of residence, interior shots of his Warsaw study, and occasional photos of the writer "on location"; (3) a sequence of articles highlighting his international fame, including profiles of his American translator, Jeremiah Curtin, and Wilson Barrett, a British playwright and actor intent on staging *Quo Vadis;* (4) a condensed "Chronicle" that lists Sienkiewicz's achievements abroad; and (5) a final sweeping bibliography of Sienkiewicz's works in foreign languages, documenting the writer's worldwide impact.

Of these features, the "visit" with Sienkiewicz, written by the popular biographer, Ferdynand Hoesick, is most expansive and comprises a particularly intriguing blend of rhapsodic tribute and celebrity interview.[62] Hoesick commences his pilgrimage with a rather long-winded assertion of Sienkiewicz's greatness "in his own lifetime," a greatness that eclipsed Mickiewicz's in its popular scope. His actual visit recalls Rouba's travelogue in its devout attention to location and artifact (the art work and family portraits in the writer's salon, the hunting gear and game trophies in his study). Depicting Sienkiewicz as a knowledgeable collector surrounded by and utilizing his various collections, Hoesick not only indicates the artist's refined sense of consumption, but also reinforces the reader's commodified appreciation of Sienkiewicz's work as writing produced by a connoisseur and connected with tangible articles of value. In Hoesick's lovingly detailed description, Sienkiewicz's study (see figure 13) seems more a gallery, a museum display, or antique shop than a workplace:

> The entire room is carpeted with a flowered rug; its doors are screened with heavy curtains; the hangings above the windows and the draperies match the crimson color of the wallpaper; in the middle of the room there is a large table covered with a tablecloth and laden with books, knick-knacks, and different writing implements; between the two windows there stands an elegant desk weighed down with a magnitude of baubles, frames, and trinkets; the fireplace, which looks like it is made from a Japanese screen, is framed by porcelain vases, bronzes, and photographs; under the main wall there is a large couch, and farther off there stands a suite of soft, upholstered furniture, tastefully arranged; by the doors there is a glassed-in bookcase packed tight with finely bound tomes; on the walls, aside from several shelves of books, there are many pictures, little scenes, sketches, deer and buffalo antlers, animal skulls, old weaponry, clubs, curved swords, pickaxes, Tatar bows and arrows. Reigning over all is a great antlered elk's head, looking as if it emerges from the wall right below the ceiling; there is also a beautiful, original-looking oriental lamp hanging from the middle of the ceiling.[63]

Yet Hoesick's account differs from Rouba's text in its ongoing citation of the master. In effect, Sienkiewicz's explanatory monologues—about his major influences, work schedule, and collections—function here as a compelling "voice-over" for the reader's perusal of his changing residences. The writer plays host and tour guide, and the reader, represented by a deferential Hoesick, assumes the role of privileged and appreciative

FIGURE 13. A corresponding photograph of Sienkiewicz's busily appointed study in Warsaw. *The Illustrated Weekly*, no. 10, 1900, 192.

guest. It is up to this sensitive reader-guest to note that Sienkiewicz does not own all the residences in which he "creates." His sojourns at the various villas photographed are said to be sponsored by affluent friends and admirers.

Extensive coverage of the jubilee resumed in the fifty-second issue, published on the very day slated for the event. The cover portrait depicts a rather formal and elegantly dressed Sienkiewicz at home, as if he is anticipating callers. The initial critical and poetic tributes, identically entitled "To Henryk Sienkiewicz," pay a more personal visit to "our master" and "my hero." (See figure 14.) A short article and series of photos portray the writer's birthplace in yet another characteristic act of commemoration. Throughout the issue, illustrations and photos convey various images and artifacts of the writer as collectors' items: a montage of photographs of Sienkiewicz "at different stages of life"; a page from his

FIGURE 14. Here the *Weekly* portrays Sienkiewicz as the sober paterfamilias, flanked by daughter and son. *The Illustrated Weekly,* no. 10, 1900, 199.

Teutonic Knights manuscript; an ornate certificate of merit awarded him by the Literary Fund (a charitable organization for writers and journalists); even a photograph of a "Sienkiewicz exhibit" on display at the prestigious A. Krywult art gallery.

Although the paper tribute offered by *The Illustrated Weekly* could not vie with the excitement and splendor of the actual jubilee, this issue exemplifies the journal's crucial eyewitness function for subscribers. An essay describing yet another Sienkiewicz-related event acknowledges the flood of reader requests for tickets to the festivities, implying that many will be denied, while *Weekly* readers will occupy ringside seats. *The Illustrated Weekly* contributed to the illusion of subscriber access by listing the day's planned events for all who attend and, subsequently, a selective account of the ceremony-packed day "to recreate the atmosphere of its main moments."

Even abridged, this report reflects the blend of worship/consumption, homage/patronage, inherent in *The Illustrated Weekly*'s packaging of both artist and jubilee. On "Sienkiewicz Day" a reverential atmosphere prevailed, established by an eleven o'clock celebratory mass in the Church of the Holy Cross, reiterated by intermittent choral performances, and confirmed by the ubiquitous Bishop Ruszkiewicz, also president of the jubilee's organizing committee. The assembly proceeded from the church to the equally ceremonial site of Warsaw's town hall. Here the jubilee got down to business. Sienkiewicz was ushered into the "first portrait hall" where the "presenting of gifts" *(wręczenie darów)* took place. Enacting ancient rituals of feudal tribute, various delegations to the jubilee had piled a table high with richly decorated testimonials and certificates—beautifully illustrated albums, steel containers, silver boxes and statuettes. But the most spectacular (and most substantial) tribute was yet to come. Once Sienkiewicz was ensconced in the main hall, on a stage surrounded by his jubilee committee and draped with wreaths of white flowers, Bishop Ruszkiewicz bestowed upon him the deed to an estate in Obłęgorek; and, in a fairy-tale flourish, four little girls dressed in white handed him four huge books signed by all those who had contributed to the purchase. Taking a page from Polish history, when kings patronized artists with titles and property, Sienkiewicz's jubilee committee had enlisted the reading public in this noble gesture, thereby transforming contributors into royal patrons and awarding the artist the most meaningful of material gifts—a creative home on Polish soil.[64] As an earlier *Weekly* issue assured would-be contributors, such a gift would pay splendid patriotic dividends:

> And we do not doubt that our great writer will draw more than one inspiration from the vale of Obłęgorek, from the tree-lined shade of this deserved retreat, and that more than one marvelous work will emanate from this luxurious residence to the glory of Polish literature.[65]

The festivities, of course, did not conclude with this grand tribute. Much of the rest of the day was spent in ceremonious give-and-take: delegates marching up to their idol with more testimonials and honorary diplomas, the idol himself responding with a speech of gratitude. Theatrical presentations—a comic sketch and "living images" representing Sienkiewicz's famous characters—underscored the spectacular and crowd-pleasing nature of the jubilee. But for all the emphasis on pomp and circumstance, it is equally striking that, by day's end, the feted guest had slipped into the role of boon companion, cavorting with his fellow writers and artists. The same relationships that *The Illustrated Weekly* implied between artist and public thus recur in its description of the jubilee. The artist was revered and patronized, ennobled and familiarized, put on a pedestal and treated to drinks. As the journal reports, Sienkiewicz's peers "observed the old Polish custom of hoisting [him] onto their shoulders and shouting his praises."[66]

For those who could not attend the celebration, did not contribute to the purchase of the Obłęgorek estate, and dared not join in the hoisting and shouting, there always remained the ultimate act of homage/patronage: the purchase of Sienkiewicz's books. *The Illustrated Weekly* seriously cited Prus's (ironic?) remark that "the sun never sets on the books of Sienkiewicz," suggesting that the act of buying Sienkiewicz was tantamount to building a Polish empire.[67] Ever helpful in this regard, the firm of Gebethner and Wolff furnished a complete price list of his works on the last page of the fifty-first issue. The most expensive of these items proved to be a "jubilee edition" of illustrations of Sienkiewicz's books. Like the "biblical" display of *Quo Vadis,* this coffee-table album featured illustrations with appropriate "scriptural" captions.

Sienkiewicz attracted the most ostentatious jubilee celebration, but he was not the only artist to receive such magnificent tribute.[68] Less than two years later, *The Illustrated Weekly* announced plans for a Maria Konopnicka jubilee that included the purchase of a villa for the writer's creative use.[69] There seemed to be some delay in its acquisition; although the Kraków-based jubilee was observed in October 1902, an account of Konopnicka's installation in her new estate at Żarnowiec did not appear until September 1903. Accompanying photos depict the villa's northern and southern exposures and Konopnicka herself on its veranda, and the text endorses the purchase in a kitschy blend of gush and brag: "So the authoress of *Mister Balcer* will be able to spin out the thread of her thoughts and the flowers of her feelings, free of care, the more so since her Warsaw admirers have given her 20,000 crowns for the estate's maintenance."[70]

With such grand gestures, the reading public not only ameliorated the artist's "hard lot," but also provided their idol with the home place they could not achieve as a nation. In so doing, they created one more important landmark, claimed one more piece of property as a symbol for a dematerialized nation. The gift estate comprised a constantly regenerating monument as the workshop of the living artist and his or her incipient museum. The artist who received such a tribute had to accept it on the costly terms of eternal display. Even as Konopnicka settled in at Żarnowiec, *The Illustrated Weekly* correspondent rather audaciously catalogued the many gifts and contributed decorations adorning her rooms; an earlier issue intruded on her privacy by photographing her collection of "jubilee gifts."

Indeed, according to the testimony of *The Illustrated Weekly*, whatever tribute the artist received obliged him or her to respond with artistic goods and services. I have already cited the stated expectations of future works dedicated "to the glory of Polish literature." Other services included charitable contributions and acts. Prus, for example, chose to link patronage directly with service by donating a fund set up in his name to the Literary Fund for charitable distribution, an arrangement heartily approved by the journal.[71] Orzeszkowa similarly channelled her jubilee funds into a pedagogical institute, which was hailed as a "light for the Church of our nation's future" and an appropriate monument for "a great defender of enlightenment."[72] The amply rewarded Sienkiewicz demonstrated a keen sense of responsibility before his national public. In one characteristic instance, he exhorted fellow writers to follow his example and *donate* their work, specifically by giving benefit readings to aid flood victims. As he argued in an open letter to *The Illustrated Weekly*, there are "extraordinary moments" that demand this sort of sacrifice and "assertion of solidarity."[73] Thus, just as royal patronage once presumed a payback in artistic form (odes, treatises, court histories), so public patronage implied its own contract—not only for accessible art (nation-inspiring entertainment now substituted for royal flattery), but also for public aid and national service.

The Illustrated Weekly weathered the First World War and Poland's emergence as an independent nation, becoming more overtly political as external conditions permitted and maintaining its considerable popularity. I contend, however, that even after the acquisition of Polish independence the reasons for the journal's success inhered in its enduring linkage of nationalism with cultural consumption. Although *The Illustrated Weekly* offered to readers a sophisticated and worldly marketplace, built with the latest technology and informed by Western European standards and fashions, it engaged and flattered them as sophisticated and worldly *Poles*, as discerning and "autonomous" Polish consumers. Its marketplace at once camouflaged and showcased the nation, cautiously materializing it through apolitical documentation and, primarily, cultural artifact. The cultural artifact, whether a work of art or the actual artist, functioned in the journal as an instant and intimate national monument—the nation made present in what Matuszewski aptly defined as a tangible, laconic synthesis. *The Illustrated Weekly* represented purchasing, commissioning, or somehow sponsoring a monument (artists "creating" on gift estates) as a means of making Poland real and making Poland great. The "autonomous" consumer could therefore buy a subjugated nation presence and power.

The text of this popular journal richly demonstrates how varied, satisfying, and binding this exchange between Polish artist and Polish reader could be. The reader-consumer of *The Illustrated Weekly* entered into a comprehensive relationship with the artist-producer, admitted into a select and sympathetic community, assured of Poland's continuing existence and greatness in the world, exalted as a co-celebrant in and an essential patron of the nation's achievements, granted an intimacy and a familiarity with native genius and offered the joys of a most rarefied form of collecting. Although this commercial publication would seem to have kicked the doors to "serious" culture wide open, it conferred a kind of nobility and exclusivity on the audience pouring in. The writer, while exposed to public scrutiny and bound to some public service, nevertheless gained a livelihood, a sinecure (in some cases), and the lofty status of speaking symbol. The artist did not sell out to commercialism, but lived happily ever after as a patronized saint.

To a great extent, this writer-reader relationship succeeded precisely because it accommodated both spiritual and material needs—the writer's isolation and financial hardships, the reader's search for meaning and pleasure, the Pole's longing for national presence. Artist and reading public tacitly formed a pact that guaranteed the former popularity, the latter prestige, and both a place on the map. Yet, perhaps above all, it was the journal's double projection of Poland as absolute value (its eternally denied or threatened reality) and cozy club (recall Mickiewicz in his dressing gown and Sienkiewicz hoisted in the air by admirers) that perpetuated this relationship. If *Vol'f Bookstore News* cultivated and complimented its reader with visions of enlightened imperialism, then *The Illustrated Weekly* inspired and jollied its reader into a noble and enjoyable conspiracy. That this strategy continued in *The Illustrated Weekly* after 1917 is not surprising, for the newly present Poland remained keenly aware of the nation's precarious global status. On the pages of *The Illustrated Weekly*, writer and reader, producer and consumer, paraded their mutual admiration society as the tightest shelter against an overwhelming world.

seven

As the Market Turns,
1890s–1990s

In Anastasiia Verbitskaia's *Keys to Happiness,* a minor character named Semen Nikolaevich debates the value of art with the aesthete and modernist Harold. Imagining a vast provincial audience, Nikolaevich warns:

> "Beware of the provinces! Don't risk taking your propaganda to the provinces. No matter how removed you are from reality, you must have noticed the astounding, strange changes of the last years. Just look at a picture of the book market after 1905. It's so interesting that it demands the pen of a sociologist . . . . They publish journals in the capital and wait trembling for the subscriptions. The provinces decide whether to be or not to be. And the reader stands to one side, just as enigmatic, opaque, and silent. The capital crowns literati and the provinces dethrone them. You throw out a slogan. The provinces will be mysteriously silent. They accept everything from you thoughtfully—tinsel with gold, glass with diamonds—and reject what's unnecessary, whatever doesn't answer their questions, slake their thirst, satisfy their quests. On occasion they even cast off pearls and diamonds, not because they don't know their worth, but because

diamonds and pearls are cold in their beauty. These may be sparkling pieces of life. But the soul of today's reader, suffering after its illusions and dreams have foundered against reality, longs for a reconciling synthesis, longs for an ideal. Form isn't necessary, understand, but essence! That's why not a single verbal artist can win the provinces. That's why they remain cold to all the new "wonderful stars" our critics rain down on them. Their light is too weak to illuminate the darkness and murk of our lives. And note that even an artist like Lev Tolstoy had to renounce literature and become a prophet in order to win the soul of the Russian reader. I repeat: what's important to the Russian reader is not *how* something is said, but *what* is said. But do you have anything to say to him?"[1]

Over the long run, Semen Nikolaevich fades from view and Harold wins Steinbach's financial support and Mania's passionate love, but Semen Nikolaevich's attack is too metatextual to be dismissed. Intimated to be a socialist and supporter of the 1905 revolution, he reenacts here the traditional role of the nineteenth-century Russian *intelligent*—first, by sensing and already revering an unknown audience beyond the hothouse of the capital, some "mysterious someone none of you knows"; second, by presuming to intuit this opaque reader's desires and aspirations; and, finally, by insisting that this reader, in contrast to the egocentric intelligentsia of the capital, seeks "ideals" and "essence" in books.

The endurance of this social type and his predictable pronouncements is notable in and of itself. But what makes Semen Nikolaevich's speech remarkable is how it conveys relations between art and the market in a novel that itself attempted to reconcile the two. Curiously enough, Semen Nikolaevich invokes the market to prove the power and implicitly superior taste of the provincial reader. The market serves him as ally rather than enemy, while the pampered capital conveniently plays the villain. Moreover, Semen Nikolaevich's characterization of the seeking reader is ultimately commandeered by the opposing "elitist" side in the novel. Although the Oscar Wildish Harold bemoans the Russian public's underdeveloped aesthetic taste, his vaunting of art above all (what Semen Nikolaevich denigrates as *"how* something is said") implies an even more transcendent, meaningful relationship between writer and reader, artist and consumer. For Harold and Semen Nikolaevich alike, the market simply cannot depreciate culture. Not coincidentally, however, both men count on Steinbach's munificent patronage.[2]

Thus, perhaps the greatest blockbuster in prerevolutionary Russian publishing history seems to assure readers, whoever they are, that nothing has changed in the writing and reading status quo, that the market that made this best-seller possible facilitates and discriminates good culture. Most important, it tacitly flatters readers into believing that they will buy right and read right. Indeed, such flattery was axiomatic in the Russian and Polish book markets at the turn of the century. What I have been identifying and analyzing throughout this book is a deft embellishment of image and role as new professions and social groups registered in the rapidly developing print culture of Russia and the Kingdom of Poland. The market promoted the rise of new publishing firms, staked out new audiences, and demanded new writers for consumption and new critics for guidance. But my selected readings indicate that the Russian and Polish publishing industries also labored hard not to disturb existing relationships between "serious" writers and "serious" readers. Rather, they made such "serious" roles more inclusive and comfortable, more accessible and consumer-oriented. They rewrote market influence so as to broaden deeply rooted cultural patterns regarding the writer's authority, the reader's quest, and literature's invariably profound meaning.

My analysis of this reaction began with "serious" writers who themselves had to cope with a more market-driven culture. Gorky, Chekhov, and Prus all approached literature as a livelihood and recognized in their work the changing constituencies they reflected and addressed. Raised in literary cultures that purportedly furnished readers with heroic types and positive role models, these men explored the mentality and life style of the new capitalists. But whatever heroic features their portraits contained derived from a reworking of established molds—in the Russian case, the paradigms of folk hero or *intelligent,* and in Prus's masterful effort, a unique reprise of the Polish Romantic leader. In the end, these talented authors seemed to sense the cultural impossibility of a capitalist hero, at least a convincing one in terms of psychological makeup and social efficacy. Indeed, the persuasiveness of their heroic portraits depended on the character's basic dissatisfaction with the limitations and inequities of capitalism.

More often than not, however, the new capitalist characters were strictly epigonic, as I demonstrate in detail in discussing Anastasiia Verbitskaia's *Keys to Happiness* and Helena Mniszek's *The Leper*. These two works represent the fascinating phenomenon of best-sellers that simply override the impact of capitalism even as they bank on market-proven formulas. The rich folk in both novels behave either like old-style aristocrats (Nelidov, Michorowski) or intellectual philanthropists burdened by the responsibility of their wealth (Steinbach). The working girls (Stefcia, Manya) either rely, without seeming to, on supportive rich people, or they pursue a lofty vocation in lieu of a money-grubbing career (Manya). Unretouched icons of the Russian intelligentsia and the Polish aristocracy triumph in these highly popular texts. Perhaps most striking is the fact that Verbitskaia and Mniszek choose to derail the happy consummation of the popular romance, full-stopping the heroine's domestic enfranchisement with suicide or death. Presumably designed for "middle" audiences, these novels nonetheless express a somewhat ambivalent disdain for a bourgeois life style and, instead of realizing middle-class happiness, in the end validate a profound angst about the possibility of personal and national fulfillment.

My analysis turns finally in part II to the market's own scripts and, consequently, to more wide-ranging instances of image enhancement. Such mass-circulation publications as *Vol'f Bookstore News* and *The Illustrated Weekly* matched the hero-making capacity of belles lettres with ingeniously attractive portraits of the writer *and* the reader. To a great extent, these publications' careful commercialization of book culture hinged on their representation of the "serious" artist—a sacrosanct figure in both societies—as professional, pragmatic, materially situated, and familiar. Journal critics managed this feat without jeopardizing the writer's authoritative status; once again, we see image and role tempered rather than fundamentally altered. As critics "materialized" and familiarized the writer, they correspondingly implied a more active, material role for the reader as critic, collector, seeker, patron, and patriot. They did indeed empower the reader as a consumer, but their conception of that role was leavened with spiritual zeal and an abiding sense of social responsibility. What these journals claimed to offer was never a guide to mere entertainment, but a kind of altruistic partnership with the reader

in a grand spiritual project—whether it constituted a general commitment to Art or a specific commitment to Nation.

My pairing of these Russian and Polish examples also exposes some
important differences in how the two literatures responded to the market. Both publishing industries appeared to resist a simple reiteration of
market-oriented value and the ranking of business over all other endeavors. The texts I have surveyed, however, suggest the existence of a Russian society that would distinguish itself advantageously *in contrast to* the
capitalist West, that asserted its moral and cultural superiority even as
it strived to achieve a Western technological sophistication. The commercialization of art required exceptional handling and qualification, of
course, for Russians tended to conflate this phenomenon with a mercenary, bourgeois, and soulless West. Against these flaws they pitched their
own supposedly national virtues of spirituality, altruism, extreme generosity, and reckless abandon. Gorky's self-made magnates are made
compelling by their grand gestures and occasional nihilism. Chekhov's
capitalists win the readers' crucial empathy through their insecurity, guilt,
and lack of complacency. Verbitskaia's flashy characters gamble all their
wealth and success in the search for the keys to happiness. Even such
trade journals as *Vol'f Bookstore News* wax defensive over Russia's combination of spiritual superiority and material underdevelopment.

For the Poles, on the other hand, a flourishing market provoked an
internal critique of a still indolent aristocracy and the growing exploitation of workers. But, significantly, it gave Poles hands-on national leverage against foreign domination. The market afforded Poles their surest
path to power and one of the very few means to national self-assertion.
It particularly linked Poles in the Kingdom with what they deemed to be
a superior, more civilized (if somewhat heartless) West, in contrast to a
brutish Russia. Although the Prussian and Austro-Hungarian empires
nominally belonged to this West, their *markets* were reported to deny or
undermine their repressive politics. Thus, in Polish literature capitalism
could function as a still imperfect, but effective, means to nationalist
ends. In Bolesław Prus's *The Doll,* a merchant can achieve noble tragedy
and be misconstrued sentimentally as a national role model because politics has failed him altogether. Mniszek's novel features an aristocrat
whose good business practices convince others of his patriotism. *The*

Illustrated Weekly, in turn, cleverly devised and promoted a specialized consumerism that popularly asserted and preserved the nation. Properly controlled, commercialization enhanced Poland's desired Western allegiance and effected a market autonomy relatively impervious to foreign oppression.

If in these cited instances the market did not realign a hallowed writer-reader dynamic in fin-de-siècle Russia and the Kingdom of Poland, what do such precedents tell us about the market transition in this region in the late twentieth century? Does there now exist a middle or upper-middle class unashamed of its pursuit of money and the good life? Are publishers willing and able to risk addressing a truly stratified market? Have belles lettres and its creators retained any prestige and authority in the ongoing political and economic transformation? Does that "enigmatic, opaque reader" still ostensibly long for ideals or settle for an easy read after an arduous day of making ends meet in post-Soviet Russia and Poland?

My response, of course, must be provisional, given the difficulty of assessing the volatile contemporary scene in the Russian and Polish publishing industry. First, there are striking similarities between the fin-de-siècle period and today: a burgeoning, diversified market; enterprising and innovative publishers; extensive relations with the global book trade; and quick import of popular Western plot formulas and designs. In fact, publishers in contemporary Russia seem explicitly aware of this analogy, for a number of firms have attempted to cash in on the presumably enduring popularity of fin-de-siècle best-sellers, reprinting such proven popular commodities as *Keys to Happiness.* Polish publishers are retrieving more recent material. Their diverse market flourished undisturbed until World War II, and even after sovietization, Polish émigré publishers produced popular works read by Poles in the diaspora and underground publishers experimented with a wide array of publications.[3] Whatever their sources, today's Russian and Polish book markets display an astounding, at times jarring, variety of publications ranging from sumptuous coffee-table collectors' editions to gossipy tabloids and porn magazines.[4]

What differentiates today's publishing scene from that of a century ago is the extremely politicized experience of the intervening decades—

some seventy years for Soviet Russians and forty years for Poles under Soviet domination. This experience at once compromised the standing of "serious" literature and obscured the stigma of being bourgeois. Soviet rule brought with it political regimentation and persecution, executions, jail and camp terms for millions targeted as "enemies of the people." It enforced a surface egalitarianism belied by the state patronage enjoyed by certain select groups, including "loyal" members of the unions of Soviet or Polish writers. More than ever before in Russian and Polish history, the production of "serious" literature demanded a constant vetting for what was deemed ideologically correct—of the writer's beliefs, behavior, and associations, the text's content *and* form, and the reader's political discernment. That vetting applied directly to all official publications, but it bears remembering that dissident literature evolved in ideological and sometimes formal opposition to the state-sponsored canon and therefore was written and/or read with the same emphasis on political message. The cold war between the Soviet bloc and the West sustained this sort of binary assessment of Russian and Polish literatures in the West as well.

Thus, the "enigmatic reader" in today's Russia and Poland differs from the reader of a century ago in initially welcoming and increasingly responding to a stratified market. The growth of a free book market above ground, commencing during the Gorbachev era, symbolized the general freedoms of speech and the press for the reading public. Cold war binarism for a time made the market a desirable *political* phenomenon. In fact, the alliance of the market with the West at first appeared to be a salutary rather than ambiguous development, as Poles and Russians alike sought to cast off moribund Soviet institutions and patronage systems in enthusiastic exchange for Western "enterprise." Far more revolutionary, however, has been Russia's and Poland's acceptance of entertainment. Decades of puritanical prohibition and censored or inadequate production have generated a backlash among Russians and Polish consumers. Not only are these much-thwarted shoppers eager for popular literature, but also they feel vindicated politically and ethically in indulging themselves. As they see it, they had endured the abuses, falsehoods, and inequities of a corrupt political state far too long and, as a result, had been deprived artificially of the good life apparently available to the average

Western consumer. To a great extent, the cultural choices made for them seemed tainted by an implicit state-sponsored classism and a totalitarian system that constantly saddled them with the dictates of authority—including, of course, the authority of "serious" literature. These beleaguered citizens, in a sense, feel that they have suffered their way to consumer empowerment.

Consumer empowerment is likewise being abetted by the high visibility of conspicuous consumers and bold entrepreneurs in these societies. The emergence of the so-called "new Russians," an unabashed nouveau riche, and similar groups in Poland herald a radically changing class configuration—if not the birth of the middle (for these new groups tend to be wealthy), then the positive embrace of a bourgeois mentality and life style intent on material acquisition, pursuit of pleasure, and financial security. More and more, the Russian and Polish publishing markets seem geared to serve rather than dictate to readers, to privilege the consuming public over the presuming artist in cultural production.

Do these changes spell an end to the power of "serious" literature in Russia and Eastern Europe? Certainly, gloomy predictions of this sort abound among writers who feel "deposed" and among observers, both native and foreign, who lament the supposed vulgarization and commercialization of their once great national literatures.[5] Certainly, the lot of the "serious" writer has become harder, given the dismantling of the all-providing writers' unions and the waning of reader interest and respect. Yet, whatever the sociopolitical allure and economic power of Western models, we should not underestimate the role of national pride and long-term cultural conditioning in shaping these societies' literary expression and self-image. After the deluge of Western popular literature and the chaotic experimentation of the market in the early 1990s, sales indicate that a significant percentage of readers are retracing the old pattern of buying for enlightenment and prestige.[6] Detective novels, science fiction, and romances still corner the lion's share of the market, but rank commercialism is waning and yielding some ground to purveyors of "serious" specialties—for example, general reference books, literary "classics," and beautifully produced children's fiction.[7] The future book trade likely will accommodate more such specialized niches, and "serious" literature will remain desirable and influential on a much smaller, self-selecting scale.[8] Whether that scale will exceed Western proportions is unclear. It may be that today's Russian and Polish readers still prefer Harlequin romances to Chekhov and Prus, and perhaps even the now dated Verbitskaia and Mniszek, yet I suspect that tomorrow's writers and publishers, like their predecessors of a century ago, will take ever greater pains to best the West by reworking the "superior" models of their national past.[9]

notes

Note: Unless otherwise indicated, all translations are by the author.

Preface

1. Staroi, *Per i Natasha.*
2. Spolar writes, "Sales of romance novels—or rather, translations of Harlequin paperbacks and hardback versions of anything by authors like Danielle Steel—have soared in Poland, Hungary and the Czech Republic, filling up the windows of street-side kiosks and shelves at some local libraries" ("Romance by the Book in Poland").
3. Ibid.
4. "In a letter to Harlequin, Grażyna, from Poznań, wrote: 'Your books are a break from everyday boredom and drabness, when my husband doesn't notice me and my children don't listen to me. Your books let one forget. It doesn't matter that this isn't exactly top-notch literature and that men ridicule it. Don't stop writing for women—they need that'" (Święcka, "Romance Novels: Fairy Tales for Big Girls").
5. Of the three Polish partitions, the Russian-administered Kingdom of Poland, which included the Polish capital city of Warsaw and the major industrial center of Łódź, exerted by far the strongest influence, both qualitative and quantitative, on Polish literature and publishing. The appellation *Kingdom of Poland* lingered as a wholly fictional title after the partitions and especially after the failed insurrection of 1863. Blobaum alternately uses the terms *Kingdom of Poland* and *Russian Poland*, but notes that "'Vistulaland' supplanted the 'Kingdom of Poland' in Russian bureaucratic parlance as the country's official designation" (*Rewolucja. Russian Poland*, 4).
6. The spectrum of cultural production and representation covered here best illustrates, to my mind, the extensive and almost invariably hybridizing interaction that took place between high and consumer cultures. Historians of the Western book trade have made similar observations. In *The Cultural Uses of Print in Early Modern France*, Chartier repeatedly disproves that there are "strict correspondences between cultural cleavages and social hierarchies," and Davidson similarly points out the error of segregating what often proved

to be overlapping reading communities ("Toward a History of Books and Readers," 9).

7. Cf. Brooks, *When Russia Learned to Read;* Levitt, *Russian Literary Politics;* Clowes et al., *Between Tsar and People;* McReynolds, *The News Under Russia's Old Regime;* Engelstein, *The Keys to Happiness.*

8. Polish scholars at Wrocław University are producing excellent pioneering work; their journal, *Literatura i kultura popularna,* commenced publication in 1991.

9. Kolbuszewski, *Od Pigalle po kresy: Krajobrazy literatury popularnej,* 11; Tompkins sums up this approach with regard to American literature: "It is the notion of literary texts as doing work expressing and shaping the social context that produced them, that I wish to substitute finally for the critical perspective that sees them as attempts to achieve a timeless, universal ideal of truth and formal coherence" (*Sensational Designs,* 200).

Chapter 1. The Publishing Business in Russia and Poland

1. Brooks, *When Russia Learned to Read,* 4.

2. Kenez characterizes the Russian distribution system as "elementary" and compares the ratio of one periodical for every 167,000 Russian citizens in 1899 with the contemporary ratio of one for every 8,000 German citizens (*The Birth of the Propaganda State,* 22).

3. *Istoriia knizhnoi torgovli,* 99. Circulation figures are found in Makhonina, *Russkaia dorevoliutsionnaia pechat,* 52, which notes that Suvorin bought the company its own forests to keep paper costs down.

4. Makhonina (*Russkaia dorevoliutsionnaia pechat',* 97–100) attributes the decline of the thick journal to the growth of a newly literate, less sophisticated readership; a contemporary emphasis on topicality and quick turnover of information; and a new, specialized interest in art over social commentary.

5. Brooks writes that the thin magazines "provided a source of light reading, serious fiction, and news" and could be construed as "the forerunner of a daily newspaper" (*When Russia Learned to Read,* 111). Circulation figures are cited in Makhonina, *Russkaia dorevoliutsionnaia pechat',* 68, 86. The top figure of 800,000 reflects the circulation of *Ogonek's* supplement; *Ogonek (Little Light)* was the most successful of the thin magazines in prerevolutionary Russia.

6. I am indebted to Susan Larsen's unpublished manuscript, "Girl Talk," for information on the format and contents of the *Heartfelt Word.*

7. Balzer traces the genesis of these professional journals back to the 1860s in his introduction to *Russia's Missing Middle Class,* 12; Brower remarks on the muckraking and local gossip functions of the Russian penny press, which

"was creating a new genre of writing by dramatizing the world of the ordinary Russian townsperson" ("The Penny Press and Its Readers," 152).

8. One gauge of this growing market is the first congress of publishers and booksellers in 1909, cited in *Istoriia knizhnoi torgovli*, 122.

9. Kenez, *The Birth of the Propaganda State*, 23–24.

10. Zieliński, *Historia Polski 1864–1939*, 219.

11. Kmiecik et al., *Prasa polska w latach 1864–1918*, contains an overview of the mass-circulation Polish press at the turn of the century. See also Kmiecik, *Prasa warszawska w latach 1908–1918*, 14–15.

12. Kmiecik et al., *Prasa polska w latach 1864–1918*, 13.

13. Kmiecik lists this top figure for the paper, and a recorded 884,544 inhabitants in 1914 Warsaw (*Prasa warszawska w latach 1908–1918*, 22, 15).

14. On *Bluszcz*, see Czyszkowa-Peschler, "She Is—A Nobody Without a Name." Czyszkowa-Peschler remarks that despite *Ivy's* "suspect" intellectual reputation as a publication for women, "the fact is there is scarcely a single author of the nineteenth century whose work did not appear in its pages at some time or other" (119).

15. See Brooks, *When Russia Learned to Read* (111–14) on the Russian *Niva*: "*Niva* was a large publication almost the size of a tabloid newspaper. . . . Serial fiction by respected writers made up the bulk of the text in each issue. There were also short accounts of events at home and abroad, ethnographic essays, and notes on developments in science and technology. The emphasis on the Russianness of its offerings was characteristic of *Niva*, and this was evident early in the magazine's career" (ibid., 113) According to Kmiecik et al., the Polish *Literary Repast* was the cheapest illustrated magazine available to Polish readers and included fiction, criticism, and articles on science, art, and political events (*Prasa polska w latach 1864–1918*, 85).

16. Zenon Przesmycki's pen name was Miriam.

17. *Dahl's History of the Book* lists the linotype, along with paper manufacture and the steam-driven printing press, as the major technological advances that facilitated the rise of the mass media in the nineteenth century (217). On the line block and halftone, see ibid., 226.

18. In *Discovering the News*, Schudson notes the widespread use of illustrations and headlines in American publications by the 1870s (95–96).

19. *Dahl's History of the Book* cites Edward Burne-Jones, Daniel Gabriel Rossetti, and William Morris as leaders in the reaction of the 1880s and 1890s "against poor illustrations and typography" (230).

20. Kmiecik directly ascribes the greater popularity of illustrated magazines to the growth of a middle class in Poland and the general enlightenment of Polish society (*Prasa warszawska w latach 1908–1918*, 432).

21. Blobaum, *Rewolucja*, 30.

22. Brooks (*When Russia Learned to Read*), McReynolds (*The News Under*

Russia's Old Regime), and Makhonina *(Russkaia dorevoliutsionnaia pechat')* all remark on the non–upper-class or non-Russian background of the major Russian publishers of this era. See also Belov and Tolstiakov, *Russkie izdateli,* for individual sketches of prominent publishers at this time.

23. Wilson describes the role of the immigrant publisher in America in "The Rhetoric of Consumption," 45. See Schudson on the immigrant's adaptability in the newspaper business *(Discovering the News,* 97–98). There also may be a connection between these immigrant publishers at the turn of the century and the American immigrant filmmakers whose orientation so strongly shaped Hollywood films in the first half of this century. In both cases, outsiders less constrained by in-country prejudices and better positioned to discern the contours of what was for them an alien culture succeeded in identifying and articulating popular desires.

24. Kenez remarks, "In the large industrial city of Kharkov, for example, there were only two newspaper vendors in 1903. In Moscow and Saint Petersburg, though newspapers were easily available in the central district, the suburbs were not well supplied" *(The Birth of the Propaganda State,* 22).

25. On the separate development of the railroads in partitioned Poland, see Zieliński, *Historia Polski,* 29–30.

26. McReynolds notes, for example, the leading edge maintained by Moscow and Saint Petersburg over the provinces in publishing commercial newspapers *(The News Under Russia's Old Regime,* 135–36). Various Polish sources repeat the same litany of big city publishing centers—Warsaw and Łódź in the Kingdom of Poland, Kraków and Lwów in Galicia, Gdańsk and Poznań in the Prussian partition. See Maleczyńska, *Książki i biblioteki w Polsce okresu zaborów,* 85; see also Szwejkowska, *Wybrane zagadnienia z dziejów książki xix–xx wieku,* 16, 19. Kołodziejczyk notes the centralization of Polish industry in Warsaw and Łódź *(Miasto, mieszczaństwo, burżuazja w Polsce w XIX w.,* 70).

27. Kenez judges most of "the products of the provincial press" to be "remarkably primitive in their language and analysis of politics," and he admits that many of the provincial papers, while valiantly attempting to educate and inform their readers, were "hopelessly amateurish" *(The Birth of the Propaganda State,* 22–23).

28. Brower asserts that the city in Russia was not a place of settled townspeople, but of "railroads, merchants, and migrants" *(The Russian City between Tradition and Modernity,* 90–91); Kołodziejczyk describes the waves of Jewish settlement in Warsaw and especially Łódź *(Miasto, mieszczaństwo, burżuazja w Polsce w XIX w.,* 77–79).

29. Brooks describes *lubki* as "lively illustrations similar to European broadsides" in which short texts are printed below the featured pictures *(When Russia Learned to Read,* 62–63).

30. On Sytin's progress, see Ruud, *Russian Entrepreneur;* Brooks, *When Russia Learned to Read* 97–101; and Belov and Tolstiakov, *Russkie izdateli,* 71–90.

31. In Brooks's view, the "culturalists" embraced and promoted culture as shared values that "were expressed primarily through the Russian literary tradition, which consisted of a pantheon of respected authors and critics and of the judgment that the true function of belles lettres was to illuminate social reality and transform readers" (*When Russia Learned to Read,* 318).

32. Ibid., 355–56; Zorkaia remarks how new readers reacted negatively to Tolstoy-sponsored *Posrednik* publications that attempted to "teach" them (*Na rubezhe stoletii,* 136).

33. Brooks, *When Russia Learned to Read,* 356.

34. See Balzer, introduction to *Russia's Missing Middle Class,* 9–10; Bailes comments: "Certainly the radical intelligentsia and professionals shared at least one major ideological point: their ethos defining their role in terms of service to society rather than service to the state per se. Where they may have differed was in the nature of that service and the degree to which one could work for the state or with the state, while 'serving society'" ("Reflections of Russian Professions," 52).

35. *Istoriia knizhnoi torgovli* translates this shift of interest into predictably Soviet terms, noting the new book trade's special appeal to the "bourgeois and technical intelligentsia" (92). Focusing on Russian newspapers, McReynolds argues that factmindedness distinguished "upstarts" from opinion-preferring intellectuals (*The News Under Russia's Old Regime,* 115).

36. Brooks counts middle-class and educated readers among the audience for serialized novels, which appealed "to those of more modern, cosmopolitan, urban, and secular interests" (*When Russia Learned to Read,* 109).

37. McReynolds, *The News Under Russia's Old Regime,* 3, 5.

38. Bourdieu posits, in his study of late twentieth-century French society, that the petit bourgeoisie and the middle class (he uses the terms interchangeably) express and enact an undifferentiated, anxious, and often mistaken reverence for what they presume to be legitimate culture (*Distinction,* 318–28).

39. See Davies, *God's Playground,* on the russification of the schools in the Kingdom (2:231–37): "After 1864, the absurd situation was reached in Warsaw where Polish teachers had to use Russian as the means of instruction for teaching Polish to Polish children (in accordance with the official myth that Polish was a 'foreign' language)" (ibid., 2:99).

40. The Positivists are renowned in Polish history for their concept of a positive Polish-Jewish alliance, but that alliance always presumed Jewish assimilation.

41. Dunin remarks in *Papierowy bandyta* that abridged versions of these authors' works were bought up more eagerly than specially composed popular

novels (8–9). Maleczyńska notes that the true record-breakers in terms of publication were the "classic" writers Józef Kraszewski and Henryk Sienkiewicz
(*Książki i biblioteki w Polsce okresu zaborów*, 23).

42. Kolbuszewski, *Od Pigalle po kresy*, 21.

43. Kolbuszewski, "Powieść popularna," 97.

44. Kolbuszewski, *Od Pigalle po kresy*, 36–44.

45. Kolbuszewski argues that popular literature succeeded in schematizing
the "high" for popular consumption (ibid., 43–44); see chapter 4.

46. In *The Printing Press as an Agent of Change*, Eisenstein remarks that
printing effected a kind of leveling of authority between masters and disciples,
teachers and students (688–89).

47. Anderson, *Imagined Communities*, 76–77.

48. In *The Cultural Uses of Print*, Chartier observes: "When printed matter
underwent this process of diffusion, some old distinctions became less clearly
drawn. The printed work was no longer a rare possession. Consequently, it
lost some of its symbolic value and became an object for a somewhat nonchalant consumption" (238). *Dahl's History of the Book* dates the appearance of
the disposable book to the mid-nineteenth century (220). With regard to
the author as producer, Denning describes the most extreme example of this
phenomenon—the writer of American dime novels who had to produce in
haste and bulk (*Mechanic Accents*, 21, 23).

49. Chartier, *The Cultural Uses of Print*.

50. Rubin, *The Making of Middlebrow Culture*, 17–22.

51. Steinberg observes the same tendencies in the writing of "worker poets"
in "Worker-Authors and the Cult of the Person." See also the caustic remark
by Kornei Chukovskii, one of the self-appointed guardians of elite culture,
that Russian pornography differs from the Western variant in that it boasts
"ideas" (cited in Zorkaia, *Na rubezhe stoletii*, 147).

52. Focused on "serious" texts, the first two chapters of part I to a certain
extent echo Bowlby's analysis of Western "highbrow" readings of capitalism
in *Just Looking*.

Chapter 2. The Problem of the Merchant in Russian Literature

1. In *Tradefull Merchants*, McVeagh recognizes "a distinct tone of mercan-
tile and patriotic ebullience" in the writings of the late seventeenth and early
eighteenth centuries. The apotheosis of the merchant hero, he contends, is found
in the works of Daniel Defoe (55–61). An interesting exception to the Russian
merchant's erasure is the tale of Sadko, which emerged during the commercial
heyday of Novgorod, one of Russia's northern trading cities and a member of
the Hanseatic League.

2. Rieber, *Merchants and Entrepreneurs in Imperial Russia,* 54. Rieber remarks that Polish merchants, like other non-Russian merchants, even enjoyed certain advantages over their Russian counterparts: the imperial government made it a practice to win over elites of newly conquered territories with economic concessions (52).

3. I use the term *intelligent,* rather than intellectual, to designate an individual member of the intelligentsia, a specifically Russian group that emerged in the nineteenth century and was distinguished by public prominence, intellectual endeavor, commitment to (usually radical) social reform, and antipathy to the tsarist government.

4. My discussion of the *sosloviia* is based on Freeze, "The *Soslovie* [Estate] Paradigm and Russian Social History."

5. Ibid., 35.

6. Pipes, *Russia Under the Old Regime,* 217.

7. Clowes, "Social Discourse in the Moscow Art Theater," 274. Pipes addresses the issue of representation in *Russia Under the Old Regime:* "In the historical and belletristic literature one occasionally encounters a Russian merchant who meets the bourgeois ideal. But these are rare exceptions. The nineteenth-century Russian merchant is much more frequently depicted as a conceited boor interested only in money, devoid of any sense of personal calling or public responsibility, both ignorant and scornful of learning. . . . The author of an important study of the Moscow merchant class, and himself a descendant of one of its more prominent families, says that in all Russian literature written by the 'intelligentsia' he knows only of one place where a private entrepreneur is treated in a favourable light" (217). See also Rieber on the dearth of firsthand evidence about merchant life (*Merchants and Entrepreneurs in Imperial Russia,* 120).

8. Fitzlyon, "Russian Society in the Reign of Nicholas II," 36.

9. See Frierson, *Peasant Icons.* Fanger, who notes "the almost complete absence of works depicting peasant life from inside," argues that "the story of the peasant in Russian literature is the story of the changing moods and attitudes of the most influential segment of educated society" ("The Peasant in Literature," 231–32).

10. Dunham comments on the changing valence of this initially neutral designation and footnotes the role played by such fin-de-siècle intellectuals as Ivanov-Razumnik and Nikolai Berdiaev in opposing the "crass" *meshchanstvo* to the enlightened intelligentsia (*In Stalin's Time,* 19, 258).

11. Rieber, *Merchants and Entrepreneurs in Imperial Russia,* 78, 81.

12. In *The Businessman in American Literature,* Watts demonstrates "that American writers produced works with anticapitalistic tendencies from the very beginning, despite our current cliches about the Puritan work ethic and the economic motives of the Founding Fathers" (5).

13. Perlman, *Russian Literature and the Business Man,* 201.

14. Ibid., vi.

15. Mathewson, *The Positive Hero in Russian Literature,* 13–14.

16. Ibid., 15.

17. In "Domestic Porkbarreling in Nineteenth-Century Russia," Goldstein argues that Saltykov-Shchedrin's villains wield provision punitively. Dostoevsky's work begs for a close investigation of his spiritual evaluation of the classes—particularly a variegated aristocracy that alternately sinks into money worship and depravity or evinces nobility of spirit.

18. Leblanc develops this point in "Dinner with Chichikov." Gogol's link of consumption with spiritual torpor interestingly parallels Charles Dickens's use of metaphors of consumption to "illustrate his concern over the way competitive economics reduce people to purely 'object' status" (Smith, "The W/hole Remains").

19. There were a few notable exceptions to this rule. Perlman bitterly remarks that an enormous fortune could tip the literary scales in a merchant's favor; he particularly damns Gogol and Turgenev as hypocrites who make fictional allowances for the wealthiest businessmen (*Russian Literature and the Business Man,* 50). Notwithstanding Perlman's charges, it is intriguing that Gogol toyed with the concept of the rich as positive heroes (the wealthy merchant Kostanzhoglo, the millionaire Murazov) in the ill-fated second volume of *Dead Souls.* Veblen's concept of "meritorious wealth," developed in *The Theory of the Leisure Class,* would seem to apply sporadically to Russian culture as well; a merchant gained in respect as he increased his fortune and decreased his daily involvement in his trade.

20. Even Dostoevsky's kindly Prince Myshkin in *The Idiot* shows little charity for the merchant type, as he remarks to Rogozhin. "'Well, it occurred to me that if this misfortune had not befallen you, if this love hadn't happened, you'd perhaps have become just like your father, and in a very short time, too. You'd have settled down quietly in this house alone with your mute and obedient wife, hardly ever opening your mouth even to utter a stern word, trusting no man and having no need to, and merely making money in gloomy silence. At the most you'd occasionally have praised the old books and taken an interest in the Old Believers' custom of crossing themselves with two fingers, and that, too, only in your old age'" (245).

21. See, among other discussions, Heldt, *Terrible Perfection;* Gheith, "The Superfluous Man."

22. Dobroliubov, "Luch sveta v temnom tsarstve" ("A Ray of Light in the Kingdom of Darkness").

23. See Kobiakova, "An Autobiography," in *Russia Through Women's Eyes.*

24. Hoisington, "Melnikov-Pechersky," 690.

25. See Hoover, *Alexander Ostrovsky.*

26. Dobroliubov is responsible for the coinage and attribution of *samodur.* See "Temnoe tsarstvo."

27. Ibid.

28. Hoover, *Alexander Ostrovsky,* 9, 132.

29. See Holmgren, "Questions of Heroism in *Oblomov.*"

30. Ehre argues otherwise in *Oblomov and His Creator,* accentuating the positive power of Oblomov's imagination and poeticizing.

31. Goncharov, *Oblomov,* 182. All quotations are from *Oblomov,* trans. Duddington, with my occasional revisions based on the Russian text in Goncharov's *Sobranie sochinenii,* vol. 4. Further references are given in the text in parentheses.

32. Dobrolyubov, "What Is Oblomovitis?," 121.

33. Ehre, *Oblomov and His Creator,* 219.

34. See Mathewson's summation of this contemporary verdict: "Goncharov's Stolz (in *Oblomov*), one of the most deliberate efforts to create a wholly positive, emblematically good man, is dismissed on two counts: the limited, mundane quality of his morality, and the abstractness of his literary portrait. The self-disciplined, practical businessman represents an advance, in some ways, over earlier types, but the practicality of his concerns denies him participation in loftier matters of social principle" (*The Positive Hero in Russian Literature,* 54–55).

35. Perlman, *Russian Literature and the Business Man,* 41.

36. Ibid., vi.

37. Rieber, *Merchants and Entrepreneurs in Imperial Russia,* 50.

38. See, for example, Kean, *All the Empty Palaces;* see also West, "The Riabushinsky Circle"; Norman, "Pavel Tretiakov and Merchant Art Patronage, 1850–1900"; Bowlt, "The Moscow Art Market."

39. Fitzlyon, "Russian Society in the Reign of Nicholas II," 36.

40. Rieber, *Merchants and Entrepreneurs in Imperial Russia,* 170.

41. The support of national culture especially characterizes the select group of "Moscow entrepreneurs" composed of former peasants of the Old Belief (e.g., the Morozovs and Soldatenkov); "partially Europeanized" Slavophil merchants (e.g., the Tret'iakovs); and fallen nobility (e.g., Chizhov and Delvig) (ibid., 165–66).

42. Bowlt, "The Moscow Art Market," 110.

43. By his own admission, the novelist Aleksandr Amfiteatrov dealt with the rushed tempo of the times by historicizing his subjects: "'When Goncharov and Turgenev wrote about events ten years past, they made them into contemporary novels, but we have to present these as history'" (Griakalova, foreword to the reprint of Amfiteatrov's *Mertvye bogi,* 14).

44. In his idiosyncratic fashion, Mirsky quickly catalogues, on the one hand, the "considerable output of Russian fiction" in the 1880s and 1890s that was

"not of a very high quality," citing specific examples of "journalistic" literature. He approves, on the other hand, the works by the "literary lawyers" who "won an all-Russian reputation by their eloquence" and contributed substantially to Russian literary criticism (*A History of Russian Literature,* 351–53, 358–60). Many writers who achieved "serious" status in this period worked simultaneously as feuilletonists for the press; their stints as reporters and commentators supported them creatively as well as financially. See also Balzer, "The Problem of Professions in Imperial Russia," which posits a considerable overlap between professionals and the intelligentsia (186).

45. Perlman, in *Russian Literature and the Business Man,* approves these writers, along with S. A. Naidenov, as sympathetic to the new merchant. Although he generally attributes their sympathy to a "bourgeois" background, he specifically remarks that Amfiteatrov was the son of a priest, Naidenov the son of a merchant, and Boborykin the son of a wealthy nobleman.

46. Quotation from Boborykin, "Letters about Moscow" (*Pis'ma o Moskve),* cited in Chuprinin's introduction to Boborykin, *Kitai-gorod. Proezdom,* 9.

47. Perlman claims, without irony, that the merchant hero of *Vasilii Tiokin* represents "a perfect gentleman" (*Russian Literature and the Business Man,* 139).

48. In "Social Discourse in the Moscow Art Theater," Clowes concentrates on these two "*meshchanstvo* writers" and their important innovations on standard Russian theater scripts.

49. Rieber, *Merchants and Entrepreneurs in Imperial Russia,* 121–22.

50. While Gorky's radical political reputation prevented his entry into the tsarist literary establishment, symbolized by the Academy of Sciences, it ensured his acceptance by such prominent writers as Tolstoy and Chekhov.

51. Clowes argues that such non-noble writers "experienced a traumatic disjunction of social identity as they crossed from the small-business milieu to the world of popular literary circles filled with lively social and moral debate and reform-oriented journals" ("Social Discourse in the Moscow Art Theater," 274). Note that Perlman wholly misreads Gorky as a product of the lower class and hence sees no possible similarity between the two writers (*Russian Literature and the Business Man,* 109).

52. Clowes traces Gorky's revision of the standard "conflict between fathers and sons" script in his dramatic work ("Social Discourse in the Moscow Art Theater," 281–83).

53. See Mathewson's comment on Gorky's search for heroes: "He did not limit his search to a single class or look for a single set of admirable qualities through the range of castes and classes in Imperial Russia" (*The Positive Hero in Russian Literature,* 166). Hare is quick to point out that Gorky did not even favor tramps as a group, but patterned his heroes on the most exceptional among them (*Maxim Gorky,* 14).

54. Scherr sums up this frequent critical observation in *Maxim Gorky*, 29.

55. Scherr argues that the tramps' "chief merit lies in their rejection of contemporary bourgeois society," but he does not identify which estates constitute this bourgeoisie (ibid.). Gorky, however, is quite specific in his distaste for the peasant: "Time and again, I had heard and read that life in the country was more wholesome and more genial than in the city. Yet I saw the peasants engaged in unceasing and backbreaking toil. . . . The peasants' life did not seem to me a simple one. It required a constant strained attention to the soil and a great degree of crafty shrewdness in dealing with one's fellows. Nor was there anything genial about this intellect-starved existence. All the village people I could see went through life gropingly, like sightless creatures. They were all afraid of something, each mistrusted the others, and there was something of the wolf in them" (from *My Universities*, in *Collected Works*, trans. Altschuler, 493–94, with my emendations based on the Russian original in *Polnoe sobranie sochinenii*, vol. 16).

56. See the cycle of three plays—*Summerfolk* (*Dachniki*, 1904), *Children of the Sun* (*Deti solntsa*, 1905), and *The Barbarians* (*Varvary*, 1905)—in which Scherr observes an increasingly negative depiction of the intelligentsia (*Maxim Gorky*, 65).

57. Hare, *Maxim Gorky*, 27.

58. Mathewson, *The Positive Hero in Russian Literature*, 167–76, 227–32.

59. Mathewson remarks that Gorky felt a "generalized need" for the heroic "throughout his creative life" (ibid., 165).

60. Mathewson notes that Gorky "found a successful tragic design . . . in the career of the energetic, self-made bourgeois who was destroyed by the wealth he accumulated" (ibid., 166).

61. Gorky, *Foma Gordeev*, 7. Citations are from Gorky, *Foma Gordeev*, in *Collected Works in Ten Volumes*, trans. Wettlin, vol. 2, with my emendations based on the Russian original in *Polnoe sobranie sochinenii*, vol. 4.

62. Hare, *Maxim Gorky*, 49.

63. Scherr, *Maxim Gorky*, 37–38, specifically names *The Zykovs* and *The Old Man*.

64. Ibid., 38.

65. Holtzman concludes, "Although, as we have observed, young Gorky's search for a potent hero was directed to the great Russian masses, his most artistic and most striking creations came from the ranks of the capitalist class —the Gordeevs, the Shchukovs, the Maiakins" (*The Young Maxim Gorky*, 163). Such later works as *The Artamonov Business* (1924–1925) and the sketch "Bugrov" in *Fragments from My Diary* (1922) reflect much the same pattern.

66. Quotation from Hare's unidentified citation of Gorky: "The features distinguishing our big bourgeoisie from that of the West are clear and plentiful. Our historically younger bourgeois, springing as a rule from the peasantry, got rich quicker and more easily than the historically older bourgeoisie of the

West. Our industrial magnate, untrained by the fierce competition prevailing in the West, preserved in himself, almost to the twentieth century, traits of the eccentric and the playboy" (*Maxim Gorky,* 109). In his portrait of the real-life Nizhnii-Novgorod merchant, Bugrov, Gorky declares that he felt "a tense curiosity together with an instinctive hostility" toward this old millionaire who had read his *Foma Gordeev,* and this ambivalence is borne out by subsequent meetings and conversations. After a three-way conversation among Bugrov, the famous "enlightened" industrialist, Savva Morozov, and himself, Gorky relates: "It was strange to know that this man [Bugrov] lived on the work of many thousand people and at the same time to hear that this work was of no use to him, meaningless in his eyes. I could not help thinking: 'Only Russian people can live and feel in that way'" ("Bugrov," in *Fragments from My Diary,* trans. Budberg, 256–57).

67. For example, in Gorky's play *Vassa Zheleznova* (1910; rev. ed. 1935), Vassa's son Pavel is said to have been crippled when his father beat his pregnant mother.

68. It is intriguing, however, that Vassa favors her daughter and daughter-in-law and maneuvers her male children out of the family business.

69. "As a group, the children of both the old and new wealthy, of successful businessmen, seem to follow self-destructive paths or else refuse to follow their fathers into business. The children suffer and their families disintegrate. New money or old money, the children are doomed, and the authors do not suggest any reason other than money" (Watts, *The Businessman in American Literature,* 71).

70. Scherr notes that Gorky first attempted to write about his life in 1893, but when he returned to this topic two decades later, he could not find his early work and so began a new draft (*Maxim Gorky,* 75).

71. Scherr traces the "indirect evidence" of Gorky's artistic license with autobiographical data and posits that the author "apparently idealized some of the people in the family while making others still more negative" ("Gor'kij's *Childhood*").

72. Scherr, *Maxim Gorky,* 80.

73. Gorky, *My Universities,* in *Collected Works,* trans. Altschuler, 463–64.

74. See, for example, his portrait of the love-preaching Tolstoyan Klopsky, who "smacks his thick lips" when he is treated to raspberries and milk, drinks to excess, and proposes to two women at once (ibid., 458–63).

75. During a conversation with Iakov the stoker, a man to whom he told stories by Pushkin and Dumas, Gorky suddenly realized, "The overwhelming majority of books I had read said absolutely nothing at all about how those noble heroes worked or how they earned their living" (*My Apprenticeship,* trans. Wilks, 214).

76. In "Redefining the Intellectual's Role," Loe examines Gorky's behav-

ioral and programmatic impact on his literary circle, a group of young men who similarly hailed from the lower strata of Russian society. These writers, however, largely broke with Gorky over the issue of revolutionary commitment.

77. Loe maintains that Gorky would tolerate "no compromise between the intellectuals and the middle class" (ibid., 300).

78. Bruford penetrates the pleasant facade of the Chekhov family and its talented father and sons: "Everyone envied their parents then, Chekhov said later, but the boys themselves felt like little convicts. An overdose of compulsory religion in youth probably helped to turn them against it later, especially as they associated it with their father's general 'despotism,' scenes at table because the soup was oversalted, free use of the rod and the like" (*Chekhov and His Russia*, 3).

79. Karlinsky concludes: "The size limitations and requirements imposed by various humor magazines were particularly important in training Chekhov to rely on careful organization rather than on the traditional eventful plot for producing the impact he wanted" (introduction to *Letters of Anton Chekhov*, trans. Heim and Karlinsky, 40). See Chudakov, *Poetika Chekhova*, for a description of the changing characteristics of Chekhov's narrators.

80. Shekhtel' himself could serve as an advertisement for class mobility. His mother kept house for the progressive merchant family, the Tret'iakovs, who sponsored his training as an architect. See the exhibition catalogue, *The Twilight of the Tsars*.

81. On Suvorin, one of the first Russians to create a publishing empire (complete with its own paper factory), see Makhonina, *Russkaia dorevoliutsionnaia pechat'*, 53–57.

82. Letter to Dmitrii Grigorovich, March 28, 1886; Grigorovich was a once renowned writer who recognized Chekhov as the outstanding talent of his era and beseeched him to devote more care to his art (*Letters of Anton Chekhov*, trans. Heim and Karlinsky, 58–59). Karlinsky remarks that Chekhov's recognition by Grigorovich and Nikolai Leskov was symbolically effective, but the man "who backed his recognition of Chekhov's talent with concrete action and who did more than anyone else to launch him on a major career in serious literature was the writer and publisher Alexei Suvorin" (ibid., 54).

83. Maegd-Soep makes this observation in *Chekhov and Women*, 205, noting especially Chekhov's early satire of the "petty bourgeois housewife," whom he ridicules for "shallowness, mediocrity, and intellectual backwardness" (ibid., 220).

84. Hingley remarks, "Each of these three works presents some facet of a milieu which we are amazed to find the mature Chekhov portraying so rarely, since he had sprung from it himself" (introduction to *The Oxford Chekhov*, trans. and ed. Hingley, 7:3).

85. Chekhov, "A Woman's Kingdom," in *The Oxford Chekhov*, trans. Hingley, 7:57. Citations are from this edition, with my emendations based on the Russian original in *Polnoe sobranie sochinenii i pisem*, vol. 8. Further references will be given in the text.

86. Jackson argues that the lower half of Anna's house constitutes a woman's kingdom where people are "preoccupied with chance and fate" ("Chekhov's 'A Woman's Kingdom,'" 95), and he faults Anna for yielding to its ethos of passivity and fatalism.

87. Ibid., 96, 92.

88. Anna's bequests to the poor do no good: the thousands she spends on the workers' barracks result in no improvements and the small sum she bestows on a penitent transforms him into a permanent pest.

89. Chekhov, "A Case History," in *The Oxford Chekhov*, trans. Hingley, 9:78.

90. Chekhov, *Three Years*, in *The Oxford Chekhov*, trans. Hingley, 7:215. Translations, with a few emendations based on the Russian original in *Polnoe sobranie sochinenii i pisem*, vol. 9.

91. Ibid., 7:157.

92. As the doctor reflects: "'The Lyalikov woman and her daughter are unhappy—they look pathetic—and the only one to enjoy life to the full is Miss Christine: an elderly, rather silly old maid with a pince-nez. So what does it all come down to? What are these five mills working for? To what end is cheap cotton sold in eastern markets? Just so that Miss Christine can eat her sturgeon and drink her Madeira!'" ("A Case History," in *The Oxford Chekhov*, trans. Hingley, 9:74). Chekhov constantly toys with the prejudged boundaries of flesh and spirit: e.g., the inveterate womanizer and club-goer Gurov falls unexpectedly and sincerely in love in "The Lady with the Lapdog," and the famous thinker Professor Serebriakov tyrannizes his family and monopolizes his estate with his financial and physical needs in *Uncle Vanya*.

93. Clowes reads *The Cherry Orchard* as Chekhov's ironic revision of the enduringly popular "nest of gentlefolk" script in Russian dramaturgy, and she remarks that Chekhov's directors insisted on interpreting his innovative work along just these traditional lines ("Social Discourse in the Moscow Art Theater," 277, 279).

94. Hoover notes the thematic parallels between Ostrovskii and Chekhov in *Alexander Ostrovsky*, 135–36.

95. Chekhov, *The Three Sisters*, in *Plays*, ed. Fen, 318.

96. Marina Majdalany, "Natasha Ivanovna," 305, 307.

97. Chekhov, *The Cherry Orchard*, in *Plays*, ed. Fen, 334.

98. Ibid., 359.

99. Interestingly, Chekhov's appeal and influence resurged in post-Stalin Soviet culture with the emergence of a de facto middle class of consuming professionals.

100. Bruford, *Chekhov and His Russia*, 198, 206.

101. Morson, "Prosaic Chekhov, Metadrama, the Intelligentsia and *Uncle Vanya*," seems to be addressed to a latter-day leftist intelligentsia as well.

102. In a complementary observation, Clowes notes the prevailing negative image of the middle in the Moscow Art Theater ("Social Discourse in the Moscow Art Theater," 287).

103. In *Doctor Zhivago*, Boris Pasternak gives his hero, Iurii Zhivago, a millionaire father and his heroine, Lara Antipova, affluent patrons.

Chapter 3. The Doll-Nation of Polish Capitalism

1. Davies, *God's Playground*, 2:22.

2. Kołodziejczyk, among many others, makes this point in *Miasto, mieszczaństwo, burżuazja w Polsce w XIX w.*, 9.

3. This is Miłosz's composite portrait in *The History of Polish Literature*, 282.

4. Blobaum remarks that "many bankrupt Polish noblemen migrated to the cities in the 1880s," where they found work and "made up the majority of the recruits for a newly emerging urban intelligentsia" (*Rewolucja*, 31).

5. Markiewicz estimates that at least 50 percent of the Polish writers in the Russian and Austrian partitions belonged to the landed gentry and another 25 percent came from the families of bureaucrats, teachers, and free tradesmen (*Literatura pozytywizmu*, 15–16.

5. Markiewicz estimates that 15 percent of all writers in the Kingdom of Poland were women (ibid., 16). In *Życie literackie Warszawy*, Kulczycka-Saloni quotes Bolesław Prus at length on the writer's terrible material situation in this period (24–26, 31–38).

7. Kulczycka-Saloni more generally names "literature and theater" as the sanctuaries for Polish language (ibid., 13).

8. Markiewicz, *Literatura pozytywizmu*, 19.

9. Kulczycka-Saloni observes that the new writing intelligentsia felt themselves to be above class and party affiliation and committed to national service. They also expressed scorn for the bourgeoisie and remaining wealthy landowners (*Życie literackie Warszawy*, 14). Markiewicz confirms the writer's strong sense of a national role and duty in this period (*Literatura pozytywizmu*, 20).

10. Markiewicz, *Literatura pozytywizmu*, 24.

11. Miłosz, *The History of Polish Literature*, 284.

12. Kulczycka-Saloni, *Życie literackie Warszawy*, 16.

13. Rieber notes that at the beginning of the nineteenth century "the most formidable challenge to the economic well-being of the Moscow merchants arose in the kingdom of Poland"; by the mid-1880s, this region "where only slightly more than 7 percent of the total population lived, was producing one-

quarter of the steel, two-fifths of the coal, one-fifth of the sugar, and just under one-fifth of the value of all textiles in the Russian empire. On top of this, 50 percent of all products made in Poland were sold in Russia" (*Merchants and Entrepreneurs in Imperial Russia*, 62, 66). See also Davies, *God's Playground*, 107. Blobaum tempers this assessment by noting that the kingdom's industrial output still "lagged far behind" that of Western Europe and was diminished significantly by the beginning of the twentieth century (*Rewolucja*, 26–27).

14. I am indebted to Markiewicz for this catalogue of types and works (*Literatura pozytywizmu*, 56–57).

15. Opalski outlines both admission and assimilation in "The Concept of Jewish Assimilation in Polish Literature of the Positivist Period."

16. This literary era was also marked by the bold emergence of Polish modernism in the specific movement retroactively named "Young Poland." In its critical recovery of romanticism and review of national themes, "Young Poland" represented an intriguing variation on the pattern of elite art resisting market regimentation and the dominance of middlebrow or lowbrow production.

17. Szweykowski declares that *The Doll* emerged in a period when Prus was suffering his most serious crisis of belief (*Twórczość Bolesława Prusa*, 181).

18. Some critics describe Wokulski as Prus's alter ego. Kulczycka-Saloni maintains that Prus so loved his hero that he lost his sense of humor in portraying him (*Bolesław Prus*, 293). See also Szweykowski, *Twórczość Bolesława Prusa*, 176; Miłosz, *The History of Polish Literature*, 298.

19. See Grzeniewski, *Warszawa w "Lalce" Prusa*, for a description of Prus's painstaking recreation of Warsaw. Grzeniewski's first attempt at "mapping" *The Doll*, prompted in part by a sense of loss after the city's wartime destruction, appeared as "Warszawskie realia *Lalki*." Curiously, Prus airbrushed this city portrait for all signs of its russification. My thanks to Bożena Shallcross for this important observation.

20. The other two centers were Łódź and Sosnowiec (Kołodziejczyk, *Miasto, mieszczaństwo, burżuazja w Polsce w XIX w.*, 83).

21. In *Bolesław Prus*, Kulczycka-Saloni cites the opinion of the eminent sociologist, Jan Szczepański (332). Szweykowski asserts that he knows of no other novel that provides such an expressive, richly detailed image of national reality (*Twórczość Bolesława Prusa*, 192).

22. Miłosz, *The History of Polish Literature*, 285.

23. Miłosz asserts that the Positivists "turned their anger mostly against the second wave of the Romantics, particularly against the craze for messianic ideas" (ibid., 284).

24. Markiewicz suggests a veiled Russian influence on the post-1880 Polish novel: "Less apparent due to political reasons was the inspiration of the great Russian novel (Turgenev, Tolstoy), especially in terms of deepening psychological analysis and the creation of peasants from the folk" (*Literatura pozyty-*

wizmu, 70). Tsybenko draws a more specific comparison between *The Doll* and Tolstoy's *Anna Karenina* in "'Kukla' Boleslava Prusa i 'Anna Karenina' L'va Tolstogo."

25. Prus, "Słówko o krytyce pozytywnej," 84.

26. Miłosz remarks that Prus "employed his humor as a tool. His aim was to combat and to educate. He compared the public to a fish, which can be caught only with the bait of jokes" (*The History of Polish Literature,* 292). Markiewicz reports that critics could not fathom *The Doll*'s construction and so pronounced it "a non-masterpiece." See *"Lalka" Bolesława Prusa,* ed. Markiewicz, 62.

27. Two prominent writers of the Positivist period, the journalist and editor Aleksandr Swiętochowski and the literary critic Piotr Chmielowski, pass these judgments. Selections from their criticism on *The Doll* are cited in *"Lalka" Bolesława Prusa,* ed. Markiewicz, 558–59, 566–67.

28. Brzozowski, "Bolesław Prus," 414.

29. Markiewicz, *"Lalka" Bolesława Prusa,* 6–7, 9; Kulczycka-Saloni, *Bolesław Prus,* 319; Szweykowski, *Twórczość Bolesława Prusa,* 190.

30. On the defining "heteroglossia" of the nineteenth-century novel in Bakhtin's criticism, see Morson and Emerson, *Mikhail Bakhtin,* 344–48.

31. Prus, *The Doll,* 155. All citations are from Prus, *The Doll,* trans. Welsh, with my emendations based on the original in *Lalka,* ed. Markiewicz. Further references will be given in the text.

32. Ibid., 195. Elsewhere Szuman recapitulates these terms, remarking that "like a miser, [Wokulski] has hoarded his heart's capital and now we see the results of this economy" (ibid., 326).

33. It is also noteworthy that the duchess delegates Wokulski to erect a romantic monument to her old lover's memory.

34. Markiewicz makes this observation in his introduction to *Lalka,* 17.

35. In the episode that provides the novel's title, Baroness Krzeszowska accuses Stawska of stealing her dead daughter's doll, a charge Wokulski disproves before the court by revealing the doll's trademark and therefore its purchase in his store.

36. I have borrowed this term from Williams, *Dream Worlds.*

37. Veblen says of the discriminating shopper: "High-bred manners and ways of living are items of conformity to the norm of conspicuous consumption" (*The Theory of the Leisure Class,* 64).

38. Bela articulates this philosophy in a debate with Wokulski (*The Doll,* 451).

39. During the Easter collection, volunteers set up stations in the church for collecting offerings; this event constituted something on the order of a charity ball for upper-class young women—a forum for doing good works and being seen.

40. Wokulski muses, "If she [the child] were mine, then surely I'd regain control of my senses which I'm losing day by day. And her mother is a pretty woman, too. Her hair, profile, eyes" (ibid., 98).

41. See Świętochowski's abridged essay, "Bohaterowie Prusa," in *"Lalka" Bolesława Prusa,* ed. Markiewicz.

42. It is intriguing that this dream is embodied in yet another goddess figure whose face, significantly enough, is not revealed: "He recalled Geist in his wooden sandals, and his strange house surrounded by its wall. And suddenly it seemed to him that the house was the first step of a huge staircase, at the top of which stood a statue disappearing into the clouds. It represented a woman, whose head and bosom were out of sight, only the brass folds of her robe could be seen. It seemed to him that there was an inscription 'Unchangeable and pure' on the step which her feet touched. He did not understand what this was, but felt that from the statue's feet there flowed into his heart some greatness full of tranquillity" (*The Doll,* 625).

43. When Wokulski moves his shop into larger quarters, Rzecki is delighted with the new store but regrets the loss of his room. He is moved to tears when he discovers that Wokulski has replicated his old cell in the new location, although he finds the addition of a fine drawing-room "disagreeable" (ibid., 139–40).

44. Kott, "Kariera kupca," in *"Lalka" Bolesława Prusa,* ed. Markiewicz.

45. Markiewicz, introduction to *"Lalka" Bolesława Prusa,* 19. Kulczycka-Saloni (*Bolesław Prus,* 298–99) identifies Prus's particular attack on the aristocratic characters who scorn work.

46. Kulczycka-Saloni enumerates these sins in "Czytając Prusa," 306–07.

47. Another telling characterization: the handsome clerk Mraczewski, eventually the husband of Mrs. Stawska, flirts with socialism even as he hones his skills as clerk and manager.

48. Szweykowski notes this sequence of German-Polish-Jewish shop ownership, concluding that "the Poles only constituted a transitional phase" (*Twórczość Bolesława Prusa,* 187).

49. Whereas the old clerk would defend the equal rights of Jews in principle, he mouths bigoted views aplenty about Jewish stinginess and clannishness.

50. When his tavern buddies claim that Wokulski must be involved in arms dealing, Rzecki hotly protests, presuming that "Stas's interests must be honest!" (*The Doll,* 482–83).

51. This excised scene is given in the appendix to *Lalka,* ed. Markiewicz, 2:515.

52. Wokulski waits on tables at a restaurant owned by the German Hopfer and inherits Mincel's shop by marriage.

53. Opalski and Bartal, *Poles and Jews,* 134–35.

54. See, for example, Szweykowski, *Twórczość Bolesława Prusa,* 176.

55. Sienkiewicz, *Rodzina Połanieckich* and *Bez Dogmatu*. Lednicki sees in *Without Dogma* a reprise of the Russian plot of "a morally firm, strong, and pure woman confronting a weak, capricious, superfluous man" (*Henryk Sienkiewicz*, 45).

56. Markiewicz, introduction to *"Lalka" Bolesława Prusa*, 83.

57. Miłosz, *The History of Polish Literature*, 314; Miłosz maintains that *The Połaniecki Family* "indicated Sienkiewicz's *rapprochement* with the ideology of the National Democratic Party and its program of capitalist prosperity under the protection of czarist Russia" (ibid.).

58. Chekhov, letter to Aleksei Suvorin, April 13, 1895. "It's a Polish cottage-cheese cake with saffron. Add a little Potapenko to Paul Bourget, sprinkle with Warsaw eau-de-cologne, divide in two, and there you have Sienkiewicz.... It is clear that Sienkiewicz has not read Tolstoy and is unfamiliar with Nietzsche, he talks about hypnotism like a philistine, but on the other hand every one of his pages is swarming with Rubenses, Villa Borgheses, Correggios, and Botticellis—the better to show off his culture to the bourgeois reader and covertly stick out his tongue at materialism. The novel's goal is to lull the bourgeoisie in its golden dreams" (*Letters of Anton Chekhov*, trans. Heim and Karlinsky, 275–76).

59. Markiewicz cites Marian Gawalewicz's "optimistic novel" *Warsaw* (1901) as one example (*"Lalka" Bolesława Prusa*, 60).

60. Koc weighs Borowiecki's similarity to Wokulski in terms of "intelligence, ability, energy, and will" against his very different aspirations (*O "Ziemi Obiecanej" Reymonta*, 30–31).

61. *Ziemia obiecana*, in Reymont, *Dzieła wybrane*, 7:322.

62. With regard to the unconvincing ending, Koc notes: "Spiritual bankruptcy only appears in the 'Epilogue' of *The Promised Land*. For that reason, too, it surprises the reader who is unprepared for an internal shift in a man indifferent to everything but money" (*O "Ziemi Obiecanej" Reymonta*, 31).

63. Opalski and Bartal, *Poles and Jews*, 108. For evidence of the spider image, see Junosza-Szaniawski, *Pająki* (*The Spiders*, 1894); *Pająki wiejskie* (*Village Spiders*, 1895); and *W pajęczej sieci* (*In the Spider's Web*, (1896).

64. Ibid., 111.

65. See ibid., 111–19.

66. Slotnick concludes that what *The Family Moskat* "reveals and condemns is the evolution and existence of that world of chaos and decay in which Auschwitz was possible" (*"The Family Moskat"*).

67. Singer, *The Brothers Ashkenazi*, 407. Norich generalizes the authority of this passage: "No other voice counters this perspective—to which, indeed, the entire novel has led—and it remains the only possible conclusion that Jews of any period can draw" (*The Homeless Imagination in the Fiction of Israel Joshua Singer*, 45).

68. Markiewicz notes this treatment in works by Wiktor Gomulicki, Or-Ot, Baliński, and Antoni Słonimski (*"Lalka" Bolesława Prusa,* ed. Markiewicz, 60).

69. *Śladami Wokulskiego,* ed. Godlewski et al., borrows Godlewski's title and amplifies his "topographical" research with essays by Grzeniewski and Markiewicz and photographs of *The Doll's* "realia." I am indebted to George Suboczewski for the loan of this fascinating volume.

70. In his "Posłowie" to the postwar *Śladami Wokulskiego,* Grzeniewski notes the disappearance of the plaques during and immediately after the war and Godlewski's wartime arrest and death in Auschwitz (193–94).

71. Cited from Andrzej Wierzbicki, "Wokulski żyje!" in *"Lalka" Bolesława Prusa,* ed. Markiewicz, 267–70.

Chapter 4. The Birth of the Middlebrow?

1. See Brooks, *When Russia Learned to Read.* On Polish popular literature, see Dunin, *Papierowy bandyta;* see also Chruściński, "Powiastka 'dla ludu.'"

2. Dunin specifically refers to the "good spiritual food" social activists and pedagogues wanted to deliver to the people (*Papierowy bandyta,* 6).

3. Dunin comments on the relative unpopularity of specially composed "popular" works as opposed to the popularity of abridged versions of Sienkiewicz's and Prus's texts (ibid., 8–9). Markiewicz notes that popular adaptations of works by Kraszewski, Orzeszkowa, Prus, and Sienkiewicz were being issued by the 1880s (*Literatura pozytywizmu,* 189). See Brooks's survey of Russian publishers of "good literature" for the folk (*When Russia Learned to Read,* 337–45); and Belov and Tolstiakov, *Russkie izdateli,* 36–63, on Florentii Pavlenkov, publisher of a popular biography series of famous people and of popular editions of the classics.

4. Markiewicz, *Literatura pozytywizmu,* 189. Chruściński notes that authors of literature "for the folk" *(dla ludu)* were most often journalists, teachers, and priests ("Powiastka 'dla ludu,'" 217). Dunin implicitly disagrees with Markiewicz's notion of the intelligentsia's control, noting the successes of a "separate market" developed by publishers keen on making money (*Papierowy bandyta,* 9).

5. Dunin, *Papierowy bandyta,* 10. Dunin lists the following Polish writers in this category: Maria Rodziewiczówna, Irena Zarzycka, Paweł Staśko, Tadeusz Dołęga-Mostowicz, and Antoni Marczyński. He comments that "all of this work—perhaps too familiar to an older and middle generation of readers—is terrain that has yet to be studied" (ibid., 11).

6. Martuszewska cites the critic Cezary Jellenta on the derivative, yet undeniably Positivist nature of Rodziewiczówna's work ("W stronę powieści popularnej," 201–15).

7. Aside from Rieber, *Merchants and Entrepreneurs in Imperial Russia,* see the following essays in *Between Tsar and People,* ed. Clowes et al.: Kassow, West, and Clowes, "Introduction: The Problem of the Middle in Late Imperial Russia"; Gleason, "The Terms of Russian Social History"; Monas, "The Twilit Middle Class of Nineteenth-Century Russia"; West, "The Riabushinsky Circle"; Rosenthal, "The Search for a Russian Orthodox Work Ethic"; Owen, "Impediments to a Bourgeois Consciousness in Russia."

8. Kassow, West, and Clowes, introduction to *Between Tsar and People,* 4.

9. Ibid., 4–5.

10. Davies relates that "the new middle stratum . . . contained a high proportion of Germans, Jews, Russians, and even Czechs and Hungarians: some assimilated, some not: some who were native born, and some who arrived from distant regions of the three partitioning Empires. Its activities were most in evidence in the towns of Russian Poland, less so in Prussia or in Galicia" (*God's Playground,* 194).

11. Kołodziejczuk notes that Jews numbered 46.5 percent of the urban population in 1865, in contrast to 13.5 percent in all of partitioned Poland (*Miasto, mieszczaństwo, burżuazja w Polsce w XIX w.,* 77). Davies claims that "the Jews of Warsaw stood fair to attain the position of an absolute majority in the first decades of the twentieth century" (*God's Playground,* 206).

12. Davies concludes that the middle groups in Polish society "were united only by their common desire to be distinguished from the toiling masses" (*God's Playground,* 196).

13. I am indebted to Rubin, *The Making of Middlebrow Culture,* for these definitions and a history of the middlebrow in the United States.

14. Marker traces this gap to the beginning of modern Russian literature in the eighteenth century: "Even in the very realm that they had taken a hand in creating, the literati were finding themselves outflanked by an unfavorable convergence of hacks, merchants, and public taste" (*Publishing, Printing, and the Origins of Intellectual Life in Russia,* 235).

15. For one important historical example, see Debreczeny's discussion of the "middlebrow" literary production that so irked and challenged Pushkin in the 1820s and 1830s (*Social Functions of Literature,* 110–23).

16. This notion of selective consumption as education is epitomized by the American business venture, the Book-of-the-Month Club, founded in 1926. A subscriber obtained that all-important "image of being au courant" by consuming the Club's guaranteed high-quality selections (Rubin, *The Making of Middlebrow Culture,* 99–101).

17. The socioeconomic conditions fostering a cult of personality are described in Susman, *Culture as History.* On the cult of personality as it was manifested in late imperial Russia, see McReynold's essay on the cabaret singer, Anastasiia Vial'tseva ("'The Incomparable' Anastasia," 273–94).

18. Such was the case for certain American middlebrow critics who guaranteed an audience for their journal through their personalized writing persona. Rubin points out examples of this personalized engagement in the writings of Christopher Morley and Heywood Hale Broun (*The Making of Middlebrow Culture*, 136–40).

19. Helena Mniszek, born Mniszek-Tchorznicka, is generally known in Poland as Mniszkówna.

20. The romance flourished as a serious genre in medieval and Renaissance Europe; a more formulaically written and derivative variant evolved from roughly the late eighteenth century up to the present day. For information on the evolution of the romance, see Jensen, *Love's Sweet Return*. For discussions of woman's elaboration as consumer and commodity in the Western mass-circulation press, see Garvey, *The Adman in the Parlor*. Other analyses of the connection between middle-class women and the production of fiction appear in Douglas, *The Feminization of American Culture*; Showalter, *A Literature of Their Own*; Armstrong, *Desire and Domestic Fiction*.

21. Modleski, *Loving with a Vengeance*, 17.

22. Ibid., 58; see also Radway, *Reading the Romance*, 55, 61, 113. The notion of a "feminized" hero is certainly subject to dispute, as many Harlequin romance heroes are distinguished by the quite opposite stereotypes of aggressiveness and "hardness." I'm grateful to Helena Goscilo for this important counter-observation.

23. For a history of the modern-day commodification of romance, see Radway, *Reading the Romance;* and Jensen, *Love's Sweet Return*. See also appendixes to Thurston, *The Romance Revolution*, for the editorial guidelines that romance publishing houses provide prospective authors. The guidelines for "Harlequin American Romance" specify that the heroine "should typify the average middle-class American woman so that the reader can identify with her more easily"; while the hero need not be rich, "he should be an achiever and upwardly mobile in his job" (223). I should note that, given its very set formulas and cheap marketing, the popular romance today represents a more lowbrow than middlebrow product. In the early twentieth century, however, the romance occupied a more ambiguously "classed" position for its writers and readers, a position I argue to be roughly equivalent to the middlebrow.

24. Kalita, *Mniszkówna*, 12–13.

25. Brooks observes: "What distinguished Verbitskaia's work from other types of Russian popular fiction was her presumption that her writing was the equal of serious literature" (*When Russia Learned to Read*, 154). Dunin points out Mniszek's attempt at a classical drama, *Pluto and Persephone. A Fairy Tale from Mythology* (1919) and concedes that she "was not without literary ambition" (*Papierowy bandyta*, 11).

26. Brooks, *When Russia Learned to Read*, 156. Attempting to characterize Verbitskaia's audience, Brooks deduces in it a strong "middling component":

"Her fantasies of upward mobility could appeal to a very wide audience, but her long-winded and naive pronouncements about culture suggest a readership willing to accept such digressions as the price of a little learning on the cheap. Her readers were probably people who had escaped wholly or partially from lower-class origins and had a smattering of education" (*When Russia Learned to Read*, 159).

27. Walas remarks on the extraordinary and unexpected popularity of *The Leper (Trędowata)*: "It was read in palaces and shanties, ridiculed in editor's offices and salons, and copied out by hand in school notebooks. It became a fetish *à rebours,* and the legend that grew up around it increased its success" (afterword to *The Leper,* 307). Dunin concurs, citing the critic Julian Krzyżanowski on the telltale success of *The Leper:* "Mniszek's success signalled the new and widespread demands of readers who were not yet able to appreciate the works of the most programmatically proletariat writers, but were not satisfied by strictly traditional literature, oral literature, or even the penny dreadfuls" (*Papierowy bandyta,* 11). Citing the evidence of one bookseller, Dunin notes that *The Leper* probably also attracted "experienced novel readers" (ibid., 12). Mniszek's sequel to *The Leper, Lord Michorowski* (1910), also enjoyed incredible popularity. See the entry for Mniszek in *Literatura polska. Przewodnik encyklopedyczny,* 1:679.

28. Kalita asserts that Mniszek's governess "fed" her an earlier variant of Harlequin romances in the Hachette edition of *Bibliothèque Rose.* He also notes that Mniszek was a great fan of Sienkiewicz (*Mniszkówna,* 8–9).

29. Engelstein, *The Keys to Happiness.* Brooks first identifies this form of consumer education in *When Russia Learned to Read,* 157–58.

30. Walas, afterword to *The Leper,* 311.

31. See Engelstein, *The Keys to Happiness.* Comparing Verbitskaia with an English romance novelist, McReynolds claims that "both were pioneering in that they wrote about sex for other women" ("Anastasiia Verbitskaia and Elinor Glyn," 1), Glyn came to this emphasis "from a wealthier tradition of female literature" (19).

32. Walas, afterword to *The Leper,* 309.

33. Huyssen, *After the Great Divide,* 49. See also Holmgren, "Why Russian Girls Loved Charskaia."

34. Speaking of Harlequin romances, Jensen observes: "The main focus of attention is on the heroine, whose appearance, personality, socioeconomic background, thoughts, emotions and even bodily sensations are described in detail. The heroine is the character with whom readers are expected to identify, no matter how different she or her experiences may be from themselves and their lives" (*Love's Sweet Return,* 83).

35. Verbitskaia, *Keys to Happiness* (*Kliuchi schast'ia: Roman daidzhest*), 1:13. Further references are given in the text.

36. Manya's attraction to aristocratic artifacts, gestures, and life styles also

serves to reinforce the sense of her aesthetic superiority. On the "classing" of aesthetic taste and distinction, see Bourdieu, *Distinction*, 2, 18–96.

37. As part of proving Stefcia's "equality" and satisfying the fashion-conscious reader, the narrator almost always remarks on the heroine's tasteful and effective dress when she enters a scene.

38. There is only one passage in the novel where the narrator admits that Stefcia may have grown a bit too accustomed to aristocratic life: "It is easy to live without comfort if you have not known it, but it is hard to get unused to it. Stefcia did not show this, but something was missing" (Mniszek, *The Leper*, 2:37). All citations are translated from this edition. Further references will be given in the text.

39. At one point, the "splendor and magnificence" of Głębowicze so overwhelm Stefcia that she anticipates Wokulski's fate: "She felt so crushed that it seemed the huge castle had fallen on her" (Mniszek, *The Leper*, 1:394).

40. "In both Harlequins and Gothics, the heroines engage in a continual deciphering of the motives for the hero's behavior. The Harlequin heroine probes for the secret underlying the masculine enigma, while the reader outwits the heroine in coming up with the 'correct' interpretation of the puzzling actions and attitudes of the man" (Modleski, *Loving with a Vengeance*, 34).

41. Over the last several decades, of course, Harlequin romances reflect drastically altered sexual mores.

42. Goscilo argues in the introduction to the English translation of *Keys* that Steinbach's and Verbitskaia's notions of gender roles must be drawn from Otto Weininger's influential 1903 treatise, *Sex and Character*, which defined "masculine" as the "Aryan" qualities of rationality and creativity and allied the "feminine" with irrationality, wantonness, fecundity, and Jewishness.

43. In her sampling of these panaceas, Manya typifies a general trend in Russian literature following the aborted revolution of 1905. See Engelstein, *The Keys to Happiness*, 359–96.

44. Walas, afterword to *The Leper*, 308.

45. Martuszewska remarks that Mniszek patterned her novel to a significant extent on two works by Rodziewiczówna—*Magnat (The Magnate)* and *Błękitni (The Bluebloods)*—in which Rodziewiczówna uncharacteristically made her protagonists aristocrats ("W stronę powieści popularnej," 208).

46. In *The Commodity Culture of Victorian England*, Richards argues that the first such exhibition held in London in 1851 "was responsible for synthesizing what can be seen as the six major foundations of a semiotics of commodity spectacle: the establishment of an autonomous iconography for the manufactured object; the use of commemoration to place objects in history; the invention of a democratic ideology for consumerism; the transformation of the commodity into language; the figuration of a consuming subject; and the invention of the myth of the abundant society" (58–59).

47. Michorowski declares that he would so intern the Jews on his estate that they would do him and "the people" no harm: "I'll use them in certain areas—under strict supervision and not on the farms or in the villages, because then they will have a harmful effect on the people. . . . I'll contain them and keep them firmly in line. Then they won't hurt me" (Mniszek, *The Leper*, 2:231).

48. *The Leper* features one such scene in which Stefcia and her aristocratic "betters" listen intently to Pan Maciej's stories of his days in the Polish army: "These people now possessed no great names or titles, but they shared a single passionate blood. They were bound together by love for the fatherland, and its historic drama filled their souls with sadness. All of those present were children of their nation, and its wounds hurt them more than their own—like the wounds of a dying mother. Etiquette disappeared, concealed in the rich wall tapestries and carvings. In its place there appeared the quiet angel of peace, who united them into a single family, protected by the wings of the gray old patriarch" (1:243).

49. In her survey of romance readers, Radway found that a substantial majority felt "a happy ending" was the work's "most important ingredient" (*Reading the Romance,* 67). Jensen notes the lengths to which a Harlequin romance will go for a happy ending: "Harlequins conform to many classic tales of romantic love in which the lovers are constantly stymied by insurmountable obstacles—for example, Tristan and Isolde, Orpheus and Eurydice, Romeo and Juliet. Love is denied by death in these stories but Harlequins, like most contemporary formula fiction, always feature a happy ending. Sometimes the great mimetic romances of the past are adopted by Harlequin writers, who rewrite the objectionable tragic endings" (*Love's Sweet Return,* 76).

50. For example, unlike American films, many Russian silent films ended with the heroine's death. Martuszewska argues for the popularity of the unhappy ending: "Although it is generally accepted (and probably rightly so) that the consumer of mass culture very much values a fairytale optimism, we should remember that he also likes melodrama. This explains the enormous popularity of such works as *The Leper* and *Love Story*" ("W stronę powieści popularnej," 213). Walas also notes that Stefcia's death adheres to the folk tradition of renouncing this sorry world for heavenly transcendence (afterword to *The Leper,* 314–15).

51. Engelstein proposes this reading: "In the end, however, this 'new woman' cannot tear herself from the bosom of traditional Russian society, from the fatal power of the impoverished nobleman who ultimately triumphs over the crafty, capitalistic Jew and the allure of modern pleasures. Freedom is too much for her. She does not want to be a man" (*The Keys to Happiness,* 413).

52. Manya's ending is a telling contrast not only to the happy domestication of the popular romance heroine, but also to common plot resolutions in other Western middle-class women's fiction. Garvey observes: "In the middle-

class magazine stories, authorship offers women the possibility of finding satisfaction and fulfillment as productive workers before marriage. The plots, however, foreclose the continuation of such work and suggest that having and spending money are ultimately superior pleasures" (*The Adman in the Parlor*, 144).

53. As Waldemar's grandmother displays these jewels to Stefcia and tells their sad stories, Stefcia's "eyes hurt from looking at them and shivers played on her nerves and shook her body" (Mniszek, *The Leper*, 2:186).

54. Bronfen summarizes this commonly recurring shift from imperfect life to perfect death: "The creation of beauty allows us to escape from the elusiveness of the material world into an illusion of eternity (a denial of loss), even as it imposes on us the realisation that beauty is itself elusive, intangible, receding. Because it is created on the basis of the same elusiveness it tries to obliterate, what art in fact does is mourn beauty, and in so doing mourns itself" (*Over Her Dead Body*, 64). Stefcia's everlasting purity also suggests her connection with the potent image of the Virgin Mary, whose feminized ideal, Bronfen argues, "is a representation of alterity, of Woman as an ethereal being, to be venerated in her intact splendour" (ibid., 68).

55. For another example of a Polish hybrid text that appealed to readers on patriotic and emotional grounds, see Martuszewska's analysis of Rodziewiczówna's prose: "The main basis of understanding between the reader of Rodziewiczówna's novels and the implied author is their shared belief in patriotism and an authentic, all-encompassing love" ("W stronę powieści popularnej," 214–15).

Chapter 5. The Icon and the Ad

1. In *The Magazine in America*, Tebbel and Zuckerman cite the impressive circulation figures for American magazines at the turn of the century, noting the one million subscribers for *The Ladies' Home Journal* (68).

2. Wilson argues that "the change in the reading process derived essentially, although not exclusively, from a 'consumerist' reorientation implemented by a group of men well versed in the verbal, communicative, and organizational skills of a sales economy" ("The Rhetoric of Consumption," 43).

3. On the press's challenge to both the intelligentsia and the autocracy in its contents and mode of reporting, see McReynolds, *The News Under Russia's Old Regime*, 73, 97, 161–62.

4. Davidson approaches this model from the opposite direction, advocating the replacement of the "capitalistic diadic model of producer and consumer" with the three-way relations between writer, reader, and book trader ("Toward a History of Books and Readers," 20).

5. *Vol'f Bookstore News* 8 (January 1905), features these self-promotional credos.

6. Testimony about the influence of *Vol'f Bookstore News* comes from no less an authority than Vladimir Lenin, who valued this publication for its complete and reliable information (*Istoriia knizhnoi torgovli [History of the Book Trade]*, 93).

7. Ibid., 92. Makhonina sees Vol'f's progress as paradigmatic of other publishers who worked their way up through the trade as sales clerks, store owners, and eventually publishers (*Russkaia dorevoliutsionnaia pechat'*, 113).

8. *Istoriia knizhnoi torgovli*, 92.

9. Ibid., 93.

10. *Vol'f Bookstore News* 8 (January 1905), 1.

11. Introduction to "Chronicle of Books and Literature," ibid., 1 (October 1897).

12. See Holmgren, "Gendering the Icon," 321–46.

13. See the bibliographic note by L. Mavrov, "Kniga v 2000 frankov," *Vol'f Bookstore News* 2 (August 1899): 244–45, in which the author ponders the "unprecedented" 2,000-franc price tag for the coffee-table book, *Znatnaia zhenshchina v proshlom stoletii*.

14. L. Serdechnev, "Novyi sopernik knig," *Vol'f Bookstore News* 8 (January 1905): 2.

15. A. Piasetskii, "Graf Dmitrii Nikolaevich Bludov, kak bibliofil," ibid., 1 (September 1898): 248–49.

16. F. Lopukhin, "Sobiranie knig—kak strast'," ibid., 4 (October 1900): 6–10. A complementary article on book stealing insists on the terrible seriousness of this crime. See N. Nadezhdin, "O vorovstve knig," ibid., 7 (1904): 56–59.

17. S. Ko-ov, "Ob ukhode za knigami" (final installment), ibid., 6 (March 1903): 41–44.

18. G. Vitkovskii, "Metod osmyslennago chteniia," ibid., 10 (January 1907): 19–20.

19. N. P-v, "Gigiena chteniia," ibid., 7 (November–December 1904): 109–10.

20. Mariia Gertsfel'd, "Iskusstvo chitat," ibid., 7 (July 1904): 70–72.

21. It is intriguing that the *Vol'f Bookstore News* was able to enlist the services of a prominent young writer, Maxim Gorky, in conveying this message about reading. His sketch, "O bezpokoinoi knige" narrates, in first person, the story of a forty-year-old man accustomed to light reading who is unexpectedly agitated and transformed by a recommended book (ibid., 4 [March 1901]: 69–71).

22. Oktav Iuzan, "Konets knige!," ibid., 3 (November 1899): 26–30. This citation refers to the article's last installment.

23. Ibid., 27–28.

24. Viktor Rusakov, "Literaturnyi zarabotok Pushkina, neskol'ko dannykh o gonorarakh, poluchennykh poètom," ibid., 2 (April–May 1899): 155.

25. Ibid.

26. Ibid., 163, italics in the original.

27. See, for example, a similar treatment of Chekhov's "business": S. F. Librovich, "Literaturnyi zarabotok Chekhova," ibid., 10 (July–August 1907): 157–68.

28. N. Chernov, "Gonorary frantsuzskikh pisatelei," ibid., 2 (June–July 1899): 194.

29. Staryi literator (Old man of letters), "Novyi tip izdatel'stva, opyt proekta pereustroistva v oblasti nashego knizhnago dela," ibid., 3 (October 1899): 9–12.

30. Viktor Rusakov, "Muzei pamiati F. M. Dostoevskago," ibid., 7 (January 1904): 11–15.

31. See Holmgren, "Gendering the Icon."

32. See, for example, the announcement of a new book, *Kak zhivet i rabotaet L. N. Tolstoi,* in the "Chronicle" section, *Vol'f Bookstore News* 1 (May–June 1898).

33. For example, the *News* devoted assorted articles to Turgenev's beloved —"Podruga velikago pisatelia. K konchine Poliny Viardo-Garchia," *Vol'f Bookstore News* 13 (June 1910): 159–61; Tolstoy's son, also a writer—"Po primeru velikago ottsa," ibid., 10 (April 1907): 80–82; and Tolstoi's wife— "Dnevnik grafini S. A. Tolstoi," ibid., 10 (November 1907): 225–28.

34. This bottle, along with candy boxes featuring Gogol's portrait on the top, are displayed in the catalogue, *Torgovaia reklama i upakovka v Rossii XIX–XX vv.*

35. Rubin describes a similar strategy devised by such middlebrow specialists as the Book-of-the-Month Club: Books were advertised as a means of enhancing the reader's social image (*The Making of Middlebrow Culture,* 143–44). Wilson also notes that American magazines sold on the premise of keeping their readers "informed" ("The Rhetoric of Consumption," 63).

36. Viktor Rusakov, "Zhivaia biografiia L. N. Tolstogo," *Vol'f Bookstore News* 6 (October 1903): 101–04.

37. Ibid.

38. M. Vasil'evskii, "Vozmozhno-li izdavat' v Rossii khudozhestvennyi zhurnal?," ibid., 10 (February 1907): 37–42.

39. P. Sivkov, "Soiuz chitatelei," ibid., 4 (August 1901): 123.

40. K. S-kii, "Znachenie, pol'za i nedostatki periodicheskoi pechati," ibid., 2 (August 1899): 209–16.

41. A typical report summarizes the results of a survey of student readers and concludes, "In general, [our] youth are on the right track" (M. N. Vasil'evskii, "Chto chitaet uchashchaiasia molodezh'?," ibid., 13 [June 1910]: 166–68). A similar report published in 1904 comes to much the same conclusion. Cf.

L. L'vov, "Chto chitaet sovremennaia uchashchaiasia molodezh'?," ibid., 7 (July 1904): 65–66.

42. For one such statement, see "Nashi molodye poety. Kratkaia kharakteristika eno," ibid., 3 (July–August 1900): 127–31.

43. Such apparently was Gorky's situation. Viktor Rusakov, "Maksim Gor'kii. Ocherk literaturnoi kar'ery pisatelia," ibid., 3 (April 1900): 91–93.

44. Pavel Rossiev, "Na mogile P. I. Mel'nikova. (Iz zapisnoi knizhki)," ibid., 6 (January 1903): 1–2.

45. A. Nalimov, "Velikosvetskaia poetèssa. Pamiati E. P. Rostopchinoi," ibid., 11 (October 1908): 208–11.

46. Viktor Rusakov, "Kak zhil i rabotal avtor 'Soborian.' Listki iz literaturnykh vospominanii," ibid., 3 (March 1900): 79–84.

47. Rusakov piques the reader's interest with his description of Leskov's passion for "autographs, little pictures, old engravings, pocket watches, ivory statuettes and so forth." The writer adorned his study with these objects and often smuggled them into his work.

48. Viktor Rusakov, "Po povodu pornograficheskago napravleniia v belletristike," *Vol'f Bookstore News* 10 (April 1907): 92–96.

49. Viktor Rusakov, "Bol'nye pisateli," ibid., 10 (May 1907): 109–13.

50. Vsevolod Borisov, "V gost'iakh avtora Sanina," ibid., 11 (April 1908): 73–75.

51. Viktor Rusakov, "Sanin—kriticheskaia zametka," ibid., 11 (April 1908): 75–78.

52. N. Zorech, "'Kliuchi schast'ia'—samaia iunaia kniga tekushchago goda," ibid., 12 (July 1909): 171–73.

53. A reviewer of the *Diary of Mariia Bashkirtseva* (reissued in Russian in 1911) makes much the same argument. Although this diary of a young Russian artist exposed its subject's colossal egotism and encouraged its young readers not to follow suit, the reviewer nevertheless expresses admiration for the *phenomenon* of Bashkirtseva's personality. L. Kostina, "Novyia stranitsy samoi zamechatel'noi knigi," ibid., 14 (November 1911): 276–79.

54. McReynolds notes the extraordinary popularity of *Wrath of Dionysus:* "The modest print run of 1,000 copies, priced at a ruble and a half apiece, made it simply one of dozens of other so-called 'boulevard' novels targeted at Russia's expanding audience for topical, quasi-sensational fare. By the time the book appeared in its tenth edition in 1916, however, the price had almost doubled, the print run tripled, and it had been translated into French, Italian, German, and Latvian" (introduction to *Wrath of Dionysus*, vii).

55. S. Dorotin, "Gospozha Nagrodskaia i eia roman," *Vol'f Bookstore News* 14 (November 1911): 273–75.

56. McReynolds notes that the Russian press generally conveyed culture as the empire's mainstay (*The News Under Russia's Old Regime*, 46).

57. In "Reklama v literature," *Vol'f Bookstore News* 3 (July–August 1900): 132–33, A. Shvarov discusses the suit brought by the American journal *Cosmopolitan* against Tolstoy after the Russian writer withdrew his work from their pages. Apparently Tolstoy called a halt to *Cosmopolitan's* publication of his novel *Resurrection* after that journal had badly mangled its translation and censored its contents. Shvarov believes that *Cosmopolitan* undertook this action "less to win the suit than to advertise its publication in a completely American way."

58. The very notion of a hygiene of books and reading conveyed the impression of necessary care for the body rather than fussing over one's possessions.

59. D. M. Filosofov, "O knige i eia vneshnosti," *Vol'f Bookstore News* 7 (June 1904): 51–56. This citation covers the first part of the article. The conclusion appears in ibid., 7 (July 1904): 67–70.

60. Staryi bibliofil (Old bibliophile), "Novaia stranitsa v istorii vneshnosti knig," ibid., 1 (December 1897): 65–71.

61. Cf. ibid., 1 (February 1898).

62. Ibid., 6 (April 1903).

63. M. Glovskii, "Velikoe serdtse. Po povodu smerti Elizy Orzheshko," ibid., 13 (June 1910): 168–71.

64. Viktor Rusakov, "Uspekh Senkevicha—v Rossii i za granitseiu. (K dvadtsatipiatiletiiu deiatel'nosti pisatelia)," ibid., 4 (November 1900): 17–20; see "Senkevich o Geine," in ibid., 7 (May–June 1904): 59. For more on Sienkiewicz in the Polish press, see chapter 6.

65. For another example of "reporting" Russo-Polish conflicts, see the sketch of the "Russian" writer K. S. Barantsevich (half Polish and half French) in I. P. Mertsalov's "Glavnye predstaviteli sovremennoi russkoi belletristiki," ibid., 1 (May–June 1898): 178–88. The author tersely informs us that Barantsevich's grandfather "took part in the 1831 Polish uprising and was hanged in the presence of his wife and two small children" (ibid., 188).

66. V. V. Chuiko, "Velikii poèt-romantik Mitskevich i ego znachenie," ibid., 2 (February 1899): 93–100.

67. McReynolds identifies the tendency in the Russian mass-circulation press to contrast the beneficent Russian empire with its exploitative and mercenary European counterparts (*The News Under Russia's Old Regime,* 183, 196–97).

68. Brooks posits that the Russian classics were not linked with the autocracy in this period, but it is significant that the "apolitical" classics depicted in the *News* nevertheless function as empire builders ("Russian Nationalism and Russian Literature," 323).

69. Viktor Rusakov, "Uspekh Senkevicha—v Rossii i za granitseiu," *Vol'f Bookstore News* 4 (November 1900): 17.

70. Ibid.

71. For a discussion of relations between market and empire in Western Europe, see Richards, *The Commodity Culture of Victorian England,* 120–34.

Chapter 6. Patronized Saints

1. Kulczycka-Saloni observes that the new merchant-publishers in post-1863 Polish society viewed literature as a "commodity" *(towar)* (*Życie literackie Warszawy,* 75).

2. Słomkowska, *Dziennikarze Warszawscy,* 9, 11.

3. According to Słomkowska, Kraszewski by 1861 ceased appealing to the Polish aristocracy, began popularizing the images of the merchantry, and cited "work as the highest criterion of human value" (ibid., 241).

4. Kulczycka-Saloni observes how the press and other publications crossed these borders (*Życie literackie Warszawy,* 82–83).

5. Słomkowska, *Dziennikarze Warszawscy,* 12.

6. Kmiecik et al., *Prasa polska w latach 1864–1918,* 85.

7. Kmiecik remarks that Warsaw readers' interest in illustrated magazines grew sharply after the 1905 revolution, a fact he attributes to a rising middle class (*Prasa warszawska w latach 1908–1918,* 432).

8. Cf. Kmiecik et al., *Prasa polska w latach 1864–1918,* 85–89.

9. Kmiecik, *Prasa warszawska w latach 1908–1918,* 404.

10. Muszkowski describes Józef Wolff as a quick study, an excellent organizer, and an editor eager to transform a rather stodgy journal into an innovative publication (*Z Dziejów Firmy Gebethner i Wolff,* 23).

11. For information about circulation, see ibid.; see also Kmiecik et al., *Prasa polska w latach 1864–1918,* 85. In an interesting discrepancy, *The Illustrated Weekly* boasted in 1899 that it had a million subscribers (no. 45, 1899, 877–78). Kmiecik provides a more detailed history in *Prasa warszawska w latach 1908–1918,* 381–404.

12. Kmiecik, *Prasa warszawska w latach 1908–1918,* 386–87.

13. *The Illustrated Weekly,* no. 8, 1898, 143.

14. Kmiecik et al., *Prasa polska w latach 1864–1918,* 107, notes that the first color reproduction appeared on the cover of an 1892 issue of *The Illustrated Weekly;* color reproduction did not become widespread in the Kingdom of Poland until 1910.

15. Ibid., 45.

16. "Week by week" announces this special issue policy in no. 40 for the year 1900; that issue focused on Kraków's famous Church of St. Mary.

17. In this famous 1410 battle, a combined Polish and Lithuanian army finally repelled the Teutonic Knights.

18. Kmiecik asserts the *The Illustrated Weekly*'s implicitly anti-Russian and proindependence platform (*Prasa warszawska w latach 1908–1918,* 401).

19. For sample responses, see *The Illustrated Weekly,* no. 33, 1900, 655–56, in which Ignacy Matuszewski summarizes Polish national characteristics as part of a review of a new history of Polish literature; see also the editorial, ibid., no. 16 (1903), 304, which castigates Poles for their egoism and failure at collective action.

20. Bertold Mertury, "Literatura przekładowa za granicą," *The Illustrated Weekly,* no. 37, 1904, 707–08.

21. Ibid., no. 11, 1900, 219; no. 18, 1901, 353.

22. Ibid., no. 20, 1906, 390.

23. It is no accident that Sieroszewski's work is highly praised in *The Illustrated Weekly* and pronounced more sensitive and comprehensive than the empire-mongering "Eastern" tales of Rudyard Kipling.

24. "Rosya i Japonia," *The Illustrated Weekly,* no. 8, 1904, 145.

25. Władysław Nawrocki, "Alexander Puszkin," ibid., no. 24, 1899, 467–68.

26. Artur Górski, "Mickiewicz żywy i umarły," ibid., no. 8, 1906, 152–54.

27. Ibid., no. 32, 1905, 595–96; no. 41, 1905, 762–63; no. 14, 1905, 258.

28. On the *wieszcz*'s national role, see Holmgren, "Witold Gombrowicz Within the *Wieszcz* Tradition."

29. "Odezwa 'Komitetu jubileuszowego Henryka Sienkiewicza,'" *The Illustrated Weekly,* no. 52, 1899, 1031.

30. Ignacy Matuszewski, "Mickiewicz," ibid., no. 9, 1902, 169–72.

31. Ibid., no. 16, 1899, 739; no. 51, 1901, 999.

32. Bakhtin, *Problems of Dostoevsky's Poetics,* 196–99. Predictably, *The Illustrated Weekly* (no. 39, 1898, 758) also proclaimed its "equality" with European publications, advertising that its volume matched that of the largest journals in Europe. This defensive posture may well be characteristic of other "smaller" nations that sense their marginal world status.

33. The "Chronicle" regularly featured such rubrics as "Translations from the Polish" ("Przekłady z polskiego") and "World renown" ("Sława u obcych"). "Week by week" enthusiastically alerted readers to an artist's auspicious debut or well-deserved jubilee. In his analysis of American mass-market magazines in the same period, Wilson identifies similar narrative strategies: a style approximating a sales "pitch"; the cultivation of a personable, persuasive persona; the presumption of exclusivity by which an editor "inscribed a circle around himself and invited the reader in ("The Rhetoric of Consumption," 49–50).

34. Krzywoszewski, journalist and editor of *Świat,* indicates in his memoir, *Długie życie (A Long Life)* the importance of such gatherings for the develop-

ment of Polish culture (38, 42). Kulczycka-Saloni remarks on the influence of a number of different social circles in the absence of institutionalized forums (*Życie literackie Warszawy,* 90–107).

35. In a typical notation, the "Chronicle" records, along with general news of the world, that two articles on the writer Maria Konopnicka had recently appeared in a Viennese journal and a Parisian bimonthly (1903). *The Illustrated Weekly* pounced on any such external attention paid to Polish "greats."

36. Konstancya Skirmuntt, "Jeszcze słówko o rodowodzie Mickiewicza," *The Illustrated Weekly,* no. 3, 1903, 53.

37. For his article "Mickiewicz w Lozanne," Hen. Ced. visits the poet's Swiss residence and learns about his domestic life from his former neighbors (ibid., no. 36, 1900, 703). Gustaw Doliński's piece on the hunting Mickiewicz, "Mickiewicz jako myśliwy," is cleverly illustrated by Konstanty Górski (ibid., no. 10, 1899, 190–92). "Genealogia Mickiewicza" appears complete with a family tree (ibid., no. 33, 1902, 649–53). Górski's article deduces Mickiewicz's hunting knowledge from passages in his pastoral epic, *Pan Tadeusz.*

38. Leopold Meyet, "Z kart żałobnych rodziny Słowackich," ibid., no. 13, 1899, 252–53.

39. The author defends Poles from a voyeuristic interest in their artists' private lives: "Our society is distinguished by its sincere and positive homage to its geniuses. We don't yet indulge in that sort of 'cultural combing' through the ashes in order to spread scandal and satisfy the masses." *The Illustrated Weekly,* no. 42, 1899, 819–20.

40. Rajmund Stanisław Kamiński, "Z nieznanych listów poety," ibid., no. 24, 1898, 475.

41. Hieronim Łopaciński, "'Pieśń o grzybach' wspomniana w Panu Tadeuszu," ibid., no. 27, 1899, 523–24; Adam Boruta, "Paderewski u siebie," ibid., 4, 1899, 65.

42. Napoleon Rouba, "Śladami wieszcza," ibid., no. 6, 1898, 107; see also ibid., no. 7 (1898), 136.

43. It is intriguing that one such article series on "Polish landmarks in Paris" ("Pamiątki polskie w Paryżu") was written by Władysław Mickiewicz, son of the famous Adam.

44. "Pomnik Aleksandra Gierymskiego w Rzymie," *The Illustrated Weekly,* no. 31, 1903, 616. This sort of commemoration represents an interesting variation on the national tradition of cenotaphs and tombs of Unknown Soldiers noted by Anderson in *Imagined Communities,* 10. In this case, a known body is required to assert national glory in a foreign land.

45. In keeping with a general interest in historic restoration, *The Illustrated Weekly* devoted many articles and illustrations to such specific projects as the restoration of Wawel Castle in Kraków and various churches and cathedrals in

Warsaw. See also the proprietary series on Polish flora and fauna—"Nasze drzewa" by Edmund Jańkowski and "Nasze zwierzęta i ptaki w podaniach" by Józef Ryszkiewicz.

46. Ignacy Matuszewski, "Psychologia pomników," ibid., no. 12, 1898, 1022.

47. Stanisław Libicki, "Uroczystości Krakówskie," ibid., no. 27, 1898, 519–20.

48. This repeated implication of individual engagement with and contribution to monument-building distinguishes fin-de-siècle Polish practice from general concepts of the monument as an untouchable, superhuman landmark. Yampolsky observes that a monument "keeps the worshipper at a distance," a distance "inscribed into its function, and therefore approaching the monument is always a sort of transgression of a sacral zone . . . when we look upon workers installing or dismantling a monument, their physical contact with the object subconsciously shocks us" ("In the Shadow of Monuments," 94).

49. These items, the product of the firm of Wacław Sułkowski, are advertised as the "latest novelty" (supplement to *The Illustrated Weekly*, no. 50, 1903, 1).

50. For example, the "Chronicle" reprinted a tantalizing plug for Kazimierz Tetmajer's *Na skalnym Podhalu*, which appeared in the *Przegląd zakopiański (Zakopane Review)* and concluded with a clever invitation: "This can't be described. It has to be read" (*The Illustrated Weekly*, no. 17, 1903, 338).

51. The back page of *The Illustrated Weekly* was reserved for advertisements; by the early 1900s illustrated and quite varied ads gave readers a foretaste of the journal's advertising supplement.

52. See *The Illustrated Weekly*, no. 28, 1902, and no. 51, 1902, for the Sienkiewicz-Stachiewicz collaboration. Garvey notes a similar practice in the American mass-circulation press, whereby "respected artwork and respected artists" were enlisted to uplift visual advertisement (*The Adman in the Parlor*, 102–05).

53. *The Illustrated Weekly*, no. 39, 1898, 757.

54. Tebbel and Zuckerman describe the premiums offered by American magazines in the late nineteenth century: "Premiums became so widespread and so popular that the *Literary World* half seriously advised its readers that young couples could furnish their first house entirely with premiums if they only subscribed to enough magazines" (*The Magazine in America*, 60).

55. See Williams, *Dream Worlds*, 65–66; Debord, *The Society of the Spectacle*, 115. Even though commemorative souvenirs are designed to "annihilate history" (Richards, *The Commodity Culture of Victorian England*, 60–61), the commemorative packaging of Polish history also fulfilled a cathartic role, purveying in idealized form what could not be disseminated in other, noncommercial ways.

56. See Debord's characteristically philosophical description of this attitude:

"The spectator's alienation from and submission to the contemplated object (which is the outcome of his unthinking activity) works like this: the more he contemplates, the less he lives; the more readily he recognizes his own needs in the images of need proposed by the dominant system, the less he understands his own existence and his own desires" (*The Society of the Spectacle*, 23).

57. *The Illustrated Weekly*, no. 52, 1898; ibid., no. 5, 1899, 99.

58. See, for example, the note about Kraków's youth raising money to bring Słowacki's remains back to Poland (ibid., no. 41, 1899).

59. For all his carping about a parochial Polish nationalism, the twentieth-century writer Witold Gombrowicz proved to be most appreciative of Sienkiewicz as a "first-rate second-rate writer" (Gombrowicz, "Sienkiewicz").

60. Sienkiewicz presided over the Mickiewicz jubilee committee in Warsaw and served as the key speaker at the more private Słowacki celebration in Miłosławie (*The Illustrated Weekly*, no. 40, 1899, 780).

61. Ignacy Matuszewski, "Sława u obcych" ("World Renown"), ibid., no. 10, 1900, 182.

62. Ferdynand Hoesick, "U Henryka Sienkiewicza," ibid., no. 10, 1900, 185–92. Hoesick's biographies of such figures as Słowacki were criticized in *The Illustrated Weekly* for their overabundance of details at the expense of any sort of synthesizing vision.

63. Ibid., 188; for photos of this amazing room, see 190–92; see also figure 13. Hoesick's account imitates a general trend of describing artists' homes, and while Sienkiewicz's study resembles that of other "academic artists," it also flaunts a conservative defiance of the new minimalist decors of "Young Poland." I am grateful to Bożena Shallcross for situating this decorative phenomenon historically.

64. Thanks to Madeline G. Levine for recognizing the royal provenance of this act—particularly in the case of the writer Mikołaj Rej.

65. *The Illustrated Weekly*, no. 29, 1900, 560.

66. Ibid., no. 52, 1900, 1021.

67. Ibid., 1020.

68. See the coverage of Sienkiewicz's receipt of the Nobel Prize, for which he expressed thanks for "this crowning of Polish work and creative power" (*The Illustrated Weekly*, no. 18, 1906, 339–40).

69. Ibid., no. 25, 1902, 497.

70. Ibid., no. 38, 1903, 744.

71. Ibid., no. 24, 1903, 475. Even the reporting on this fund took on a moral tone. *The Illustrated Weekly* noted that most of the contributions consisted of "widows' mites" from the provinces and that this fact had a moral significance in and of itself (ibid., no. 45, 1903, 896).

72. These are Konopnicka's words, cited in ibid., no. 28, July 14, 1906.

73. Ibid., no. 34, 1903, 663.

Chapter 7. As the Market Turns

1. Verbitskaia, *Kliuchi schast'ia* 6 VOLS . . . . issued by Kushnerev in Moscow, 1910, pp. 173–75.

2. It is significant that Steinbach, the ultimate patron, supports both radical politics and modernist art with equal fervor and generosity.

3. In Polish publishing history, the development of an underground independent press during the 1970s and 1980s merits special and separate study. It was during this period that a number of publishers mastered models of the Western book trade, managed to smuggle in some advanced print technology for production, and expanded that production in innovative and sometimes nonideological directions. See Lopiński, *Konspira: Solidarity Underground.*

4. The Polden' v Moskve (Noon in Moscow) publishing house is currently issuing a 200-volume collection of world literature, each issue bound in leather, brocade, and gold, and selling for $200–300 (Henry, "200 Classics for the Rich Bibliophile").

5. One observer characterizes this change somewhat differently, arguing that the writer has become a truly "private person who works for a living" as opposed to "a national tutor who teaches society the rules of political and moral decorum" (Buida, "Russia Is Reading Again").

6. A report entitled "The Polish Giant Stirs," *Publishers Weekly,* September 5, 1994, quotes Andrzej Rosner, the Polish deputy for literature, books, and libraries, on this sea change: "'Commercialization is now slowing and the huge wave of imported rubbish is receding.'" Babakian, "Fair Flaunts Publishers' Progress," notes that "Russia's publishing industry is starting to rebound from the backslide it experienced in the early 1990s," featuring "fewer bodice-ripping covers and more of an emphasis on fiction, scholarly and reference materials." Ivanov observes that publishing has rebounded as Russia's "second largest" industry (after vodka production), even though it has not regained Soviet-era circulations ("What Is Russia Reading," 16, 21).

7. Mitlyng admits the market predominance of "thrillers and romances" but points out that "small publishers are emerging to cater to niche markets and tiny, but devoted audiences," including intellectuals ("Russian Readers Move Past Pulp Fiction"). *Publishers' Weekly* notes the current Polish interest in "popular science, self-help, and foreign-language instruction" and discusses "the big official success story" of Polish Scientific Publishing, the leading publisher of scientific works run by Grzegorz Boguta, a former underground publisher.

8. Mitlyng observes that the "serious" book has become a luxury item for once avid and now impoverished members of the intelligentsia. There now exist, however, examples of such successful "niche" publishers as the Russian Ad Marginum (publishers of philosophy, history, and literature) and the

Sabachnikov Press, which sold out its 3,000 print run of Blaise Pascal's philosophical meditations within several months (Ivanov, "What Is Russia Reading," 21).

9. According to Ivanov, even now Russian readers, quantitatively at least, prefer domestic detective fiction to Western imports. He lists five Russian detective writers as the best-selling authors of 1996 (ibid., 17–18).

bibliography

Adburgham, Alison. *Shopping in Style: London from the Restoration to Edwardian Elegance.* London: Thames and Hudson, 1979.

Anderson, Benedict. *Imagined Communities: Reflections on the Origin and Spread of Nationalism.* Rev. ed. London: Verso, 1991.

Armstrong, Nancy. *Desire and Domestic Fiction: A Political History of the Novel.* New York: Oxford University Press, 1987.

Babakian, Genine. "Fair Flaunts Publishers' Progress." *Moscow Times,* September 5, 1996.

Bailes, Kendall E. "Reflections of Russian Professions." In *Russia's Missing Middle Class: The Professions in Russian History,* ed. Harley D. Balzer, 39–54. Armonk, N.Y.: M. E. Sharpe, 1996.

Bakhtin, Mikhail. *Problems of Dostoevsky's Poetics.* Ed. and trans. Caryl Emerson, with an introduction by Wayne C. Booth. Minneapolis: University of Minnesota Press, 1984.

Balzer, Harley. "The Problem of Professions in Imperial Russia." In *Between Tsar and People,* ed. Clowes et al., 183–98.

———. Introduction to *Russia's Missing Middle Class: The Professions in Russian History.* Ed. Harley D. Balzer. Armonk, N.Y.: M. E. Sharpe, 1996.

Belov, S. V., and A. P. Tolstiakov. *Russkie izdateli kontsa XIX–nachala XX veka.* Leningrad: Nauka, 1976.

Blobaum, Robert E. *Rewolucja: Russian Poland, 1904–1907.* Ithaca: Cornell University Press, 1995.

Boborykin, Piotr. "Letters about Moscow" ("Pis'ma o Moskve"), in Chuprinin, introduction to *Kitai-gorod.*

Bourdieu, Pierre. *Distinction: A Social Critique of the Judgement of Taste.* Trans. Richard Nice. Cambridge: Harvard University Press, 1996.

Bowlby, Rachel. *Just Looking: Consumer Culture in Dreiser, Gissing and Zola.* New York, London: Methuen, 1985.

Bowlt, John E. "The Moscow Art Market." In *Between Tsar and People,* ed. Clowes et al., 108–30.

Brilliant, Richard. *Portraiture.* Cambridge: Harvard University Press, 1991.

Bronfen, Elisabeth. *Over Her Dead Body: Death, Femininity and the Aesthetic.* New York: Routledge, 1992.

Brooks, Jeffrey. "Russian Nationalism and Russian Literature: The Canonization of the Classics." In *Nation and Ideology: Essays in Honor of Wayne S. Vucinich,* ed. Ivo Banac, John G. Ackerman, and Roman Szporluk, 315–34. New York: Columbia University Press, 1981.

————. *When Russia Learned to Read: Literacy and Popular Literature, 1861–1917.* Princeton: Princeton University Press, 1985.

Brower, Daniel R. *The Russian City between Tradition and Modernity, 1850–1900.* Berkeley and Los Angeles: University of California Press, 1990.

————. "The Penny Press and Its Readers." In *Cultures in Flux: Lower-Class Values, Practices, and Resistance in Late Imperial Russia,* ed. Stephen P. Frank and Mark D. Steinberg, 147–67. Princeton: Princeton University Press, 1994.

Bruford, W. H. *Chekhov and His Russia: A Sociological Study.* New York: Oxford University Press, 1947.

Brzozowski, Stanisław. "Bolesław Prus." In *Eseje i studia o literaturze,* vol. 1. Wrocław, Warsaw: Biblioteka Narodowa, 1990.

Buida, Iurii. "Russia Is Reading Again, Without Tutors." *Moscow Times,* November 6, 1996.

Chartier, Roger. *The Cultural Uses of Print in Early Modern France.* Trans. Lydia G. Cochrane. Princeton: Princeton University Press, 1987.

Chekhov, Anton. *Letters of Anton Chekhov.* Trans. Michael Henry Heim, with Simon Karlinsky. Ed. and intro. Simon Karlinsky. New York: Harper and Row, 1973.

————. *The Oxford Chekhov.* Vols. 7 and 9. Trans. and ed. Ronald Hingley. Oxford: Oxford University Press, 1975, 1978.

————. *Plays.* Trans. and intro. Elisaveta Fen. Harmondsworth: Penguin, 1978.

————. *Polnoe sobranie sochinenii i pisem v tridtsati tomakh.* Moscow: Nauka, 1974–1987.

Chruściński, Kazimierz. "Powiastka 'dla ludu': Z badań nad 'literaturą trzecią' 2. połowy XIX w." In *Problemy Literatury Polskiej Okresu Pozytywizmu 1,* ed. Jańkowski and Kulczycka-Saloni, 217–31. Warsaw: PAN-IBL, 1980.

Chudakov, Aleksandr. *Poetika Chekhova.* Moscow: Nauka, 1971.

Chuprinin, Sergei. Introduction to Piotr Boborykin, *Kitai-gorod. Proezdom.* Moscow: Moskovskii rabochii, 1985.

Clowes, Edith. "Social Discourse in the Moscow Art Theater." In *Between Tsar and People*, ed. Clowes et al., 271–87.

Clowes, Edith, Samuel D. Kassow, and James L. West, eds. *Between Tsar and People: Educated Society and the Quest for Public Identity in Late Imperial Russia.* Princeton: Princeton University Press, 1991.

Czyszkowa-Peschler, Małgorzata. "She Is—A Nobody Without a Name: The Professional Situation of Polish Women-of-Letters in the Second Half of the Nineteenth Century." In *Women in Polish Society*, ed. Rudolf Jaworski and Bianka Pietrow-Ennker, 113–42. New York: Columbia University Press, 1992.

Dahl's History of the Book, 3rd ed. Bill Katz. Methuen, N.J.: Scarecrow Press, 1995.

Davidson, Cathy N. "Toward a History of Books and Readers." In *Reading in America*, ed. Davidson.

Davidson, Cathy N., ed. *Reading in America: Literature and Social History.* Baltimore: Johns Hopkins University Press, 1989.

Davies, Norman. *God's Playground: A History of Poland in Two Volumes.* New York: Columbia University Press, 1982.

Debord, Guy. *The Society of the Spectacle.* 3rd ed. New York: Zone Books, 1994.

Debreczeny, Paul. *Social Functions of Literature: Alexander Pushkin and Russian Culture.* Stanford: Stanford University Press, 1997.

Denning, Michael. *Mechanic Accents: Dime Novels and Working-Class Culture in America.* London: Verso, 1987.

Dobrolyubov, N. A. "What Is Oblomovitis?" in *Belinsky, Chernyshevsky and Dobrolyubov: Selected Criticism.* Ed. and intro. Ralph E. Matlaw, 133–75. Bloomington: Indiana University Press, 1976.

———. "Temnoe tsarstvo." In *Sobranie sochinenii v trekh tomakh*, 2:305–448. Moscow: Khudozhest vennaia literatura, 1987.

———. "Luch sveta v temnon tsarstve." In *Sobranie sochinenii v trekh tomakh*, 3:268–348.

Dostoevsky, Fyodor. *The Idiot.* Trans. and intro. David Magarshack. Harmondsworth: Penguin Books, Ltd., 1979.

Douglas, Ann. *The Feminization of American Culture.* New York: Avon Books, 1977.

Dunham, Vera. *In Stalin's Time: Middleclass Values in Soviet Fiction.* Durham, N.C.: Duke University Press, 1990.

Dunin, Janusz. *Papierowy bandyta. Książka kramarska i brukowa w Polsce.* Łódź, 1974.

Ehre, Milton. *Oblomov and His Creator: The Life and Art of Ivan Goncharov.* Princeton: Princeton University Press, 1973.

Eisenstein, Elizabeth L. *The Printing Press as an Agent of Change: Communications and Cultural Transformations in Early Modern Europe.* Cambridge: Cambridge University Press, 1979.

Engelstein, Laura. *The Keys to Happiness: Sex and the Search for Modernity in Fin de Siècle Russia.* Ithaca, N.Y.: Cornell University Press, 1992.

Fanger, Donald. "The Peasant in Literature." In *The Peasant in Nineteenth Century Russia,* ed. Wayne Vucinich, 231–62. Stanford: Stanford University Press, 1968.

Fitzlyon, Kyril. "Russian Society in the Reign of Nicholas II." In *Before the Revolution: A View of Russia under the Last Tsar,* ed. Kyril Fitzlyon and Tatiana Browning, 15–70. Woodstock, N.Y.: Overlook Press, 1977.

Freeze, Gregory L. "The *Soslovie* (Estate) Paradigm and Russian Social History." *American Historical Review* 91 (1986): 11–36.

Frierson, Cathy. *Peasant Icons: Representations of Rural People in Late Nineteenth-Century Russia.* Oxford: Oxford University Press, 1993.

Garvey, Ellen Gruber. *The Adman in the Parlor: Magazines and the Gendering of Consumer Culture, 1880s to 1910s.* New York: Oxford University Press, 1996.

Gheith, Jehanne. "The Superfluous Man and the Necessary Woman: A 'Revision.'" *Russian Review* 55 (April 1996): 226–44.

Gleason, Abbott. "The Terms of Russian Social History." In *Between Tsar and People,* ed. Clowes et al., 15–27.

Godlewski, Stefan. "Śladami Wokulskiego." In *Śladami Wokulskiego: Przewodnik literacki po warszawskich realiach "Lalki,"* ed. Godlewski et al.

Godlewski, Stefan, Ludwik B. Grzeniewski, and Henryk Markiewicz, eds. *Śladami Wokulskiego: Przewodnik literacki po warszawskich realiach "Lalki."* Warsaw: Czytelnik, 1957.

Goldstein, Darra. "Domestic Porkbarreling in Nineteenth-Century Russia, or Who Holds the Keys to the Larder?" In *Russia.Women.Culture,* ed. Goscilo and Holmgren, 125–51.

Gombrowicz, Witold. "Sienkiewicz." In *Diary. Volume One,* trans. Lillian Vallee, 223–30. Evanston, Ill.: Northwestern University Press, 1988.

Goncharov, Ivan. *Oblomov.* Trans. Natalie Duddington. New York: E. P. Dutton, 1953.

———. *Sobranie sochinenii.* Vol. 4. Moscow: Khudozhestvennaia literatura, 1979.

Gorky, Maxim. *Collected Works in Ten Volumes.* Trans. Margaret Wettlin. Moscow: Progress Publishers, 1978.

———. *Collected Works in Ten Volumes.* Trans. Helen Altschuler. Moscow: Progress Publishers.

———. *Foma Gordeev.* In *Collected Works in Ten Volumes,* trans. Margaret Wettlin, vol 2.

———. *Fragments from My Diary.* Trans. Moura Budberg. London: Penguin Press, 1972.

———. *My Apprenticeship.* Trans. and intro. Ronald Wilks. Harmondsworth: Penguin, 1974.

———. *My Universities.* In *Polnoe sobranie sochinenii.* Vol. 16. Moscow: Nauka, 1973.

———. *Polnoe sobranie sochinenii. Khudozhestvennye proizvedeniia v dvadtsati piati tomakh.* Moscow: Nauka, 1968–1982.

Goscilo, Helena, and Beth Holmgren. Introduction to *Keys to Happiness.* Bloomington: Indiana University Press, 1999.

Goscilo, Helena, and Beth Holmgren, eds. *Russia. Women. Culture.* Bloomington: Indiana University Press, 1996.

Gray, Camilla. *The Russian Experiment in Art, 1863–1922.* Rev. ed. London: Thames and Hudson, 1962.

Griakalova, N. Iu. Foreword to Aleksandr Amfiteatrov, *Mertvye bogi.* Moscow: Sovremennik, 1991.

Grzeniewski, Ludwik Bohdan. "Posłowie." In *Śladami Wokulskiego: Przewodnik literacki po warszawskich realiach "Lalki,"* ed. Godlewski et al., 181–205.

———. *Warszawa w "Lalce" Prusa.* Warsaw, 1965.

———. "Warszawskie realia *Lalki.*" In *Śladami Wokulskiego,* 89–179. Warsaw: Czytelnik, 1957.

Hare, Richard. *Maxim Gorky: Romantic Realist and Conservative Revolutionary.* London: Oxford University Press, 1962.

Heldt, Barbara. *Terrible Perfection: Women and Russian Literature.* Bloomington: Indiana University Press, 1987.

Henry, Patrick. "200 Classics for the Rich Bibliophile." *Moscow Times,* July 26, 1996.

Hingley, Ronald. Introduction to *The Oxford Chekhov,* trans. and ed. Ronald Hingley, vol. 7. Oxford: Oxford University Press, 1975.

Hoisington, Thomas H. "Melnikov-Pechersky: Romancer of Provincial and Old Believer Life." *Slavic Review* 33 (December 1974): 679–94.

Holmgren, Beth. "Witold Gombrowicz Within the *Wieszcz* Tradition." *Slavic and East European Journal* 33 (1989): 556–70.

———. "Why Russian Girls Loved Charskaia." *Russian Review* 54 (January 1995): 91–106.

———. "Gendering the Icon: Marketing Women Writers in Fin-de-siècle Russia." In *Russia.Women.Culture.*, ed. Goscilo and Holmgren, 321–46.

———. "Questions of Heroism in *Oblomov.*" In *Goncharov's "Oblomov": A Critical Companion,* ed. Galya Diment, 77–89. Evanston, Ill.: Northwestern University Press, 1998.

Holtzman, Filia. *The Young Maxim Gorky 1868–1902.* New York: Columbia University Press, 1948.

Hoover, Marjorie L. *Alexander Ostrovsky.* Boston: Twayne Publishers, 1981.

Huyssen, Andreas. *After the Great Divide: Modernism, Mass Culture, Postmodernism.* Bloomington: Indiana University Press, 1986.

Istoriia knizhnoi torgovli. 2d ed. Ed. A. A. Govorov, M. A. Vinogradov, S. B. Liublinskii, and E. A. Silant'ev. Moscow: Kniga, 1982.

Ivanov, Mikhail. "What Is Russia Reading?" *Russian Life,* July 1997.

Izvestiia knizhnykh magazinov tovarishchestva M. O. Vol'f (Vol'f Bookstore News).

Jackson, Robert Louis. "Chekhov's 'A Woman's Kingdom': A Drama of Character and Fate." In *Critical Essays on Anton Chekhov,* ed. Thomas A. Eekman, 91–102. Boston: G. K. Hall, 1989.

Jańkowski, Edmund, and Janina Kulczycka-Saloni, eds. *Problemy Literatury Polskiej Okresu Pozytywizmu 1.* Warsaw: PAN-IBL, 1980.

Jensen, Margaret Ann. *Love's Sweet Return: The Harlequin Story.* Bowling Green, Ohio: Bowling Green State University Popular Press, 1984.

Junosza-Szaniawski, Klemens. *Pająki (The Spiders,* 1894).

———. *Pająki wiejskie (Village Spiders,* 1895).

———. *W pajęczej sieci (In the Spider's Web,* 1896).

Kalita, Tomasz. *Mniszkówna.* London and Warsaw: Unicorn Publishing Studio, 1993.

Kassow, Samuel D., and James L. West, Edith W. Clowes. "Introduction: The Problem of the Middle in Late Imperial Russia." In *Between Tsar and People,* ed. Clowes et al., 3–14.

Kean, B. *All the Empty Palaces: The Merchant Patrons of Modern Art in Prerevolutionary Russia.* London: Barrie and Jenkins, 1983.

Kenez, Peter. *The Birth of the Propaganda State: Soviet Methods of Mass Mobilization, 1917–1929.* Cambridge: Cambridge University Press, 1985.

Kmiecik, Zenon. *Prasa warszawska w latach 1908–1918.* Warsaw: Państwowe Wydawnictwo Naukowe, 1981.

Kmiecik, Zenon, Jerzy Myśliński, et al. *Prasa polska w latach 1864–1918.* Warsaw: PAN-IBL, 1976.

Kobiakova, Aleksandra. "An Autobiography." In *Russia Through Women's Eyes: Autobiographies from Tsarist Russia,* ed. Toby W. Clyman and Judith Vowles, 60–74. New Haven: Yale University Press, 1996.

Koc, Barbara. *O "Ziemi Obiecanej" Reymonta.* Wrocław, Warsaw, Kraków: PAN, 1990.

Kolbuszewski, Jacek. *Od Pigalle po kresy: Krajobrazy literatury popularnej.* Wrocław: Wydawnictwo Uniwersytetu Wrocławskiego, 1994.

———. "Powieść popularna: na prełomie XIX i XX wieku," *Literatura i kultura popularna* 1 (1991): 97–110.

Kołodziejczyk, Ryszard. *Miasto, mieszczaństwo, burżuazja w Polsce w XIX w.* Warsaw: Państwowe Wydawnictwo Naukowe, 1979.

Kott, Jan. "Kariera kupca." In *"Lalka" Bolesława Prusa,* ed. Markiewicz, 272–80.

Krzywoszewski, Stefan. *Długie zycie: Wspomnienia (A Long Life . . .).* Warsaw: "Biblioteka Polska," 1947.

Kulczycka-Saloni, Janina. *Bolesław Prus.* Rev. and enl. ed. Warsaw: Wiedza Powszechna, 1967.

———. "Czytając Prusa." *Prace polonistyczne* 41 (1985): 297–309.

———. *Życie literackie Warszawy w latach 1864–1892.* Warsaw: Państwowy Instytut Wydawniczy, 1970.

Larsen, Susan. "Girl Talk: Lidiia Charskaia and Her Readers." Unpublished manuscript, University of California, San Diego.

Leblanc, Ronald. "Dinner with Chichikov: The Fictional Meal as Narrative Device in Gogol's *Dead Souls.*" *Modern Language Studies* 18 (fall 1988): 68–80.

Lednicki, Wacław. *Henryk Sienkiewicz: A Retrospective Synthesis.* The Hague: Mouton, 1960.

Levitt, Marcus C. *Russian Literary Politics and the Pushkin Celebration of 1880.* Ithaca, N.Y.: Cornell University Press, 1989.

Literatura polska. Przewodnik encyklopedyczny. Warsaw: Państwowe Wydawnictwo Naukowe, 1984.

Loe, Mary Louise. "Redefining the Intellectual's Role: Maksim Gorky and the *Sreda* Circle." In *Between Tsar and People,* ed. Clowes et al., 288–307.

Lopiński, Maciej. *Konspira: Solidarity Underground.* Trans. Jane Cave, with an afterword by Lawrence Weschler. Berkeley and Los Angeles: University of California Press, 1990.

McReynolds, Louise. "Anastasiia Verbitskaia and Elinor Glyn: A Novel Perspective on Russia and the West." Unpublished manuscript, University of Hawaii.

———. "'The Incomparable' Anastasiia Vial'tseva and the Cult of Personality." In *Russia. Women. Culture.*, ed. Goscilo and Holmgren, 273–94.

———. Introduction to Evdokia Nagrodskaia, *The Wrath of Dionysus*, trans. and ed. Louise McReynolds. Bloomington: Indiana University Press, 1997.

———. *The News Under Russia's Old Regime: The Development of a Mass-Circulation Press.* Princeton: Princeton University Press, 1991.

McVeagh, John. *Tradefull Merchants: The Portrayal of the Capitalist in Literature.* London and Boston: Routledge and Kegan Paul, 1981.

Maegd-Soep, Carolina de. *Chekhov and Women: Women in the Life and Work of Chekhov.* Columbus, Ohio: Slavica Publishers, Inc., 1987.

Majdalany, Marina. "Natasha Ivanovna, the Lonely Bourgeoise." *Modern Drama* 26 (September 1983): 305–09.

Makhonina, S. Ia. *Russkaia dorevoliutsionnaia pechat' (1905–1914).* Moscow: Izd. Moskovskogo universiteta, 1991.

Maleczyńska, Kazimiera. *Książki i biblioteki w Polsce okresu zaborów.* Wrocław: Ossolineum, 1987.

Marker, Gary. *Publishing, Printing, and the Origins of Intellectual Life in Russia, 1700–1800.* Princeton: Princeton University Press, 1985.

Markiewicz, Henryk. Introduction to *"Lalka" Bolesława Prusa,* ed. Markiewicz. Warsaw: Czytelnik, 1967.

———. *Literatura pozytywizmu.* Warsaw: IBL-PAN, 1986.

Markiewicz, Henryk, ed. *"Lalka" Bolesława Prusa.* Warsaw: Czytelnik, 1967.

Martuszewska, Anna. "W stronę powieści popularnej: Pisarstwo Marii Rodziewiczówny w latach 1887–1904." In *Problemy Literatury Polskiej Okresu Pozytywizmu 1,* ed. Jańkowski and Kulczycka-Saloni, 201–15.

Mathewson, Rufus W., Jr. *The Positive Hero in Russian Literature.* Stanford: Stanford University Press, 1975.

Mazanek, Anna. *Literackie drogi wielkiej emigracji do kraju przez wielkopolską prasę (1832–1848).* Wrocław, Warsaw, Kraków, Gdańsk, Łódź: PAN, 1983.

Miller, Michael Barry. *The Bon Marché: Bourgeois Culture and the Department Store, 1869–1920.* Princeton: Princeton University Press, 1981.

Miłosz, Czesław. *The History of Polish Literature.* Berkeley: University of California Press, 1982.

Mirsky, D. S. *A History of Russian Literature from Its Beginnings to 1900.* Ed. Francis J. Whitfield. New York: Vintage Books, 1958.

Mitlyng, Victoria. "Russian Readers Move Past Pulp Fiction." *Moscow Times,* March 4, 1997.

Mniszek, Helena. *Trędowata (The Leper).* 2 Vols. With an afterword by Teresa Walas. Kraków: Wydawnictwo Literackie, 1972.

Modleski, Tania. *Loving with a Vengeance: Mass-Produced Fantasies for Women.* Hamden, Conn.: Archon Books, 1982

Monas, Sidney. "The Twilit Middle Class of Nineteenth-Century Russia." In *Between Tsar and People,* ed. Clowes et al., 28–37.

Morson, Gary Saul. "Prosaic Chekhov, Metadrama, the Intelligentsia and *Uncle Vanya.*" *Triquarterly* 80 (winter 1990–91): 118–59.

Morson, Gary Saul, and Caryl Emerson. *Mikhail Bakhtin: Creation of a Prosaics.* Stanford: Stanford University Press, 1990.

Muszkowski, Jan. *Z Dziejów Firmy Gebethner i Wolff, 1857–1937.* Warsaw, Kraków, Łódź, Poznań, Wilno, Zakopane: Gebethner and Wolff, 1938.

Nagrodskaia, Evdokia. *The Wrath of Dionysus.* Trans. and ed. Louise McReynolds. Bloomington: Indiana University Press, 1997.

Norich, Anita. *The Homeless Imagination in the Fiction of Israel Joshua Singer.* Bloomington: Indiana University Press, 1991.

Norman, John O. "Pavel Tretiakov and Merchant Art Patronage, 1850–1900." In *Between Tsar and People,* ed. Clowes et al., 93–107.

Opalski, Magdalena. "The Concept of Jewish Assimilation in Polish Literature of the Positivist Period." *Polish Review* 32 (1987): 371–83.

Opalski, Magdalena, and Israel Bartal. *Poles and Jews: A Failed Brotherhood.* Hanover, N.H.: Brandeis University Press, 1992.

Ostrovskii, A. N. *Polnoe sobranie sochinenii.* Vols. 1, 2, 5, 10. Moscow: Khudozhestvennaia literatura, 1950–1953.

Owen, Thomas C. "Impediments to a Bourgeois Consciousness in Russia, 1880–1905: The Estate Structure, Ethnic Diversity, and Economic Regionalism." In *Between Tsar and People,* ed. Clowes et al., 75–89.

Perlman, Louis. *Russian Literature and the Business Man.* New York: Columbia University Press, 1937.

Pipes, Richard. *Russia Under the Old Regime.* New York: Charles Scribner's Sons, 1974.

"The Polish Giant Stirs." *Publishers Weekly,* September 5, 1994.

Prus, Bolesław. *The Doll.* Trans. David Welsh. New York: Twayne Publishers, Inc., 1972.

———. *Lalka (The Doll).* Edited, with an introduction by Henryk Markiewicz. Warsaw: Państwowy Instytut Wydawniczy, 1973.

———. "Słówko o krytyce pozytywnej." Rpt. in *"Lalka" Bolesława Prusa,* ed. Markiewicz.

Radway, Janice A. *Reading the Romance: Women, Patriarchy and Popular Literature.* Rev. ed. Chapel Hill: University of North Carolina Press, 1991.

Reymont, Władysław. *Dzieła wybrane.* Vol. 7. Kraków: Wydawnictwo Literackie, 1957.

Richards, Thomas. *The Commodity Culture of Victorian England: Advertising and Spectacle, 1851–1914.* Stanford: Stanford University Press, 1990.

Rieber, Alfred J. *Merchants and Enrepreneurs in Imperial Russia.* Chapel Hill: University of North Carolina Press, 1982.

Rosenthal, Bernice Glatzer. "The Search for a Russian Orthodox Work Ethic." In *Between Tsar and People,* ed. Clowes et al., 57–74.

Rubin, Joan Shelley. *The Making of Middlebrow Culture.* Chapel Hill: University of North Carolina Press, 1992.

Ruud, Charles A. *Russian Entrepreneur: Publisher Ivan Sytin of Moscow, 1851–1934.* Montreal: McGill–Queens University Press, 1990.

Scherr, Barry. "Gor'kij's *Childhood:* The Autobiography as Fiction." *Slavic and East European Journal* 23 (1979): 333–45.

———. *Maxim Gorky.* Boston: Twayne Publishers, 1988.

Schudson, Michael. *Discovering the News: A Social History of American Newspapers.* New York: Basic Books, Inc., 1978.

Showalter, Elaine. *A Literature of Their Own: British Women Novelists from Bronte to Lessing.* Princeton: Princeton University Press, 1977.

———. *Sexual Anarchy: Gender and Culture at the Fin De Siècle.* London: Penguin Books, 1990.

Sienkiewicz, Henryk. *Rodzina Połanieckich (The Polaniecki Family).* Warsaw: Państwowy Instytut Wydawniczy, 1976.

———. *Bez Dogmatu (Without Dogma).* Warsaw: Państwowy Instytut Wydawniczy, 1978.

Singer, I. B. *The Family Moskat.* New York: Farrar, Straus and Giroux, 1950.

Singer, Israel Joshua. *The Brothers Ashkenazi.* Trans. Joseph Singer, with an introduction by Irving Howe. New York: Penguin, 1993.

Słomkowska, Alina. *Dziennikarze warszawscy: Szkice z XIX wieku.* Warsaw: Państwowe Wydawnictwo Naukowe, 1974.

Slotnick, Susan A. "*The Family Moskat* and the Tradition of the Yiddish Family Saga." In *Recovering the Canon: Essays on Isaac Bashevis Singer,* ed. David Neal Miller, 24–38. Leiden: E. J. Brill, 1986.

Smith, Monika Rydygier. "The W/hole Remains: Consumerist Politics in *Bleak House, Great Expectations,* and *Our Mutual Friend.*" *Victorian Review* 19 (summer 1993): 1–21.

Spolar, Christine. "Romance by the Book in Poland." *Washington Post,* August 28, 1995.

Staroi, Vasilii. *Petr i Natasha: v prodolzhenie L. N. Tolstogo.* Moscow: Vagrius, 1996.

Steinberg, Mark D. "Worker-Authors and the Cult of the Person." In *Cultures in Flux: Lower-Class Values, Practices, and Resistance in Late Imperial Russia,* ed. Stephen P. Frank and Mark D. Steinberg, 168–84. Princeton: Princeton University Press, 1994.

Stites, Richard. *Russian Popular Culture: Entertainment and Society since 1900.* Cambridge: Cambridge University Press, 1992.

Susman, Warren. *Culture as History: The Transformation of American Society in the Twentieth Century.* New York: Pantheon, 1984.

Święcka, Agnieszka. "Romance Novels: Fairy Tales for Big Girls." *Warsaw Voice,* April 2, 1995.

Świętochowski, Aleksandr. "Bohaterowie Prusa," in *"Lalka" Bolesława Prusa,* ed. Markiewicz, 566–68.

Szwejkowska, Helena. *Wybrane zagadnienia z dziejów książki XIX-XX wieku.* Wrocław" Państwowe Wydawnictwo Naukowe, 1979.

Szweykowski, Zygmunt. *Twórczość Bolesława Prusa.* 2d ed. Warsaw: Państwowy Instytut Wydawniczy, 1972.

Tebbel, John, and Mary Ellen Zuckerman. *The Magazine in America, 1741–1990.* New York: Oxford University Press, 1991.

Terras, Victor. *A History of Russian Literature.* New Haven: Yale University Press, 1991

Thurston, Carol. *The Romance Revolution: Erotic Novels for Women and the Quest for a New Sexual Identity.* Urbana: University of Illinois Press, 1987.

Tompkins, Jane. *Sensational Designs: The Cultural Work of American Fiction, 1790–1860.* New York: Oxford University Press, 1985.

Torgovaia reklama i upakovka v Rossii XIX–XX vv. Catalogue. Moscow: Gosudarstvennyi istoricheskii muzei, 1993.

Tsybenko, E. Z. "'Kukla' Boleslava Prusa i 'Anna Karenina' L'va Tolstogo." *Vestnik Moskovskogo Universiteta,* ser. 9, 9 (January–February 1991): 33–41.

The Twilight of the Tsars: Russian Art at the Turn of the Century. Hayward Gallery, London, 7 March–19 May 1991. South Bank Centre, 1991.

Tygodnik Illustrowany (The Illustrated Weekly).

Veblen, Thorstein. *The Theory of the Leisure Class.* Intro. John Kenneth Galbraith. Boston: Houghton and Mifflin, 1973.

Verbitskaia, Anastasiia. *Moemu chitateliu. Detstvo, gody ucheniia (To My Reader. Childhood, School Years).* Moscow, 1911.

————. *Kliuchi schast'ia: Roman daidzhest (The Keys to Happiness)*. 2 Vols. Saint Petersburg: Severo-zapad, 1993.

————. *Kliuchi schast'ia*. 6 Vols. Moscow, 1910.

Walas, Teresa. Afterword to *Trędowata*, by Helena Mniszek. Kraków: Wydawnictwo Literackie, 1972.

Watts, Emily Stipes. *The Businessman in American Literature*. Athens: University of Georgia Press, 1982.

West, James L. "The Riabushinsky Circle: Burzhuaziia and Obshchestvennost'." In *Between Tsar and People*, ed. Clowes et al., 41–56.

Wicke, Jennifer. *Advertising Fictions: Literature, Advertisement and Social Reading*. New York: Columbia University Press, 1988.

Wierzbicki, Andrzej. "Wokulski żyje!" In *"Lalka" Bolesława Prusa*, ed. Markiewicz.

Williams, Rosalind H. *Dream Worlds: Mass Consumption in Late Nineteenth-Century France*. Berkeley and Los Angeles: University of California Press, 1982.

Williamson, Judith. *Decoding Advertisements: Ideology and Meaning in Advertising*. London: Marion Boyars, 1978.

Wilson, Christopher. "The Rhetoric of Consumption: Mass-Market Magazines and the Demise of the Gentle Reader, 1880–1920." In *The Culture of Consumption: Critical Essays in American History, 1880–1920*, ed. Richard Wightman Fox and T. J. Jackson, 39–64. New York: Pantheon, 1983.

Yampolsky, Mikhail. "In the Shadow of Monuments: Notes on Iconoclasm and Time." In *Soviet Hieroglyphics: Visual Culture in Late Twentieth-Century Russia*, ed. Nancy Condee, 93–112. Bloomington: Indiana University Press, 1995.

Zieliński, Henryk. *Historia Polski 1864–1939*. Warsaw: Państwowe Wydawnictwo Naukowe, 1968.

Zorkaia, Neia M. *Na rubezhe stoletii. U istokov massovogo iskusstva v Rossii 1900–1910 godov*. Moscow: Nauka, 1976.

index